Auto Empire

Eric Choi
Richard Choi

Designed and edited by Kkume Publishing studio

Auto Empire / Eric Choi & Richard Choi. —1st ed.
ISBN 978-1533334688

Contents

From the Authors...1
Empire I. Volkswagen AG..7
　Porsche Pursues Volkswagen 8
　Volkswagen Takes Over Porsche...14
　"Four Ring" Audi: An Empire Within an Empire.....................................22
　Volkswagen's Endless Thirst 31
　Car History 40
Empire II. General Motors...43
　Cars for All: The GM Odyssey 44
　Bean Counters vs. Car Guys 50
　The Fall and Resurrection of the GM Empire...56
　Car History 63
Empire III. Toyota...65
　From Looms to Cars: Toyota's 90 Years of Innovation...........................66
　The Lexus Project: The Final Piece of the Toyota Empire.......................73
　The Prius Miracle: Overcoming the mass recall and the great earthquake 80
　Inside History 87
Empire IV. Renault Nissan 89
　Renault: Misfortune of War 90
　Embracing Nissan: Rise to 4th in the World 96
　Ghosn's Magic Takes Renault Global 102
　Car History 110
Empire V. Hyundai Motor Group 113
　The Pony Miracle: Parting with Ford...114
　Growth Pains: Bromont Disaster and the 1st & 2nd Oil Shocks 121
　Kia Motors: Dream of Technological Independence 128
　Hyundai Takes Kia Under Its Wing 134
　New Beginning: Launch of the Hyundai Motor Group..........................140
　MK's Gambit: Venturing into the World 149
　Hyundai Motor Group: Lone Wolf or Busy Under the Surface.............156
　Inside History 163
Empire VI. Fiat Chrysler Automobiles 165
　Italy's Automobile Empire: From Fiat to Ferrari....................................166
　Chrysler Begins to Wobble..173
　Porsche Pursues Volkswagen 178
　Car History 187
Empire VII. Ford..189
　One Car Every 16 Seconds: The Popularization of Cars 190
　Mulally's Insight Saves Ford 196

Empire VIII. Honda 203
  Stubborn Craftsman Reaches the Pinnacle of Technology.............................204
  Inside History 211
Empire IX. Peugeot-Citroën (PSA) 213
  Pride of France Swallows its Pride to Survive 214
Empire X. Daimler AG...221
  Daimler Empire: From Mini Cars to Trucks..222
  Tri-Star Becomes Younger 228
  Inside History 235
Empire XI. BMW Group 237
  Quandt Family's Decision Saves BMW 238
  Design Innovation: Recovery from Failed Rover Acquisition 244
  Inside History 250
Empire XII. Jaguar Land Rover...253
  British Luxury Marques Recover from Brink of Collapse 254
  Car History...261
Empire XIII. SsangYong Motor 263
  The Korando Never Stops..264
  Inside History 272
Empire XIV. Renault-Samsung..275
  Samsung's Unfulfilled Dream Attempts Comeback under Renault................276
Empire XV. Daewoo Motors...283
  Daewoo Motors: The Withering Empire..284
  Car History..292
  About the Authors..295
  Reference..296
  Photo Credits 299

"Auto Empire will be an insightful guide for CEOs, executives and employees of automobile companies. It also makes a valuable economic and business management study for students aspiring to find jobs in the auto industry. Upon reading this book, I could sense the extensive research done by the authors and their attempts to approach information from various viewpoints. I am confident once you read this book, the cars cruising on the streets will never look the same."

Choong-ho Kim, former CEO of Hyundai Motor

"I sincerely hope Auto Empire provides you with insight into how cars evolved throughout history. The history of cars is also the history of freedom. If someone were to ask the authors, "What is this book?" I suspect the authors would reply, A book that gives us something we all want: Freedom."

Ji-soo Yu, President of Kookmin University

From the Authors

A record of the auto industry helps people to learn from the past

When it comes to buying vehicles, there are just a minute number of countries that have domestically manufactured automobiles that people should invest in. When looking at the top 10 vehicle manufacturers, these countries include France, Germany, Italy, Japan, Korea and the United States.

A few automobile manufacturers have popped up in other countries including China and India, and the manufacturers have made major strides in the industry thanks to the strong demand of locals. Of the countries that didn't fight in either World War I or World War II, Korea is the one country that managed to become a worldwide automobile leader.

The automotive industry is a tightly-knit web of multiple industries in an array of nations. During the early automotive industry days, war helped drive the advances, with hundreds of companies vying to be the best.

After an infinite amount of mergers and acquisitions, the industry is regarded as being monopolized so that only the strong will survive. With unique industry manufacturing products that ride a thin line between consumer goods and industrial goods, it's important that companies own more than one brand in order to compete. These kinds of changes will ensure things progress further.

Trying to put together the automobile industry's 130-year history was not an easy task. Not to say it wasn't a meaningful task for a Korean auto industry analyst, looking hard at the industry as a whole. It's my thought and belief that the efforts I put for will be a stepping stone for improvements and self-developments in the auto industry.

The past is like a magic mirror in that it can show a potential future. And, don't forget the old saying, history will always repeat itself. My hope is that this book gives people insight into a possible future, especially those folks working in the auto industry throughout the world and investors looking for any potential investment opportunities.

I especially want to be an important tool for those people in the automotive parts industry, helping them to understand each company and provide them with a fighting opportunity in the vast market. For vehicle enthusiasts, there is *Auto Empire*, which can give some insight into how the industry works.

I spent much of my year writing this book. When I wasn't working on the book, I was researching for it – using various books and reference materials. I was looking for any reference materials that could chronicle events that took place before my birth. Much of my spare time was in the National Assembly Library. There's no doubt that writing a book is difficult to do, especially a book of this nature. However, I am certain that the hard work and dedication I had improved me.

With that in mind, I would like to thank certain people for their support while I traveled this road. These folks include a large number of people who work in the auto industry as well as my co-workers for their encouragement to write it. I am appreciative to Richard, my co-author, who made sure the book was finished and saw release to the public.

A big thanks goes out to my family – my mother, father and brother. And, a heartfelt thanks to my wife Chorong Maeng who supported and loved me unconditionally throughout the process.

Eric Junghyuk Choi
Auto Industry Analyst, Shinhan Investment

A better understanding on the evolution of worldwide automobile companies

Constant motion – that's the way the automobile industry and market is going. The industry's turbulence is allowing these companies to develop, grow and potentially die in history. In a way, automobile companies are comparable to living organisms. Similar to cell growth through proliferation, companies can boost their size through mergers and acquisitions.

There are an array of stories building up to M&As between automakers. It's not uncommon for companies to merge with other companies, developing a whole new business. However, it's also common for them to downsize the company... usually due to being too big for its own good. These efforts are done for two key reasons, development and existence

Corporation histories are a testament to an intense struggle to survive and thrive, battling against competitors to attain market dominance and to ensure their stories are both amusing and thrilling. I've discovered, why looking back at the history of auto manufacturers' growth, that the majority of the information is found in pieces.

What I found was that the well-researched information came from the autobiography on Ferdinand Karl Piech, chairman of the supervisory board for Volkswagen Group along with several historical books on many other worldwide auto manufacturers such as BMW, Toyota, Porsche, etc. It's these books that helped me with the book's writing.

A key factor that affected corporations rise and fall are the historical changes. In fact, some corporations have been able to rewrite their history. This book tries showing readers about the development of automakers and how economic conditions affect their business throughout the world. Some historic events are repeatedly mentioned because these events had major impacts on each one.

This book is an accumulation of an articles series called, "Key M&A Moments that Changed the History of the Automotive Industry" published in the March 2014 issue of Hankyung Business Weekly. On top of that, the book talks about certain events that have altered the auto industry's course that led to the redefining in standards of classic cars.

There were several people who helped with the book's writing, and I want to offer them my deepest gratitude and appreciation for all their help:

First, my co-author Eric, an analyst with Shinhan Investment, who provided me with the most help. Seung-gyu Jang, for providing me with a chance to better the lacking essays for Hankyung Business Weekly. Ik-won Lee, Korea Economic Daily Head of the Industry Department, for his help in bettering my reporting and writing skills. Both Choong-ho Kim, former CEO for Hyundai Motor Company and Yu Ji-soo, president of Kookmin University, for their contributions toward reviewing the book. I want to thank Yeong-un Gong, executive director with Hyundai Motors and other automobile industry-related people for their assistance in making sure the book was made in fruition. Finally, I want to express my undying love to my family for all the support and encouragement they offered during this time.

Although I have spent close to a year writing the book, there is always room for improvement. Therefore, I welcome readers to share their advice, humbly accepting their opinions so that the book can be updated and improved upon. It's my desire that my efforts have not gone in vain, and that this will be a useful guide for students in business management and economics studies along with the general public.

I would feel great honor should the book become the start of an array of publications focused on the automotive industry.

Richard Jin-suk Choi,
Business Section Reporter for The Korea Economic Daily

EMPIRE I

Volkswagen AG

CHAPTER 1

Porsche Pursues Volkswagen

"We are going to acquire Volkswagen," Porsche CEO, Wendelin Wiedeking, announced to the Porsche family in 2005. Soon after, Porsche began buying Volkswagen shares for the sole reason of defending Volkswagen against hostile takeover attempts by foreign corporations. On the surface, Wiedeking's decision was justified, given that, in 2000, German Chancellor Gerhard Schröder was asked by Ford CEO Jacques Nasser if the German government would oppose a Ford-Volkswagen merger. Porsche increased its stake in Volkswagen to 18.5% by October 2005 and to 50.73% by January 2009. Along with AOL's acquisition of Time Warner in 2000, this was one of the most well known examples of a "David (Porsche)" attempting to takeover a "Goliath (Volkswagen)."

At the time, Porsche had accumulated around 3 billion euros in cash, following the success of its SUV, Cayenne. Unless it had other plans, Porsche was obligated to use the cash to pay dividends to its shareholders. Meanwhile, a growing consensus was that Porsche, being smaller than other multinational automobile manufacturers, needed to achieve economy of scale to continue developing new cars and technology. As a result, Porsche CFO Holger Haerter proposed a plan to acquire Volkswagen with investment banks using cash in possession, loans, and stock options, putting the Volkswagen acquisition in motion.

Wendelin Wiedeking and Ferdinand Piëch

"There were two brothers. They were not from the same mother, nor did they have the same surname: they were close relatives. They grew up together, allowing them to become closer than family. When they grew, the two became the heads of two different corporations. Unlike their close personal relationship, their companies came to engage in a feud as each company attempted to take over the other. This escalated into conflict and rivalry between the two families."

Though this may seem like a work of fiction, it is not. It is an actual M&A case that was the focus of the auto industry until 2013. It is the story of the vendetta between Volkswagen AG, the European automobile giant, and Porsche SE, one of the world's most prominent sports car companies. The clash began with Porsche's attempt to takeover Volkswagen, but ended with Volkswagen emerging victorious. At first, it seemed that David was going to defeat Goliath. In reality, Goliath picked up David and stuffed him in his pocket.

Porsche's 80-year history is a close related to Germany's history throughout the 20th century. Porsche came into existence in 1931 when the engineering genius, Dr. Ferdinand Porsche founded "Dr. Ing. h. c. F. Porsche GmbH" at Kronenstraße 24, Stuttgart, Germany. The Daimler-Mercedes Group (parent company of Mercedes-Benz) was indirectly involved in the establishment of Porsche. Dr. Porsche was the chief designer at a subsidiary of the Daimler Motor Group. He quit his job and started his own company after his design was rejected due to cost cuts. If the Daimler subsidiary had accepted the design, Dr. Porsche would not have decided to establish his own company, and if the Porsches that we all know had ever come into existence, they would have been released under a Daimler brand. The moral of this story is losing a skilled employee may present significant lost opportunity.

Dr. Porsche was not German; he was Czechoslovakian. To be exact, he was born in Maffersdorf, Bohemia, which was under the rule of the Austro-

Hungarian Empire at the time. The region is currently a part of the Czech Republic.

Dr. Porsche had a knack for developing racing cars as well as compact cars. He took part in Adolf Hitler's project to market mass-produced cars, leading to the birth of the Volkswagen Beetle. However, such contributions to the Third Reich during World War II caused Dr. Porsche to be accused of war crimes.

Aside from Ferdinand Porsche, the most noteworthy individuals in the history of Porsche are the two "brothers," Wendelin Wiedeking and Ferdinand Piëch. As the CEO, Wiedeking is the man who transformed Porsche, which was facing difficult losses, into one of the world's most prominent sports car brands. He was also the person who persuaded the Porsche family to acquire Volkswagen. In his autobiography, Piëch, whose position was the polar opposite of Wiedeking's, states that he asks himself whether he could have accomplished what Wiedeking had if he was heading Porsche. Piëch's autobiography was published in 2002, before Wiedeking attempted to acquire Volkswagen.

In order to learn about the supervisory board chairman Ferdinand Piëch of the Volkswagen Group, we need to first take a look at the Porsche family tree.

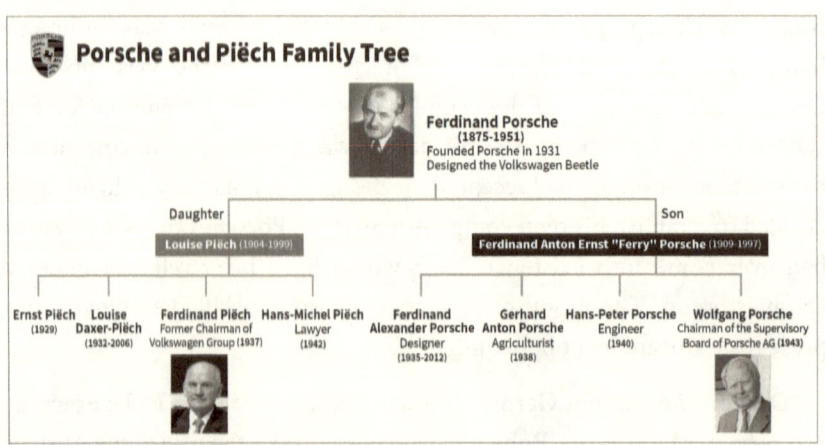

Porsche founder Ferdinand Porsche was succeeded by his son, Ferry Porsche, and his daughter, Louise Porsche, who was just as competent an entrepreneur as her brother. Louise married lawyer Anton Piëch and gave birth to four children, who includes Anton Ernst and Ferdinand Piëch. Ferdinand Piëch would grow up to compete with his cousin, Wolfgang Porsche, to gain control over Porsche and Volkswagen. Wolfgang Porsche, who placed Wiedeking in the lead to takeover Volkswagen, is currently the chairman of the supervisory board at Porsche. However, with Porsche on the verge of gaining control of Volkswagen, the tide changed in favor of Piëch. It would be impossible to imagine the devastation Wolfgang Porsche must have felt as victory slipped through his fingers. Fortunately, his company has been doing well.

On a side note, I had the opportunity to meet Wolfgang Porsche at the IAA Frankfurt Motor Show in September 2013. I noticed that Wolfgang Porsche never had a smile on his face. It was also the 50th anniversary of the Porsche 911, the company's flagship model.

The Ernst Case: Invasion of Middle Eastern Capital

Generally, the more children a founder has, the more complicated the task of selecting a successor and dividing stakes becomes. Among Porsche's second-generation CEOs, Louise Piëch took special precautions to ensure that her children did not lose their stakes in Porsche. Years later, Ferry and Louise began discussing who would head Porsche should they retire. Ferry and Louise each had four children and the 10 of them each held 10% stakes in Porsche. In principle, the siblings had agreed to entrust a member of the Porsche family with the management of Porsche in Germany and a member of the Piëch family with the management of Porsche's Austrian operations. However, the ambitious Ferdinand Piëch was not satisfied. Ferdinand Piëch began to clash with his cousins, Ferdinand Alexander Porsche, the designer of the Porsche 911, and Hans-Peter Porsche, the production chief at Porsche. It seemed that Ferdinand was going to start a rebellion to become the CEO of Porsche.

In the autumn of 1970, Ferry Porsche summoned the members of the Porsche and Piëch family to Schüttgut, a farm in Zell am See where the headquarters of Porsche's Austrian operations are located. He hired a group therapists from a company in Vienna. The session ended with the therapists advising that both families stop working at Porsche and hire outside managers to run the company. The families underwent another session in the summer of 1971 and reached the same conclusion. As of March 1, 1972, both families removed themselves from Porsche, ending the quarrel.

Despite the agreement, another clash occurred, referred to as the "Ernst case." In the 80s, Ernst Piëch secretly attempted to sell his stake to Middle Eastern investors after he suffered massive losses due to the Burgenland real estate project. However, Ernst Piëch had an ulterior motive for his decision to relinquish his shares: until both families stopped working at Porsche in 1972, Ernst Piëch was managing Porsche's Austrian operations and was confident he would become chairman of the supervisory board. Having been thwarted from achieving his ambition, he was so disheartened that he left the company and Austria. For Ernst Piëch, his stake in Porsche had become nothing but a symbol of his broken dreams.

Once news reached their ears, the Porsche and Piëch families used their pre-emption rights to acquire Ernst Piëch's shares. They did everything in their power to raise the 3 million marks to do so including turning Porsche into a publicly-traded company. Ultimately, the Porsche and Piëch families each obtained 53.6% and 46.3% of Ernst Piëch's stake. This upset the balance that had been maintained for years and became the trigger that intensified each family's efforts to control the other.

Corporations Seeking to Take Over Porsche

Along with Toyota and GM, Volkswagen is one of the world's three largest automakers. Volkswagen is currently increasing its size with aspirations of becoming the industry champion by 2018. Meanwhile, Porsche exceeded its global unit sales of 200,000 units for the first time in 2015. It is evident that both companies are taking themselves to new heights.

Turning the clock back 30 years, the situation was the exact opposite, as both companies were having difficulties. In 1977, the power balance between the Porsche and Piëch families was at an equilibrium with each holding 50% stakes. However, with the increasingly number of family members, the opportunities for disagreement increased and trouble occurred from unexpected places. In 1986, Porsche's annual unit sales fell to 54,000 units, which was only half of what it had been five years previously, due to the poor sales of the 924 and 911 follow-up models designed by Ferdinand Alexander Porsche, which were released around the time of the 928. To make matters worse, the dollar appreciation of 1987 caused unit sales to plunge again to 29,000 in 1988-89, pushing the company to the brink of bankruptcy.

By this point, rumors that the Porsche and Piëch families would sell Porsche began to emerge. Even Peter Schutz, who was the CEO of Porsche from 1981, answered that the family needed to sell when Ferry Porsche asked if there was any way to improve the company's earnings. With Porsche in crisis, companies seeking to buy Porsche began to appear. Among Japanese companies, Toyota and Honda came knocking with heaps of money – Toyota offered 1 billion marks and Honda a staggering 4 billion marks. Fiat, Ford and the Daimler Group also approached Porsche with offers. However, all offers were turned down by Ferry Porsche, who was the chairman of Porsche's supervisory board at the time.

The external threat strengthened internal solidarity. With Porsche struggling, the Porsche and Piëch families agreed to unite and save the company. The two families garnered 200 million marks from their own money to increase Porsche's capital. Once they pulled Porsche out of the slump, they began to search for a CEO. The families locked horns during their search. The Porsche family insisted on appointing Porsche's financial executive as the CEO, whereas the Piëch family wanted Porsche's production chief to head the company. Ultimately, the families gave in to Ferdinand Piëch, who was the chairman of the supervisory board at Audi. As a result, in 1992, Porsche's production chief became the CEO of Porsche, marking Wendelin Wiedeking's rise to prominence.

CHAPTER 2

Volkswagen Takes Over Porsche

It was one October day in 2005. Volkswagen supervisory board chairman Ferdinand Piëch was in an executive conference room at Volkswagen headquarters in Wolfsburg along with Volkswagen chairman Bernd Pischetsrieder and other executives. A heavy silence hung in the room.

On the table was an internal report stating that Porsche had acquired 18.53% of Volkswagen shares and was likely to continue increasing its stake to obtain management rights.

"We have failed to see the monster growing under our nose"

The executives murmured among themselves in self-deprecation, because Porsche, which had been Volkswagen's partner in technology development, business ventures, marketing campaigns and other areas, had begun to bare its teeth at them.

After a while, Piëch broke the silence and said, "We won't let them have their way."

Wiedeking: "David will beat Goliath"

In 1992, at the age of 39, Wendelin Wiedeking, who had joined Porsche as an engineer in 1983, became the CEO of Porsche. Armed with youthful energy and an adventurous spirit, Wiedeking used his own brand of aggressive business management techniques to save Porsche from bankruptcy and transform it into one of the top sports car companies in the world.

Sometimes a single exceptional individual takes over a company and changes its fate. Wendelin Wiedeking is one of those people. He is the mind behind Porsche's two volume sellers: the two-seat sports car Boxster and the SUV Cayenne. The two models revived Porsche and enabled the company to post record-breaking unit sales and profit margins year after year. When he was the CEO of Daimler Chrysler, Jürgen Schrempp predicted that "only six automobile companies would be left in the future." The Boxster and Cayenne forced Schrempp to revise his prediction and say that six companies and Porsche are likely to remain. Of course, Schrempp's prediction was wrong.

Wiedeking held the reins of Porsche for 16 years before he resigned on July 23, 2009. During his reign, he reached out beyond Porsche and waged one of the most intense M&A battles in history to obtain Volkswagen. Even before he committed to the Volkswagen acquisition, Wiedeking had been displaying his aspirations for Volkswagen. In 2012, he published a book on this business philosophy entitled *The David Principle*, invoking the story of David who fought and defeated Goliath. In his book, Wiedeking says, "If size did matter, the dinosaurs would still be alive."

The Secret Meeting between Piëch and Schröder

Just as Wiedeking had Wolfgang Porsche to back him, Ferdinand Piëch had Chancellor Gerhard Schröder to support him. Piëch and Schröder were friends since Schröder was the premier of Lower Saxony, the state where Volkswagen's headquarters are located.

One day in 2000, Schroder called Piëch and informed him that Ford CEO Jacques Nasser had called to ask if the German government would be opposed to Ford acquiring stakes in Volkswagen. If Ford became a major Volkswagen shareholder, there was no doubt that Ford would disrupt Volkswagen's management and its traditional partnership with Porsche. Hence, Schroder gave a negative response to Ford.

Piëch shared the news with his family and argued that the family should invest more money in Volkswagen. At the time, most members of the Porsche and Piëch families considered any significant investment in Volkswagen a risk; this became the reason why Porsche began buying Volkswagen stocks in 2005. By October 2005, Porsche had accumulated an 18.53% stake in Volkswagen, which Wiedeking announced was "a measure to protect Volkswagen from hostile takeovers by overseas entities."

The Volkswagen Law: Rule or Get Ruled

In order to understand Porsche's attempt to acquire Volkswagen, we need to look at the Volkswagen Law. Volkswagen was established by the Hitler administration on May 28, 1937. Under the Third Reich, Ferdinand Porsche designed the Beetle, which is the main contributor to Volkswagen's status today. The Volkswagen Law is the reason Porsche and Volkswagen maintained a close relationship for a long period.

After World War II, on October 8, 1949, the British military occupying Germany transferred ownership of Volkswagen to the German government while entrusting its management to the Lower Saxony state government. On August 22, 1960, the German government changed Volkswagen from a limited company to an incorporated company following the legislation of the so-called Volkswagen Law (law to privatize Volkswagen). In accordance with the law, 60% of Volkswagen shares were publicly offered, while the remaining 40% was retained by the federal and state governments.

According to Paragraph 1 of Article 2 and Paragraph 5 of Article 5 of the Volkswagen Law, the voting rights of shareholders owning over 20% of voting shares are capped at 20%. In short, no single shareholder is able to exercise over 20% of total voting rights, regardless of how many shares they own. Under article 4, 80% of shareholders must give their approval in order for a special resolution to pass at the Volkswagen shareholder meeting. This is stricter than the 75% requirement stipulated in Germany's Stock Operation Act. The clauses were implemented to ensure that the

Lower Saxony government, which held a 20.1% stake in Volkswagen, maintained its influence.

According to the Volkswagen Law, Porsche would be limited to only 20% of the voting rights, regardless of how much stake it garnered. However, fate had an evil twist. The European Commission stated that the Volkswagen Law violated the EEC treaty, which guarantees freedom of capital movement within the region, and filed a lawsuit against the German government to the Court of Justice of the EU on March 4, 2005. On October 23, 2007, the Court of Justice ruled in favor of the European Commission, nullifying the 20% voting rights cap and the government's right to appoint Volkswagen board members. This opened the path for Porsche to own Volkswagen. Finally, this was the opening Wiedeking had planned to exploit from the beginning.

The amusing part is that this story had a further twist. The German government found a loophole in the Court of Justice's ruling. Since it was not included in the lawsuit, the 80% approval requirement was kept unchanged. This allowed the Lower Saxony government to maintain its veto power. Ultimately, this loophole derailed Porsche's ploy, because the Lower Saxony government could prevent the signing of any control agreement, in accordance to the German Konzern Law, by voting against it. At the time, Lower Saxony was governed by Christian Wulff (10th President of Germany, 2010-2012), who was on Piëch's side.

It was unusual for the German government, which sat idly by and watched the Britain-based Vodafone's hostile takeover of Mandesman in 2001, to go as far as fighting the European Commission in court just to protect Volkswagen. Some speculate it was because the German government and IG Metall (a metalworkers' union) were deeply involved. Whatever the case, it is impossible to disregard Ferdinand Piëch's close ties with Schröder, Wulff and other people in the political ring.

The Global Financial Crisis of 2008: Wiedeking's Pipe Dream

While the European Commission was in court fighting the Volkswagen Law in 2005, things were looking good for Porsche. The European Commission's victory would pave the path for Porsche to gain full control of Volkswagen. So, Porsche continued to rake in Volkswagen stocks. In October 2008, Porsche announced its plan to secure a 75% stake in Volkswagen through stocks and stock options in 2009, revealing its intention to take over Volkswagen. After increasing its Volkswagen stake to 42.6%, Porsche purchased call options for 31.5% of Volkswagen shares.

Between 2005 and 2009, Porsche gained 8.2 billion euros though its Volkswagen options as Volkswagen's share price rallied consistently since Porsche began to acquire stocks. Since Porsche had 13 billion euros vested in Volkswagen, Porsche figured it would be able to regain the money spent to buy Volkswagen shares once the acquisition was completed. While Porsche was proceeding with its plans, Porsche's debt jumped by approximately 9 billion euros. Also, the U.S. subprime crisis broke out in September 2008, and, since the U.S. was Porsche's largest market, the company's unit sales plunged 27%. As a result, Porsche's cash flow began to deteriorate quickly.

Once Volkswagen's share price began to fall, Porsche saw its losses from financial derivatives begin to snowball. In 2008, a 10 euro drop in Volkswagen's share price caused 600 million euros in losses for Porsche. Hence, Porsche's strenuous attempt to acquire Volkswagen backfired and pushed Porsche to the brink of bankruptcy.

Staggering under the burden of its 10 billion euro debt, Porsche requested emergency relief funds to the German government, but was rejected. Porsche sought equity investment from the sovereign wealth fund, Qatar Investment Authority, which was unable to decide which company to invest in: Porsche or Volkswagen. Ironically, Porsche turned to Volkswagen for help. Piëch openly declared that an investigation would be conducted to find the person(s) responsible for establishing and proceeding with the arduous plan that endangered Porsche. In the end, Wiedeking assumed responsibility for causing Volkswagen's takeover of Porsche and resigned. During Wiedeking's resignation ceremony on July 23, 2009, Wolfgang Porsche held Wiedeking's hands and shed tears of sorrow for having to send away his friend and coworker of 16 years, and for the near-successful attempt to acquire Volkswagen, which ultimately backfired and caused Porsche to become Volkswagen's 10th brand.

Win-Win for Porsche and Piëch

Lead by the Piëch family, the Porsche and Piëch families agreed to combine the two companies in July 2009. Volkswagen purchased a 49.9% stake in Porsche AG from Porsche SE for 8 billion euros, which Porsche SE used to repay most of its debts. Through Porsche SE, the two families held a combined 50.73% stake in Volkswagen, while the Lower Saxony government maintained its 20.1% stake. The Qatar Investment Authority obtained a 17% stake.

Volkswagen desired an immediate merger with Porsche, but was met with fierce opposition from hedge funds that were concerned about losses from drops in share prices that might result should Volkswagen fully took over Porsche. As a result, the families settled for having Porsche SE transfer its Porsche AG shares to Volkswagen and Volkswagen assumed the role of a holding company. On July 4, 2012, Volkswagen purchased the remaining 50.1% stake in Porsche AG for 4.46 billion euros from Porsche SE.

Initially, Volkswagen wanted to postpone the acquisition of the remaining Porsche AG shares for tax reasons, but it proceeded with the purchase after the German tax authorities promised to deduct a portion of taxes resulting from the transaction. The Volkswagen Group exercised its Porsche call options to gain stock options, while leaving Porsche SE with one single common share, allowing the company to avoid becoming subject to the merger clause under the tax law and saving 900 million euros in tax.

On the surface, the conflict between Porsche and Volkswagen seemed like a clash between Wiedeking and Piëch. Under the surface, however, it was a feud between the Porsche and Piëch families. The 70-year Porsche-

Piëch feud, which began with the establishment of Porsche in 1937, came to a close with the Piëch family emerging victorious over the Porsche family.

Since his younger days, Ferdinand Piëch dreamed of heading Porsche. Just 40 years after both families agreed to stop involving themselves in the management of Porsche in 1972, Piëch had finally achieved his dream, after spending time as the chairman of Audi, chairman of Volkswagen and chairman of Volkswagen's supervisory board.

A long, hard look reveals that both the Porsche and Piëch clans have benefited from the Porsche-Volkswagen battle. After the lengthy feud, both families became major shareholders in Porsche as well as Volkswagen, one of the world's most prominent automobile giants. The Volkswagen Group has openly stated that it would become the best-selling brand in the world by 2018. There is no way to be sure, but Wolfgang Porsche and Ferdinand Piëch may be at their family farm in Zell am See toasting and drinking wine with satisfied smiles on their faces.

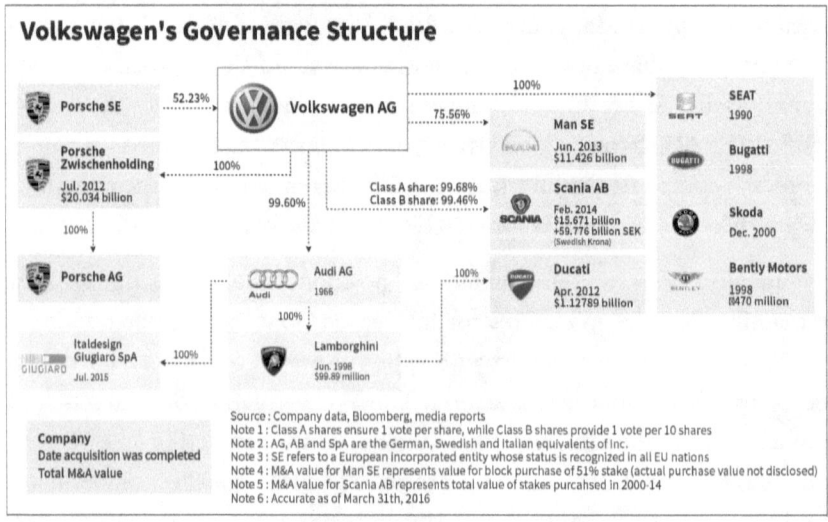

Although it has ended, the two clans' feud was not without fallout. In February 2014, seven hedge funds filed a 1.8 billion-euro lawsuit against the chairmen of Porsche and Volkswagen for investment losses. The hedge funds claimed that Porsche manipulated share prices using Volkswagen acquisition rumors, profiting wrongfully in the process. At the time, Porsche had acquired stock options for Volkswagen shares, but dismissed rumors of it attempting to take over Volkswagen. Predicting a drop in Volkswagen's share price, hedge funds short-sold Volkswagen share for quick gains. Once Porsche announced its plan to increase its stake in Volkswagen to 75%, Volkswagen's share jumped 4.4 folds from 209.3 euros on October 24, 2008, to 912.7 euros on October 28. In order to minimize their losses, hedge funds began to buy Volkswagen shares, which added more upward momentum to the shares. Because less than 5% of Volkswagen shares are traded on the market, such actions caused them to suffer losses.

Now that the two clans are on the same ship, they are likely to be able to fend off the hedge funds. Meanwhile, after buying all of Porsche's shares, Volkswagen's share price continued to rally. As a result, in late 2012, Volkswagen surpassed Siemens, SAP and other German conglomerates and became the largest company in Germany, based on market capitalization.

CHAPTER 3

"Four Ring" Audi: An Empire Within an Empire

"Audi outperformed Benz!"

In January 2012, the global automotive industry was hit hard by the news that Volkswagen's prestige brand, Audi, had sold 1.3 million cars in 2011, beating Mercedes-Benz's 1.26 million cars. Since the 1970s, Audi has been in pursuit of BMW and Benz. It took Audi over 40 years of technological innovation and quality improvement to beat its first target. Audi has since increased its lead over Benz, solidifying its position at second place. Meanwhile, Benz fell to third place six years after yielding first place to BMW.

Audi was threatening to overthrow BMW's dominance until its pursuit was thwarted by the "dieselgate" scandal in 2015. The scandal limited Audi's unit sales to 1.8 million, placing the company third after Benz's 2 million and BMW's 1.91 million. Nonetheless, Audi remains a persistent contender for the position as the leading prestige marque.

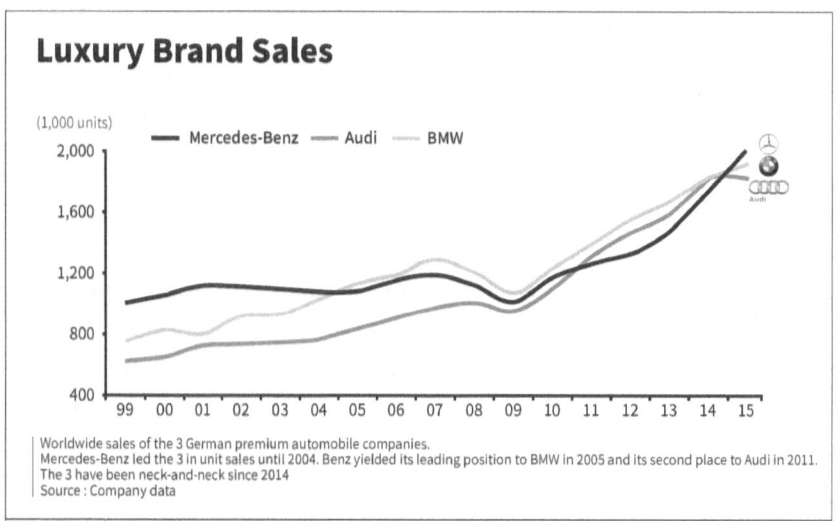

Luxury Brand Sales

(1,000 units)

Mercedes-Benz — Audi — BMW

Worldwide sales of the 3 German premium automobile companies.
Mercedes-Benz led the 3 in unit sales until 2004. Benz yielded its leading position to BMW in 2005 and its second place to Audi in 2011.
The 3 have been neck-and-neck since 2014
Source : Company data

Audi was founded with the merger of four automobile brands. Since its establishment, it has been advancing in innovative material and technology throughout its history. Some of its accomplishments are the aluminum chassis and the Quattro (AWD) system. The company proved its technological prowess by entering the Monte Carlo Rally, the 24 Hours of Le Mans and other major motorsports events. It owns the supercar brand Lamborghini, the motorcycle brand Ducati and the designing company Italdesign Giugiaro, making Audi one of the two pillars of the Volkswagen Group along with its brother Volkswagen. Audi was able to build an empire within the Volkswagen Group, thanks to the endless support of Ferdinand Piëch, the man behind Audi's rise to its current status.

Horch and the Four Rings

Audi was established in 1901 as Horch Automobil-Werke GmbH by Dr. August Horch, who left Mercedes-Benz. Despite being the founder, Horch was fired by management for focusing excessively on motor racing. Horch's situation was similar to that of Apple's Steve Jobs. While Jobs was able to return to his company, Horch was not. He established a new company also named Horch Automobile-Werke, but his previous company filed a lawsuit over the use of the Horch name. As a result, Dr. Horch changed the name of his company to Audi, the Latin equivalent of Horch, which means "to listen" in German. This amusing episode is the story of how Audi AG was established.

In 1932, Audi merged with Horsch, Dampf-Kraft-Wagen and Wanderer to form the Auto Union in an attempt to strengthen their competitive edge. Audi's four-ring emblem symbolizes the union of the four companies. The emblem upset the International Olympic Committee, as it resembled the five interlocking rings on the Olympic flag. In a stroke of brilliance, Audi used this to its advantage and began to sponsor the Olympic Games from 2013 on, appeasing the Olympic Committee also advertising its brand.

Contrary to their initial hopes of improving their competitiveness, the union of the four companies failed to produce the desired results. The Auto Union suffered financial trouble and was picked up by Daimler-Benz in 1959. In 1964, Daimler-Benz sold the trademark rights to the Auto Union and 50% of Auto Union shares to Volkswagen. Volkswagen changed the brand name of Auto Union from DKW to Audi. Two years later, Volkswagen increased its holding of Auto Union to 99.55% and fully incorporated it into the Volkswagen Group.

In 1969, Audi acquired NSU from Fiat. NSU developed the early version of the rotary engine, a rotating internal combustion engine that uses combustion gas to rotate pistons, instead of converting reciprocating motion of pistons into rotational motion; capable of producing high output with low displacement, but was discarded due to problems pertaining to fuel efficiency and durability. In 1961, it was sold to Mazda, the world's largest motorcycle manufacturer in the 50s. Before being acquired by Audi, NSU was suffering from troubles caused by negative perceptions of the reliability of rotary engines. Audi sold cars under the NSU brand until 1977. The remnants of NSU existence can be seen in Audi's ticker (NSU GR) on Bloomberg terminals.

Consisting of four companies established by skilled engineers, Audi boasted a high level of technology and took great pride in its engineering prowess. The company's focus on technology is expressed in its slogan, "*Vorsprung durch Technik*", which translates to "advancement through technology." Hence, Audi showed condescension toward its parent company, Volkswagen, and made great efforts to develop technology and cars that exceeded that of Volkswagen's. However, Volkswagen was always the decision maker.

Piëch: The Man behind Audi's Rise to Prominence

Ferdinand Piëch was one of the key people behind the growth of Volkswagen. However, he is also credited with raising Audi to its current status. After leaving Porsche, Piëch worked at Audi from 1973 to 1992. It was during this time that Audi established its brand identity as a luxury vehicle manufacturer.

After he joined Audi, Piëch produced a two-door hatchback coupe based on the successful Audi 80, which was released in July 1972, just before his arrival. The model appealed to the executives of Audi and Volkswagen. In the following year, Piëch's car was released bearing the Volkswagen emblem. This was the birth of the Passat. Piëch was the mastermind behind the diesel engine, which is the nucleus of Audi and the Volkswagen Group. He was also the drive behind the move to replace the zinc alloy chassis with an aluminum chassis. Contrary to common belief, 1994 Audi A8 was not the world's first car with a full aluminum chassis. In fact, the first car with a full aluminum chassis was Honda's legendary supercar, the NSX. Although Audi was not the first to use aluminum, the change was instrumental in enhancing Audi's position among the three German luxury car companies. Along with the aluminum bodies, another marquee feature of Audi vehicles is the Quattro, Audi's AWD system. The Quattro surprised the world when a car with the system successfully drove up a steep ski ramp. Audi was the first German luxury car manufacturer to implement an AWD system.

When he was the chief of development, Piëch began developing a passenger car with an AWD system, believing that the AWD system would provide a better driving experience, while increasing stability. By 1978, his efforts resulted in the prototype model, Audi A1. The mass production version of this prototype is the renowned Audi Quattro. Walther Treser, who led the team developing the initial AWD system, named it *quadro*, but Piëch decided that it sounded too soft and changed it to *quattro*, the Italian word for "four."

Qualitative Growth in 24 Hours of Le Mans, Quantitative Group in China

It is safe to say that Audi achieved qualitative growth through motorsports and quantitative growth in China.

Between 1981 and 1985, Audi participated in The Monte Carlo World Rally Championship, the New Zealand Rally Championship, Rallye Côte d'Ivoire and other major rally racing events and won four titles. One of the most prominent drivers on the Audi Rally Team was the legendary Walter Röhrl, who won the 1984 Monte Carlo World Rally Championship.

In the 80s, Audi participated in off-road rallies to prove the performance of its AWD system. In the 2000s, it demonstrated the prowess of its diesel engines, diesel hybrid system and other eco-friendly technologies through 24 Hours of Le Mans, which is the largest motorsports event in the world along with Formula 1 and the World Rally Championship. By 2014, Audi had won the event 13 times (Porsche has the most wins with 16). 24 Hours of Le Mansis a race in which three drivers take turns driving to see which team can cover the most distance in 24 hours. Teams that finish the race generally will have driven 4-5,000km. Audi won multiple titles with its diesel-engine sports car, the Audi R18. Since 2012, it has been winning with its diesel hybrid, the Audi R18 E-Tron.

China was instrumental in increasing Audi's unit sales. Today, car companies show a heavy reliance on Chinese sales in general. Audi ventured into the Chinese market before BMW or Mercedes-Benz and is currently leading these two in Chinese unit sales. In 2013, Audi's Chinese unit sales increased 25% from the previous year to 410,000 units, which accounts for 26.1% of Audi's worldwide unit sales (1.575 million units).

During the same year, BMW sold 210,000 units and Benz 130,000 units in China. There is no doubt that Audi benefited from establishing an early presence in the Chinese market, but another major contributor was the Chinese people's extraordinary love for Audi. Audi appealed strongly to the Chinese people because its four-ring emblem contains two number eights, which is the favored number in China because it symbolizes money.

Unlike in China, Audi is not doing well in the US. In 2013, Audi sold 158,061 vehicles in the US, nearly half of Mercedes-Benz's 312,534 units. Audi's lack of popularity in the US is attributable to the "unintended acceleration" controversy in 1986. Audi released the mid-sized sedan, Audi 100, in 1982 and exported it to the US as the Audi 5000. The vehicle was featured on a TV news program for reported incidents of sudden unintended acceleration, which critically damaged Audi's brand image in the States. The Volkswagen Group explained to its US consumers that the acceleration was caused by confusion over the location of the gas and brake pedals, but it was too late to salvage Audi's image. Nearly 30 years have passed, but Audi is still struggling in the US market, showing how important image and trust is for a brand.

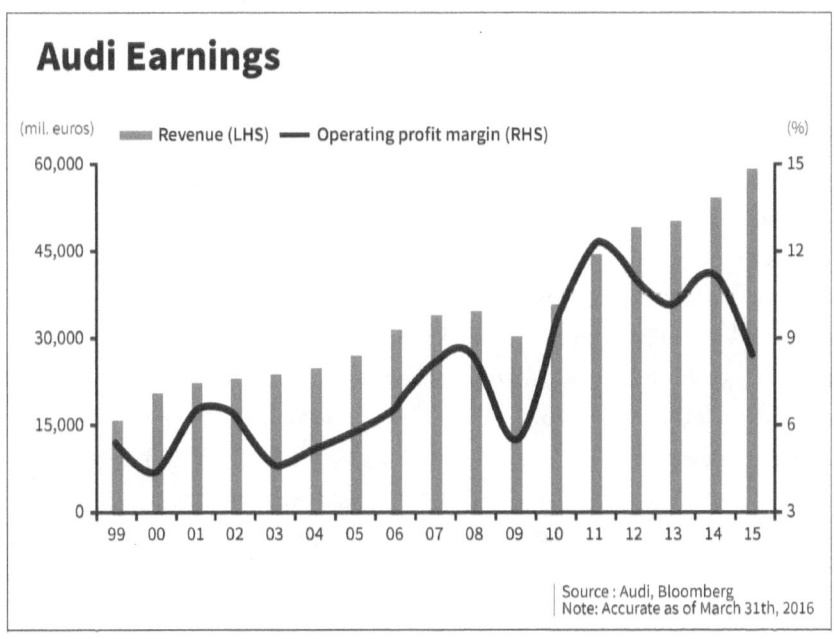

Audi Earnings

(mil. euros) ■ Revenue (LHS) ━ Operating profit margin (RHS) (%)

Source : Audi, Bloomberg
Note: Accurate as of March 31th, 2016

Acquisition of 3 Italian Companies: The Rise of a Small Empire

Audi was able to achieve inorganic growth as it was the favored company of Piëch and Volkswagen Group Chairman Martin Winterkorn. Audi was able to develop into a small empire by acquiring the Italian design firm Italdesign Giugiaro in 2010 and the Italian motorcycle manufacturer Ducati in 2012, adding to the Italian supercar maker Lamborghini, which was entrusted to the Volkswagen Group in 1998. This was the result of Audi's strategy to obtain a brand portfolio matching that of the other two German luxury vehicle makers. Audi managed to create synergy between its affiliates, which resulted in improved earnings.

In June 1998, Audi acquired Lamborghini from the Indonesian millionaire, Tommy Suharto, son of the former president of Indonesia, Suharto. Tommy Suharto acquired Lamborghini from Chrysler in 1994, but Indonesia's economic crisis in the late 90s made it difficult for Suharto to fund the development of the follow-up model to the Lamborghini Diablo. Before 2003, Audi was not considered to be on par with Mercedes-Benz or BMW. The A4 and the A6 were the main drives behind Audi's rise to prominence, but the Lamborghini Gallardo and the Audi R8 also played significant roles.

Germany is heralded as the leader in automobile performance and manufacturing quality, but Italy continues to reign as the champion in automobile design. In 2010, Audi accumulated a 90.1% stake in Italdesign Giugiaro, which was established by the Italian designer Giorgetto Giugiaro. The remaining 9.9% stake was sold off following Guigiaro's retirement in July 2015. Giorgetto Giugiaro is a high-profile designer. He was the designer of Volkswagen's mainstay models, including the first generation Golf, which is widely recognized as the standard for hatchbacks. His work also includes the Ferrari 250GT, the Maserati Ghibli and the Hyundai Pony. Piëch and Giugiaro are the same age and share a friendship. The two first met in July 1972. After leaving Porsche, Piëch wanted time to recuperate. He went to Turin to see Giugiaro and study the characteristics of Italian cars. Piëch spent about a month at Giugiaro's estate as Giugiaro's apprentice and the two became so close that Piëch learned Italian.

Being a motorcycle enthusiast, Piëch was a major influence in Audi's acquisition of the premium motorcycle, Ducati. Audi bought Ducati shares from three Italian private equity funds. Piëch once said that he had an affinity for the aesthetics of Ducati motorcycles and KTM's focus on lightweight chassis. Piëch was also a fan of Japanese motorcycles. When he became the chairman of the Volkswagen Group in January 1993, his motorcycle collection included an early Honda 750 (released in the 70s), a 135-horse power Honda VR1000 and a 4-cylinder Yamaha 500. Piëch disposed of his motorcycles only after his wife, Ursula, badgered him to choose between motorcycles and being the chairman of the Volkswagen Group.

Piëch once attempted to have Audi manufacture motorcycles. Dampf-Kraft-Wagen of the Auto Union and NSU acquired in 1969 were motorcycle manufacturers, which implies that Audi had the skill and technology to design and produce motorcycles. In 1977, Piëch assembled a team of engineers to develop a motorcycle prototype and begin mass production, but was forced to scrap the plan by Volkswagen management. This was before Honda achieved success through motorcycles. Piëch regretted the missed opportunity. Therefore, it is easy to deduce that Piëch had a significant role in Audi's acquisition of Ducati via Lamborghini in 2012. Lamborghini bought Ducati for 1.12 million dollars, which was considered to be an overpriced deal within the industry. However, the Audi management has maintained that Ducati was worth every penny.

One of the reasons Audi proceeded with the acquisition is because Ducati is one of a handfuls of motorcycle brands that is capable of competing with BMW Motorrad, BMW's motorcycle manufacturing subsidiary.

There is no doubt that the executives of the Volkswagen Group –Piëch included – wanted Audi to become the frontrunner of the German luxury car brands, but also for Audi to become as large as Volkswagen. Such hopes are likely to be the reason they placed Lamborghini, Italdesign Giugiaro and Ducati under Audi's command. Just like the Volkswagen Group, which is striving to build a greater empire, Audi has its own aspirations for growth. There is no reason to doubt Audi's growth potential, given that Piëch's right-hand man, Volkswagen Group Chairman Martin Winterkorn, was the Chairman of the Board of Management at Audi. Moreover, Piëch's most prized employee is Rupert Stadler, who has remained the CEO of Audi since his appointment in 2007 at the age of 44.

CHAPTER 4

Volkswagen's Endless Thirst

"Volkswagen and Louis Vuitton".

At a glance, these two names have virtually nothing in common. Volkswagen is an automobile company, whereas Louis Vuitton is an apparel brand. Volkswagen produces mass production vehicles intended for the general public, while Louis Vuitton is committed to expensive, high-end products. Surprisingly, the two companies do have something in common. Their holding companies, Volkswagen AG and the LVMH Group, are considered to be behemoths of their respective industries, because they have been beefing themselves up through M&As at every given opportunity.

LVMH Group closely resembles Volkswagen, which built its empire on a series of M&As

First, we need to look at Volkswagen AG. Volkswagen AG has enough brands to make it worthy of an automobile empire - a total of 12 brands, to be exact, which includes the marquee Volkswagen, Audi, Bentley, Bugatti, Lamborghini, SEAT, Škoda, Scania, the recently acquired Porsche and MAN. It also took over Ducati. As seen above, Volkswagen AG will attempt to acquire any company, as long as it is automobile-related.

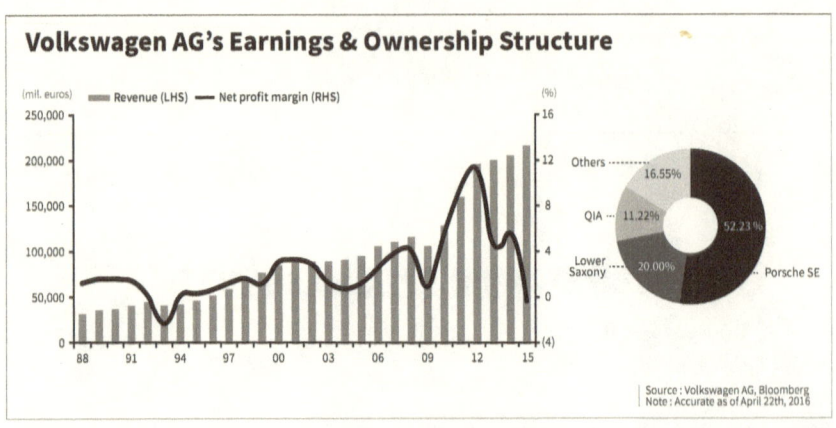

Volkswagen AG's Earnings & Ownership Structure

Source : Volkswagen AG, Bloomberg
Note : Accurate as of April 22th, 2016

The LVMH (Louis Vuitton Moët Hennessy) Group shares the same appetite. As implied by its name, the LVMH Group's business span from apparel to liquor. Thanks to the aggressive M&A efforts of Chairman Bernard Arnault, the Group owns around 60 luxury brands, which include: the prestige apparel brands Givenchy, Christian Dior, Fendi and Donna Karan and the high-end watch brand TAG Heuer, Zenith and Hublot. In 2013, the Group sought to acquire Hermès, but failed due to fierce resistance from the Hermès clan. Instead, LVMH obtained the Italian luxury brand, Bulgari. The roots of the LVMH Group lie with the high-end liquor brand, Moët Hennessy. The Group also owns Moët & Chandon, Dom Pérignon and Veuve Clicquot. LVMH also has a presence in the cosmetics sector through Guerlain, Kenzo, Make Up For Ever, Benefit, Acqua Di Parma and others.

Another common characteristic between Volkswagen AG and LVMH is that they are both still hungry for more. LVMH is currently eyeing several brands, including Hermès. Volkswagen AG is also on the lookout for potential M&A targets.

The sweet Škoda and the sour SEAT

Volkswagen AG's first acquisitions after Audi were Škoda of the Czech Republic and SEAT of Spain the, both of which are beloved automobile makers. Carl Hahn played a significant role in the acquisition of the two brands. The success story of Hahn, who headed Volkswagen for 12 years from 1982 to 1993, has become a legend among white-collar workers. Under his leadership, Volkswagen of America was able to establish a successful presence in the US. His accomplishment later got him promoted to Chairman of Volkswagen AG. When he became chairman, Hahn's focus was to make Volkswagen capable of surviving in markets other than the US. Being familiar with the US market, he was aware that Japanese automakers had risen to the mainstream in the US. Meanwhile, he acquired Škoda and SEAT to maximize output by establishing a diverse model line-up. These acquisitions also complied with the goal of establishing production facilities outside Japan.

Škoda, which was founded in 1894, has been a strong contributor since it was picked up by Volkswagen AG. In March 1991, following the collapse of communism in Eastern Europe, Škoda began its relationship with Volkswagen by forging a joint venture partnership and engaging in a share exchange, through which Volkswagen obtained a 31% stake in Škoda. By December 1994, Volkwagen had accrued a 60.3% stake in Škoda. This made Volkswagen the largest shareholder and allowed it to incorporate Škoda as its fourth brand. After increasing its stake to 70% in 1995, Volkswagen bought the remaining 30% stake from the Czech government in December, 2000, securing full ownership.

Volkswagen was entertaining the idea of buying Škoda. Renault, Fiat, GM and others were also in competition. The Czech government set forth conditions for any company that wanted to acquire Škoda : the owner must continue the Škoda brand and must not lay off any employee. Volkswagen was the only one to accept these terms.

However, Volkswagen had done its homework. At the time, the wage of a Škoda employee was 7 marks per hour, which was 10% of a Volkswagen employee's wages. Volkswagen had decided that because wages were so low, it would be cheaper to operate a large labor force than investing in plant facilities.

Soon, Škoda began establishing a market presence with prices that were cheaper than Volkswagen and with cars of outstanding quality. Volkswagen also shared chassis, engines and other inner components with Škoda, allowing it to maintain its unique identity while becoming the first automobile company in the former communist block to modernize its model line-up. Spearheaded by its flagship mid-size sedan, Octavia, Škoda began conquering the European low/mid-end automobile market, increasing its annual unit sales from 170 thousand units in 1991 to 920 thousand units in 2013.

Underneath the shadow of the flourishing Škoda, SEAT was struggling. SEAT was established as Fiat's Spanish subsidiary in 1919. It became an independent entity in 1950 and was picked up by Volkswagen before Škoda. SEAT continued to produce Fiat-licensed cars for a long time after parting with Fiat.

The relationship between Volkswagen and SEAT began with a partnership in 1982. In 1982, the Spanish government sold 75% of SEAT's shares to Volkswagen AG, who secured 99.99% ownership by 1990. In 1991, SEAT released a four-door sedan, Toledo, which was its first offering since its induction into the Volkswagen Group. The Toledo turned out to be a flop because of its inferior quality. As a result, SEAT started suffering massive losses from 1992 and became a liability for Volkswagen AG as it accounted for 93% of Volkswagen AG's losses in 1993. To make matters worse, SEAT management was constantly negligent. For instance, SEAT was operating a workforce of around 20,000 employees in 1993, but hired an additional 4,000. As a result, Piëch, who was chairman of Volkswagen AG at the time, decided to directly conduct a corporate restructuring of SEAT while establishing a task force dedicated to reviving SEAT. The restructuring resulted in unifying Volkswagen AG and SEAT's sales networks. Meanwhile, SEAT's strategic models were changed to hatchbacks and wagons, resulting in the release of the Ibiza and Cordoba in late 1993.

Soon after, SEAT welcomed Walter de Silva, who would become the design chief for Volkswagen AG and a world-renowned designer. Piëch recruited de Silva, who was working at Fiat, in 1998. De Silva designed the Leon (1999) and Ibiza (2002), which are SEAT's main sellers today. Despite the productivity of de Silva, SEAT continued to struggle, suffering subpar earnings in 2005-2006 during Spain's economic slump. Volkswagen AG announced that if SEAT was not able to generate profits by 2015, it would consider shutting down the brand and it set a global unit sales target of 800,000 by 2018. However, SEAT only manufactured 460 thousand vehicles in 2013.

There are still contradictory opinions about Carl Hahn, who was responsible for Volkswagen's acquisition of the two brands. One view holds that Hahn laid the groundwork for Volkswagen's rise into its current prominence through M&As, which allowed the Group to manufacture a wide variety of vehicles. The opposite side states that he created management issues due to strenuous M&As. Ultimately, the supervisory board voted to relieve Hahn of his post and replaced him with Piëch after Volkswagen turned in a 1.2 billion-dollar loss in 1993.

The ultimate prestige brands – Bentley and Bugatti

Unlike Škoda and SEAT, both of which cause a considerable amount of commotion, Bentley and Bugatti have been rather quiet since they joined Volkswagen AG. Bentley and Bugatti became members of the Volkswagen family in 1998.

Bentley was a company that was founded in 1912 and won France's 24 Hours of Le Mans three times in the 1920s. The company fell into troubles and was picked up by Rolls-Royce in 1931. When Vickers, which owned Rolls-Royce Motors, decided to sell Rolls-Royce in 1997, the Piëch-led Volkswagen AG engaged in a heated battle against the BMW Group to acquire the brand. After negotiations, the two agreed that the Rolls-Royce marque would go to BMW, while the Bentley marque and Rolls-Royce's plant would go to Volkswagen.

Bugatti was established in 1909, in France, by an Italian named Ettore Bugatti. Bugatti is known for the Veyron, which is recognized as the fastest car in the world after hitting a surreal top speed of 400km/h. Bugatti stopped production and closed after Ettore Bugatti passed away in 1947. The company was resurrected in 1989 as Bugatti Automobili in the hands of Italian entrepreneur, Romano Artioli, but went back out of business again in seven years. The Bugatti brand was acquired by Porsche CEO Wiedeking, but the rights were relinquished, believing it had no value. Then Piëch struck: he began buying Bugatti trademarks that had been divided and sold off at cheap prices. In May 1998, Piëch purchased Bugatti's core technology from Artioli.

After the acquisition, Volkswagen launched projects to restore Bugatti and Bentley to their former glory as ultra high-end automakers. Since then, Bugatti and Bentley have consistently contributed to improving the prestige of Volkswagen AG.

Empire adds trucks: From Scania to MAN

Even with a portfolio ranging from ultra high-end cars to low-end cars, Volkswagen AG was not satisfied. So, it expanded to trucks. One of the truck brands acquired by Volkswagen AG was the Swedish truck manufacturer, Scania. The name Scania is a reference to Skåne County (sometimes called Scania County in English) in southern Sweden, where the company was founded in 1891. Scania is the world's fourth largest truck manufacturer after Daimler AG, Volvo and Iveco.

Throughout its history, Scania has many different owners. The company merged with Vabis in 1911 and again with Saab, one of Sweden's leading automobile companies, in 1969. In 1990, Scania was separated from Saab-Scania when GM and Investor AB each accrued 50% stakes. Scania was later bought by Volvo, another one of Sweden's most prominent car manufacturers and the second largest truck marque in the world. Volvo purchased 60% of Scania shares (49% of voting rights) for 60 krona (6.926 billion dollars) in 1999. However, Volvo's attempt to merge with Scania failed as the European Commission disapproved, stating that the merger would disrupt competitive order. Later, there was a failed attempt by

Toyota to acquire Scania shares through its truck manufacturing subsidiary, Hino, in 2002. In the following year, Volvo declared it was selling a 45% stake in Scania. Toyota was again considered as a potential buyer. Unfortunately, Volkswagen had secured 18.7% of Scania shares and 34% of voting rights in 2000 as a "strategic investment," making Volkswagen the most influential shareholder. In 2008, Scania ended up in Volkswagen's hands.

MAN SE is a Germany truck manufacturer, whose origins trace back to 256 years. The company began in 1758 as the heavy industries company, St. Antony, which is recognized as the first company in history to develop and commercialize the diesel engine. The company gradually developed into MAN SE. MAN SE was one of the potential buyers of Scania, along with Toyota, in 2003 and acquired an 11.5% stake in Scania in 2006.

However, Volkswagen AG was already raking in MAN SE stakes. After a series of purchases, Volkswagen had accumulated 30.47% of MAN SE shares by 2011. In Germany, the law requires a minimum 30% stake to initiate a merger. Since MAN owned stakes in Scania, Volkswagen was able to increase its influence in both. Volkswagen went on to acquire an additional 25% stake in MAN SE in 2013. The next year, Volkswagen purchased the remaining Scania shares via tender offer, making it a fully owned subsidiary. Scania was delisted from NASDAQ and the Stockholm stock exchange in June 2014. Volkswagen AG has plans of merging Scania, MAN SE and Volkswagen's small-size truck division. Volkswagen AG is still seeking opportunities to increase its size.

The Dieselgate: Crisis befalls Volkswagen

Fueled by numerous mergers and acquisitions, the locomotive that is Volkswagen seemed to be cruising. Crisis fell upon the company in September 2015, when the US EPA ordered a recall on 482 thousand diesel-engine cars. According to the EPA, the automobile giant had been manipulating the software on its emission control system to meet US environmental regulations. The software enabled the gas reduction system only when being tested and disabled the system at other times. EPA tests revealed that actual nitric oxide substance emissions were 40 times the EPA's requirement.

One of the main causes of the scandal is the unique governance structure of German enterprises, in which the supervisory board meddled too deeply with management affairs. This created controversy over privatization of the company. The resulting dispute between the supervisory and management boards caused the problem to exacerbate. Board members were busy taking sides in internal power struggles. Many people believe that the chasm caused the lurking issue to surface and prevented management from responding quickly enough.

German enterprises have a management board comprising management officers and a supervisory board, whose members are major shareholders. The two boards would counterbalance each other and ensure transparent management – the management board runs the company, while the supervisory board keeps them in check. Volkswagen's supervisory board has 20 members – five from the Porsche and Piëch families, two from the Lower Saxony government, two from the Qatar sovereign fund and 10 from the labor union. The last member is the SEB CEO Annika Falkengren, the only member without any interest in the Group.

Ferdinand Piëch had the supervisory board under this thumb for over two decades until he resigned as chairmanship in April 2015. Piëch was attempting to oust CEO Martin Winterkorn, whose loyalty was considered to be with Piëch, when opposition from the labor union and Lower Saxony board members caused his plans to backfire. The dominant speculation is that Wolfgang Porsche's support of Winterkorn was the reason for the board opposing Piëch. However, the Dieselgate scandal forced Winterkorn to resign five months later. Winterkorn was succeeded by the Piëch-loyalist Matthias Müller, the then CEO of Porsche.

As a result of the scandal, Volkswagen decided to recall 11 million diesel vehicles suspected of manipulation. On behalf of the EPA, the US

Department of Justice filed a civil lawsuit against Volkswagen, spawning a series of class action suits around the world. Crisis had befallen the diesel empire - two months after it had fulfilled its dream of becoming the world's leading automobile manufacturer.

Industry-Altering Event #1

World War I

"Bang! Bang! Bang!"

The gun shots echoing throughout the Balkans signaled the beginning of a war that engulfed the entire world in flames. On a June day in 1914, the 19-year-old Serbian, Gavrilo Princip, shot Austrian Archduke Franz Ferdinand and his wife. A month later, Austria declared war against Serbia and thus, started World War I. WWI is a significant event in world history as well as in the automobile history.

Once war broke out, automobile companies in participating countries began manufacturing military vehicles and aircraft engines, accelerating advances in technology. One of the best examples is Germany. Daimler and Mercedes-Benz began producing military vehicles, while Dixi, which would later become the automobile division of BMW, transformed its factory into a military equipment plant. BMW was founded in 1916, during the height of the war, as a manufacturer of V12 fighter plane engines. Without WWI, BMW may have remained an aircraft engine manufacturer.

The situation was similar for France's leading automobile marques. Renault produced FT-17 tanks and other military equipment, while Peugeot operated as a defense manufacturer supplying military bicycles and vehicles, tanks, ammunition and weapons. In the US, Cadillac committed itself to manufacturing aircraft engines and machinery parts until the war ended.

In some instances, the vestige of WWI is found in emblems. For example, Ferrari's emblem, the prancing horse, originated from Baracca's Cavallino, the iconic horse painted on the fuselage of the fighter plane flown by Italian WWI fighter pilot and war hero, Francesco Baracca.

The opportunity to found Toyota came during WWI. Sakichi Toyoda, father of Toyota founder Kiichiro Toyoda, made his fortune by running a textile business during WWI. During WWI, Britain's textile exports decreased and the Japanese economy flourished by filling the void. In his will, Sakichi Toyoda left his wealth to his son Kiichiro and bade him to commit to developing automobiles.

When WWI ended in 1918, Renault of France, a member of the Allied forces that had won the war, had grown into one of the largest companies in the world. During the war, Renault had expanded its production to buses and trucks. As a result, the company enjoyed a surge in demand after the armistices were signed. On the other hand, German companies suffered from the extreme economic struggles that ensued after losing the war: financial troubles forced Daimler and Benz to merge and form Daimler-Benz AG, while BMW turned to motorcycles and automobiles to survive.

The true beneficiary was the US. While Western Europe was left in ruins, the US was able to use its massive resources and advanced technology to implement economic growth measures, allowing it to become the center of the global economy. By the late 1920s, the US had over 30 million vehicles operating, with one out of four Americans owning a car. With the US having developed into the world's largest market, it was natural for GM, Ford and Chrysler to achieve great success.

EMPIRE II

General Motors

CHAPTER 5

Cars for All: The GM Odyssey

"What's good for General Motors is good for the country." GM CEO Charles Erwin Wilson said to the Senate Armed Forces Committee during his confirmation hearing in 1952, after getting nominated as the US Secretary of Defense. This adequately summarizes GM's 108-year history in a single sentence. GM led the industry in unit sales for 77 straight years since 1931, when it first reached the top. This is a feat that no other automobile company will be able to match. The 77 years overlaps with the US's advances as the world's largest superpower.

A look into the history of GM shows that it is the true champion of M&As, not Volkswagen. Just as the US absorbed capital, cultures and corporations from around the world to grow, GM increased its size by absorbing – and, at times, discarding – dozens of automotive corporations from various corners of the globe. However, the fallout from such efforts pushed GM to the brink of bankruptcy when the US economy began to falter in the wake of the subprime meltdown of 2008. During this period, GM was forced to shut down eight of its 12 brands. The four remaining flagship brands were Chevrolet, Cadillac, GMC and Buick.

This was one of the largest restructuring efforts in the history of the automobile industry. At the time, no one in the global automobile industry foresaw the collapse of the GM empire. There was no question that the restructuring would leave the dominions of the GM empire in ruins. Yet, contrary to GM's plans, seven brands – not four - survived the crisis. As a result, GM's unit sales recovered to previous levels once the US economy began to recover.

Throughout GM's history, "car guys," who placed products - cars, in GM's case – at the center of their management strategies, and "bean counters," whose sole focus was profits, took turns heading the company. And each time the regime changed, GM underwent major ups and downs.

Born of M&As: Billy's enterprise hunt

GM was born from M&As. Its founder, William Durant (1861-1947), was the owner of Flint Road Cart Company. Durant took his first step into the automobile industry when he acquired the financially troubled Buick in 1904. Thus began Durant's near-gamble, M&A-oriented management. As the chairman of the board at Buick, Durant increased the company's capital from 75,000 dollars to 300,000 dollars. He also ordered a large increase in production. In just four years of Durant heading the company, output had increased from 28 vehicles per year to 8,820 vehicles per year, making Buick the second largest automobile manufacturer after Ford. This established the foundation for the enterprise that would become General Motors.

On September 16, 1908, GM was born with Buick at the base and the acquisition of Oldsmobile. Its stocks were soon listed on the stock market. In the following year, Durant brought in 13 automobile companies and 10 automotive parts companies, including Cadillac, Elmore, Reliance Motor Truck and Rapid Motor Vehicle (predecessor of GMC Truck), transforming GM into a conglomerate. The name General Motors is a reference to the accommodation of "all things related to motor vehicles."

Durant was a natural-born businessman with an unrivaled knack for raising funds. He used technology patents to raise funds needed for acquiring other companies and used patents owned by GM and patent registration records to issue new stocks and used them to attract more funds. In 1908, GM acquired the prestige brand Cadillac for 4.75 million dollars, which was an exceptionally high price at the time. Due to his repeated success, Durant became known as 'Automobile Billy' within the industry.

M&As are effective for increasing the size of a company in a short period. On the other hand, they have the potential of pushing the company into danger, making them somewhat of a "winner's curse" – which is an accurate depiction of Durant's business management. Durant's business expansions had no boundaries as long as it made money. In 1910, GM invested in a power company called Heany Lamp to obtain its tungsten-filament bulb patent. However, the patent proved to be worthless, causing GM to suffer 12 million dollars in losses. In response, GM's share price plunged from 100 dollars to 25 dollars. The excessive M&A attempts caused GM financial issues, forcing Durant to hand the company over to his creditors in 1910, within just two years since founding the company.

Durant was left empty handed, but refused to give up. He finally met his savior: the famous race car driver and engineer Louis Chevrolet (1878-1941). Partnering with Chevrolet, Durant founded the Chevrolet Motor Car company on November 3, 1911, to set the stage for a comeback. Durant succeeded, as the Chevrolet 490 – released in 1914 – was an immediate success. Durant used the profits from 490 sales to buy GM stocks in secret. By 1916, Chevrolet Motor Car Company had become GM's largest shareholder. Having regained the reins to GM, Durant merged Chevrolet and GM, concluding his triumphant return.

However, the glory did not last long. Durant possessed the talent for growing a business, but was in apt at running a business stably. Once again, GM began to struggle financially due to the poor sales of its new models, and for a second time in 1920, Durant had to relinquish command and was never able to return. Up until this point, Durant had acquired 39 companies.

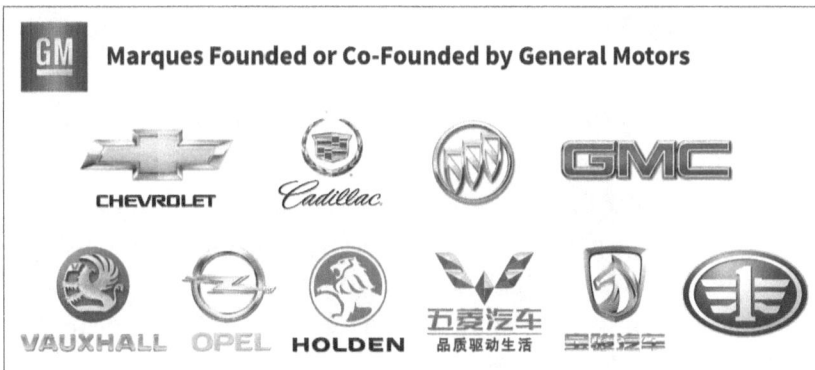

Durant established Durant Motors in 1921 to regain glory, but the company collapsed after the Great Depression broke out in 1929. In 1933, Durant liquidated Durant Motors and spent the remainder of his life running a bowling alley. Louis Chevrolet's final days were equally humble. Chevrolet left Chevrolet Motor Car after clashing with Durant, who wanted to make cars for the general public. After leaving the company, he attempted to design racing cars and airplane engines, but was unsuccessful. He died from overwork while working as an engineer at a Chevrolet plant to earn a living.

Sloanism beats Fordism

While Durant was a natural born entrepreneur, Alfred Sloan was an MIT-trained engineer who used his engineering knowledge to mold GM into the largest automaker in the world. Sloan was the closest thing to a true "car guy."

Sloan began his career at Hyatt Roller Bearings Company and was CEO by 1899. In 1918, Sloan took over Durant's GM and became the vice president. He was appointed chairman of GM when Durant left in 1923 and commanded the company until 1956, after which he remained honorary chairman until he passed away in 1966. Upon his death, Sloan donated his entire wealth, which equaled the value of 1% of GM's common shares, earning him respect until this day. MIT even has a MBA school named after him – the Sloan School. In numerous aspects, Sloan's life contrasts with Durant's.

Sloan's management prowess shone as he overcame the economic slump in the 1920s and turned in profit during the Great Depression of the 1930s. During World War II, GM doubled its cash flow and working capital by supplying military equipment. Thanks to its contributions, GM was able to increase its output from 1 million units in 1926 to over 4 million units in 1955. The company's pretax profit jumped from a mere 100 million in 1925 to 1 billion in 1949. The GM share price also reflected Sloan's skills in managing a major conglomerate. GM's share price stood at 13 dollars per share in 1922, one year before Sloan became chairman. After 25 years under Sloan's leadership, the value of GM shares had reached 112 dollars by 1947.

Sloan initiated a fundamental change within the company. He devised a strategy in which GM's weakness would become its strength. At the time, GM's main competitor was Ford. Ford was committed to a single model, the Model T, whereas GM had a variety of brands and models. Sloan defined his management principle as manufacturing "a car for every purse and purpose" and began a complete overhaul of the company's product strategy. Cadillac was designated the high-end brand, Buick and Oldsmobile the mid-end brands and Pontiac and Chevrolet the low-end brands. Fortune magazine described GM's product line-up as: Chevrolets for the common people; Pontiacs for the people with low income, but strong self-esteem; Oldsmobiles for people that are careful and capable of enjoying the better things in life; Buicks for ambitious politicians; and Cadillacs for the wealthy.

This marketing strategy created a massive sensation in the market as consumers, tired of Ford's one-size-fits-all Model T, began turning to GM. From this point on, GM entered a growth track. GM's US market share was less than half of Ford's in 1923. By 1931, GM had beaten Ford in terms of domestic market share. GM maintained a market share of at least 40% in the US between 1933 and 1985.

Sloan also made consumers wary of GM cars by continuing to roll out models with better performance and aesthetics than existing ones. This planned obsolescence strategy, which is common today, was revolutionary at the time. Scholars named Sloan's strategy Sloanism and concluded that Sloanism had beaten Henry Ford's Fordism, which focused on mass production.

Crisis relapses under the shadow of the overpowering CEO

Sloanism had changed the consumption patterns of US consumers: the average length of vehicle ownership in the US fell from five years in 1934 to two years in 1950. Automakers continued to spew out new models to lure consumers into buying automobiles. GM rolled out 55 new models in 1955 alone. The number skyrocketed to 138 by 1963. GM's Sloanism began to spread through the industry like wildfire. As a result, the number of new models released in the US market surged from 272 models in 1934 to 429 in 1963.

In addition to diversifying GMs a result, the number of new models released in the US market surged from 272 models as audacious as Durant, but never hesitated to approach M&A opportunities if needed. In particular, Sloan was eager to takeover local automobile companies to establish presences in new markets. Such attempts include the Vauxhall (UK) acquisition in 1925, the Adam Opel AG (Germany) acquisition in 1929 and Holden (Australia) acquisition in 1931.

Thanks to his legendary management skills, GM grew exponentially during Sloan's reign. As with everyone, Sloan was not without his faults. In running the company, Sloan demanded absolute obedience from subordinates, causing management to blindly focus on diversifying the company's model line-up and maximizing profits. Mid-level managers became passive and only acted upon orders from executives. As this culture began settling in, GM began to lose its competitive edge. Meanwhile, bean counters began to gain control.

CHAPTER 6

Bean Counters vs. Car Guys

Cadillac Eldorado vs. Pontiac Aztec

If someone were to ask me to name the best car among GM's vast model line-up, I would pick the 1959 Cadillac Eldorado without hesitation. As for the worst car in GM history, I would put the 2001 Pontiac Aztec at the top of my list.

The Eldorado was designed by the legendary car designer, Harley Earl, whom Sloan personally recruited. The Eldorado was five meters in length and sported an exaggerated tailfin, inspired by Lockheed's P-38 fighter plane. Meanwhile, the Pontiac Aztec was an SUV that shocked people with its bizarre frontal design, which looked as if two separate vehicles were surgically combined. Just like the Aztec Empire that fell in the 16th century, the Aztec faded into history and left GM in ruins.

The Eldorado and Aztec demonstrate the distinct difference between cars conceived when bean counters are heading the company and when car guys are running the company. After Sloan's regime ended, bean counters began running GM. The bean counters ended up endangering the very existence of the company, causing GM to file for bankruptcy protection in 2009. Ironically, Sloan was responsible for laying the foundation that led to the bean counters' rise to power.

"The curse of sloan"

Sloan succeeded GM founder Durant as the chief executive and transformed the company into a massive empire. Sloan's product strategy – having brands focus on a specific customer class and develop cars that appeal to them - has become an industry norm. Sloan was praised inside and outside the industry for his market segmentation strategy and the decentralized organization management method to support his strategy. Hence, Sloan became known as the "father of modern business management theories."

Meanwhile, GM entered its golden years in the 60s when William Mitchell succeeded Harley Earl as the chief of design at GM and designed classics, such as the Pontiac GTO and Oldsmobile 442. In 1965, a French government-run broadcasting station aired a program titled *"General Motors: le budget dela France*(the budget of France)." At the time, GM's sales were larger than France's annual budget.

Under Sloan's 44-year monarchical reign (1923-1966), GM's decision making system became rigid. In addition, the standardized work processes robbed employees of their adventurous spirits and made them complacent. Although organization management was decentralized to support Sloan's market segmentation strategy, high level executives continued to plan and allocate budgets and make important personnel-related decisions. This culture persisted after Sloan's days at GM. The culture itself may not have been an issue, but the problem was that there was no one else to lead the company with the wisdom and charisma Sloan had. As a result, the growing consensus within GM was that since GM cars were selling well thanks to the company's 40%-plus market share, the company should focus on maximizing profit. This conceit began spreading throughout the company like poison.

Bean counters endanger GM

Like Sloan, Bill Mitchell was dedicated to making cars that appealed to people. After Mitchell retired in 1977, control over product development was transferred from the design department to the product planning department, which was entirely composed of people from financial, accounting and legal departments. The product planning department placed emphasis on the results of market analyses. Based on the results of market studies, the product planning department demanded car designs comply with standards that specified the exterior and interior size of each model in millimeters. Under the glorious mission of cutting costs, the department ordered that roofs and doors of a single design be used by multiple brands, discouraging any chance of innovative and aesthetically pleasing designs.

At times, the department would intentionally lower quality, saying "Since this model was unnecessarily well made, the next model should be mediocre. Consumers will still be satisfied, and profits will increase." Any other time, this statement would have seemed asinine. But with GM on the highway to success, it may have been persuasive to the company's management because they actually decided to do so. Cutting production costs and investments did bring higher profits for a while, but GM soon lost consumers' trust. They had lost so much, to gain so little.

Internal follies were not the only cause of GM's downfall – external factors also played a role. Consumers' trust in GM was damaged in 1965 when consumer advocate Ralph Nader published "Unsafe at Any Speed," which pointed out the defects of the Chevrolet Corvair. The 1973 oil shock in 1973 was also a major hit: the US government raised mileage requirements, forcing GM to spend billions of dollars to reduce the weight and size of its cars. The efforts caused significant changes in GM cars, like the shift from rear-wheel-drive to front-wheel-drive. Given that GM managed to turn in profits during the Great Depression, one can make the case that internal follies had a larger influence than external hits.

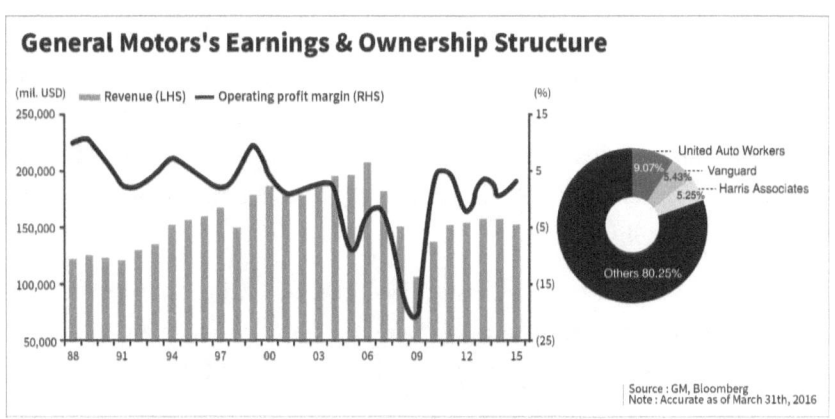

General Motors's Earnings & Ownership Structure

To make matters worse, Toyota, Honda and Nissan began to rapidly expand their presence in the US market. GM cars were unable to compete with Japanese imports. Consumers began to say that imports were better than the poorly made US cars. This was soon perceived as the truth.

GM's touch of ruin

GM and Volkswagen AG are both active pursuers of M&As. However, Volkswagen has shown caution in acquiring brands, while GM's M&A strategy has always been retain anything good and reject anything that is not. GM's approach to M&As seemed to reflect the company's tendency to focus more on the number of brands than the value and products offered by the brand.

When acquiring a company, Volkswagen AG exerts effort into imbuing life in the branding life in any, Volkswagen AG exerts effort. However, Volkoducts Volkswagen also does all it can to ensure that it is able to sell the brand off when needed, although it has never sold any of its brands.

GM shows a clear difference from the Volkswagen Group. A good example of this is Saab, which was founded in 1937 as an aircraft manufacturer. After World War II, the company transformed into an automobile company and produced its first model, 92001, in 1947. Saab made its mark in the industry with its technological prowess and reliability. It was the first in the world to use turbo charged engines in cars. In 1969,

Saab merged with the truck manufacturer Scania-Vabis and emerged as the Saab-Scania Group. However, it began to struggle from poor sales and rising wages in Sweden. Afterwards, Saab was separated from the Saab-Scania Group when it sold 50% of its shares to GM (remaining 50% held by Investor AB) in January 1990. In January 2000, GM bought the remaining shares for 640 million dollars.

In 1998, Saab released its masterpiece, the 9-3, which was a sensation among Saab enthusiasts. Ironically, Saab has yet to produce any model of significance since it became a fully owned subsidiary of GM. The 2009 9-5 TiD received positive reviews, but GM had already lost interest in Saab, as it was negotiating a deal to sell Saab to the Swedish supercar company, Koenigsegg. In the end, GM sold Saab to the Dutch car company Spyker for 74 million dollars in February 2010.

Through a controversial deals in 2002, GM acquired Daewoo Motors (currently GM Korea) for a bargain price of 136 million dollars. The Daewoo marque was discontinued after the company's name was changed in 2011. Other GM brands that vanished into history include Oldsmobile, Pontiac, Saturn and Hummer. So, it is easy to conclude that GM had a touch of ruin when it came to M&As.

GM has been equally extravagant when it comes to partnerships. GM has been a part owner of Isuzi, Suzuki, Subaru and Fiat. At one point, it formed a partnership with Toyota, which is now a strong competitor in GM's push for global hegemony. Aside from Isuzu and Fiat, which contributed to GM's diesel engine technology, most of GM's partnerships ended without any significant gains. The most recent example is GM's partnership with the French automakers PSA. In February 2012, GM purchased a 7% stake in PSA and planned approximately 40 joint projects, which included the sharing of a new compact car platform. However, plans were downsized significantly. In short, GM has been repeating this prodigal act of recklessly engaging in M&As and partnerships in pursuit of near-term gains and scrapping ties upon realizing it had made the wrong decision.

Car guy Bob Lutz steps up as reliever, but fails to save the day

GM's US market share edged near 50% at one point, but by 2000, it had plunged to 27%. In 2011, in an attempt to save the sinking ship, GM Chairman Rick Wagoner recruited a reliever: the car guy, Bob Lutz.

> "Success comes only from manufacturing outstanding products and the strategy for making outstanding products stems from a passion for the product. A company will lose its way and drift if it begins to obsess over numbers and graphs to cut costs."

This is a quote from *Car Guys vs Bean Counters: The Battle for the Soul of American Business* written by Lutz - a living legend in the auto industry, who started his career at GM during its heyday (1963-1971) and moved on become the vice chairman of BMW (1971-1974), vice chairman of Ford (1974-1986) and the vice chairman of Chrysler (1986-1998).

At the request of Wagoner, Lutz became the vice chairman of product development at GM and focused on improving the competitiveness and quality of products. Under his leadership, GM produced a number of vehicles well received by consumers, such as the Cadillac CTS, the Buick Lacrosse, the Chevrolet Camaro and the Chevrolet Equinox. Upon the 2007 release of the Volt, Chevrolet's plug-in hybrid, GM seemed to be reliving its past glory.

However, the "Car Guy" Bob Lutz was unable to save GM from the inevitable, as the financial crisis that swept through the world in 2008 threatened to erase GM's "eternal empire" from existence

CHAPTER 7

The Fall and Resurrection of the GM Empire

The most humiliating moment in GM's 106-year history came on June 1, 2009. This was the day GM filed for Chapter 11 in the New York federal bankruptcy court just before the stock market opened. At the time, GM possessed 82 billion dollars in assets, making it the fourth largest bankruptcy in US history and the largest bankruptcy for a manufacturing company. This was the fall of a giant: a company that had led the world in unit sales for 77 years (1931-2007). Inside and outside GM, "end of days" and "disintegration" were used to describe GM's situation.

We move three years forward to January 31, 2012, at the 2012 Washington Auto Show. President Barack Obama got into a GM Silverado and raised his thumb. One week before this moment, Obama said, during his Union Address, "Today, General Motors is back on top as the world's number-one automaker…. And tonight, the American auto industry is back." GM had staged a glorious comeback.

Between 2008 and 2012, GM had plunged to hell and rose back to the heavens. GM proved that it was a powerhouse by bouncing back to the world's number one automaker in just two years after filing for Chapter 11. However, during GM's struggle, bean counters had emerged into power. They dismantled Saab, Hummer, Saturn and Pontiac, closed 14 factories showing low profitability and laid off 21,000 employees. GM's restructuring is still in progress in Korea and numerous areas around the world. The company was recovering quickly, but underneath the surface, a wrecking crew was wreaking havoc faster than they could rebuild.

From General Motors to Government Motors

Once a company files for Chapter 11, it enters a court-supervised workout, during which it extends the deadline for repaying its debts and attempts to undergo restructuring to revive itself. Upon seeking Chapter 11 protection, GM was placed at the mercy of the bankruptcy court – and by extension, the federal government.

GM's collapse was not a complete surprise. It had recorded an operating loss of 31 billion dollars in 2008 and accumulated a total loss of 82 billion dollars between 2005 and 2008. GM's struggle began when the surge of oil prices (0.5 dollars/liter to 1.2 dollars/liter) undermined sales of gas-guzzling, large-sized vehicles. But, the knockout blow was delivered by the collapse of the subprime mortgage market in 2008. One may think that automobile manufacturers would not be directly affected by the subprime mortgage market, but GM was an exception, because it had invested a large amount of money in Residential Capital, the mortgage financing subsidiary of GMAC, GM's car finance unit. When the subprime mortgage market was booming, the money invested in Residential Capital was more profitable than the automobile sales division. This setup was also the brain child of the profit-focused bean counters.

The foundation of GM's very existence was threatened by the financial crisis entailed by the subprime mortgage meltdown. GM was losing 5 billion dollars in cash every three months. With its cash reserve depleting quickly, GM turned to the government for help. In exchange for a government bailout, GM released a full-page advertisement apologizing for strategic mishaps, including biasing its "product mix toward pick-up trucks and SUVs," and promising to do better. In the same year, GM yielded its position as the world's largest automaker to Toyota. This marketed the beginning of GM's mortification.

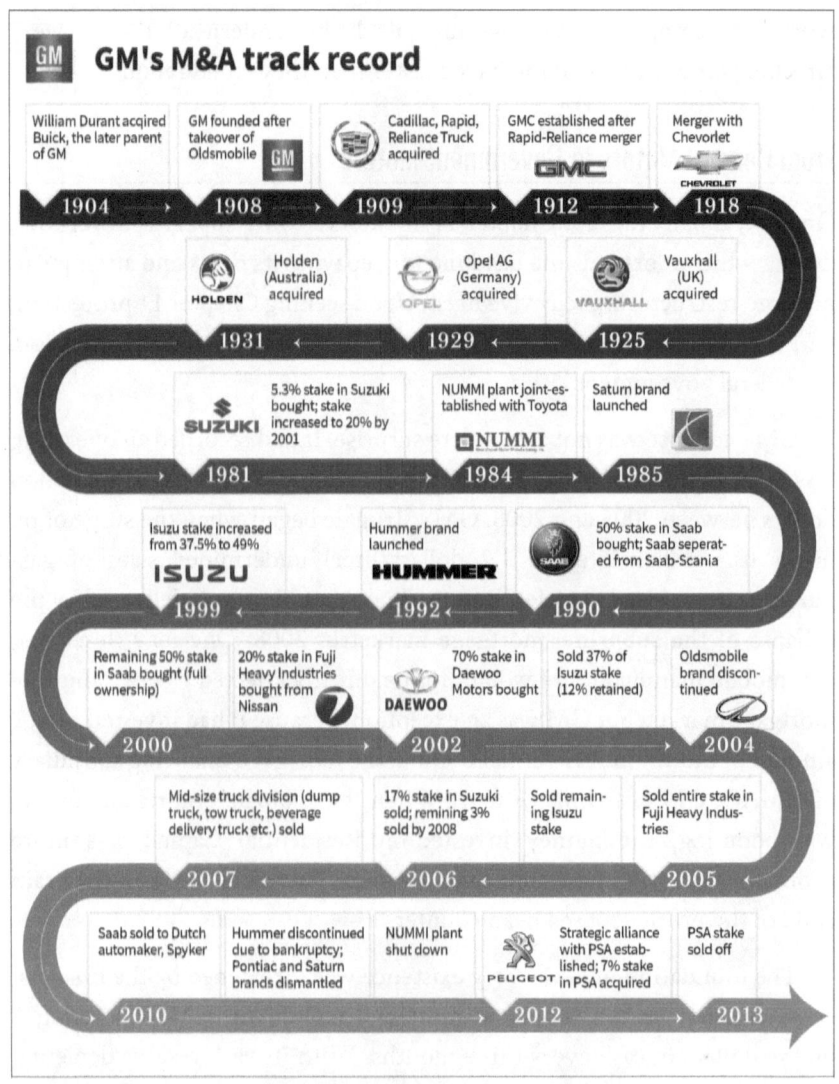

The US government supplied 52 billion dollars to GM - of which 45.3 billion was converted into stocks, giving it a 60.8% stake. The Canadian government also extended a 10 billion-dollar loan, of which 8.6 billion was converted into shares for an 11.7% ownership.

GM's creditors owned 10% of GM shares and the UAW (United Automobile Workers) Retiree Medical Benefits Trust the remaining 17.5%.

GM shares were delisted in June 2009. At the time of the delisting, GM shares were worth less than a dollar.

Throughout the industry, people mocked GM for becoming nationalized for the first time in its history, saying that GM was now an acronym for "Government Motors."

UAW and medical insurance wears down GM

The UAW was a major cause of GM's financial troubles. The headstrong UAW had been pressing GM, Ford and Chrysler every year for increase in wages and medical benefits. The labor union also demanded factories operate at 80% capacity or higher, regardless of unit sales, and that 95% of average wages be paid to any laid off employee for five years. The UAW also had a program of providing life-long annuity payment and family medical insurance coverage to retirees. During the 15 years between 1993 and 2007, GM had spent 107 billion dollars in welfare benefits to UAW members, which had earned GM the nickname Generous Motors.

With the company vulnerable, the UAW also took a step back as it decided that members would be better off forfeiting some benefits than losing their jobs altogether because the company had gone under. As a result, the UAW agreed to a revised labor contract. The new terms included the freezing of wages, forfeiting of incentives and reduction of medical benefits to retirees. The new terms were put for vote, and UAW members approved the changes on May 29, 2009. However, it was too late to save GM from its pending doom, as the company filed for Chapter 11 protection three days later.

Lightning-fast restructuring

In June 2009, the Obama Administration put the hammer down, and GM entered a swift and decisive restructuring program. In essence, the program was focused on categorizing GM assets into good assets and bad assets – the bad assets would be sold or dismantled, the good assets would be reborn as the "New GM." The government decided to sell or discontinue all GM brands, except for Chevrolet, Cadillac, GMC and Buick because they were turning profits. GM Europe sold the German brand Opel and the British brand Vauxhall to Magna, an automotive parts company based in Canada. Hummer was to be picked up by the Chinese heavy machinery company, Sichuan Tengzhong. Saab, Saturn and Pontiac were set to be sold or dismantled.

Of course, not all plans were carried out. GM was forced to retain Opel and Vauxhall because of pressure from the media and the government officials of the brands' home countries (Germany and UK). The sale of Hummer fell through due to opposition from the Chinese government – the brand was discontinued after the 2,200 stockpiled cars were sold at discounted prices. Saab, Saturn and Pontiac disappeared into history.

Labor unions also contributed to normalizing operations. New employment contracts were signed, lowering the average wages of employees from 78 dollars/hour to 45 dollars/hour, which was similar to the wages of workers at the US plants of Toyota and other foreign automakers. The unions also accepted the company's overhaul, which resulted in workforce of GM's North American plants getting cut from 90,000 to 69,000, the number of plants reduced from 47 to 31 and the dealership network streamlined from 5,900 to 3,600. Welfare benefits to retirees were also diminished significantly. As a result of such sacrifices, GM managed to reduce labor costs from 7.6 billion dollars in 2009 to 5.0 billion in 2011 and an anticipated 4.1 billion in 2014.

GM resurrects with the US, but wrecking crew still at work

While the government-led workout progressed, restructuring experts were focused on rebuilding the company's management. Wagoner, who had been chairman for eight years by this point, was pressured to resign because the corporate workout plan he submitted was considered to be insufficient. Wagoner resigned from his post on March 30, 2009. Wagoner was succeeded by GM's then chief operating officer, Fritz Henderson. After eight months as chairman, Henderson left GM on December 1st of the same year at the demand of the board of directors. Edward Whitacre, who was chairman of the board at the time, assumed the position for nine months, before yielding it to Daniel Akerson on September 1, 2010. Akerson was a finance guy that had worked as the chief of global M&As at the Carlyle Group. Recognized his prowess in financial and organizational management, he was named to the board of directors as a representative of the Department of Treasury. The man was a typical bean counter, with absolutely no experience in automobile manufacturing. However, not all bean counters that headed GM pushed the company into ruin. Akerson ran the company for three years, during which GM won back its place as the largest automobile company in the world. GM returned unit sales to previous levels by selling compact cars instead of large-sized cars. GM stocks were relisted at 33 dollars per share on November 18, 2010. Since then, the US government gradually reduced its 31% stake in GM. Finally, on December 10, 2013, the federal government sold off its remaining 2.2% stake, marking the end of GM's workout.

In order to look after his sick wife, Akerson left GM on January 14, 2014, nearly a year earlier than expected, though he would soon return as the vice chairman of the Carlyle Group. Nevertheless, Akerson was succeeded by Mary Barra, who was the then Executive Vice President of Global Product Development, Purchasing and Supply Chain and the first female CEO in GM history. Barra was an engineer and, by extension, a car woman.

During the 2014 North American International Auto Show held in Detroit in January 2014, Barra announced the 2015 GMC Canyon and promised that GM would strive to dominate in all markets and in every vehicle segment by producing new models that exceed consumer expectations.

Ironically, Barra came under fire as various vehicle defects began to arise the following month, which forced GM to recall over 30 million vehicles in 2014 alone. The number of recalls included vehicles with faulty ignition systems, of which GM was already aware, but had kept under the rug for the past decade. To summarize, Akerson got the company back on track via thorough restructuring under the protection of the Obama Administration, while Barra was left to tackle all of the vehicle defects that did not surface previously. In accordance with Akerson's road map, GM had closed the Holden's production plant in Australia, discontinued the Chevrolet marque in Europe, reduced GM Korea's output and accepted voluntary early retirement.

The decision complied with bean counters' logic of dismantling any business that was not profitable. Yet, the company retained its flexibility. GM became the first automaker to form a partnership with a car share service business in January, 2016, when it invested 500 million dollars in Lyft, a startup company competing with Uber. GM had a representative on Lyft's board of directors and gained access to Lyft's software. GM also became the primary car supplier for the startup.

With regard to the defective spark plugs used in GM vehicles, Mary Barra regained the trust of investors and employees by agreeing to pay 900 million dollars in compensation with the Department of Justice and 600 million to the families of 124 victims, while decisively stating that the issue would be resolved. Heralded as the vanguard leading GM's revival, Barra was unanimously voted as Chairwoman of GM in January 2016, a year after being appointed CEO. As a result, she etched her name in history as the first woman in GM's 105-year history to hold the position of both CEO and chairwoman at the same time. She also became the first woman to head a global automobile manufacturer.

Groundbreaking Classics #1

Karl Benz's Patent Motorwagen and Henry Ford's Model T

Only one vehicle can assume the title of "the first car in the world." The Patent Motorwagen stands at the beginning of the change from horse-drawn carriages to motorized vehicles. It also marks the genesis of the automobile industry.

The Patent Motorwagen was invented by Dr. Karl Benz. Dr. Benz established the world's first automobile factory, Benz & Cie, in Mannheim, Germany, in October 1883. The production of the Patent Motorwagen began in 1885 on the back of the mission to produce a "carriage that moves without a horse." On January 29, 1886, Dr. Benz received a patent for the vehicle in Berlin, Germany. The patent number was 37435. The name Patent Motorwagen essentially means "patented motorized wagon," which seems fitting for the name of the world's first motorized vehicle.

On July 3rd of the same year, the Patent Motorwagen underwent its first long-distance test drive - a 103-kilometer course from Mannheim to Pforzheim. Surprisingly, the driver was not Dr. Benz, but his wife, Bertha Benz, which means that the world's first long-distance drive in a motorized vehicle was done by a woman.

The Patent Motorwagen used a 954cc single-cylinder gasoline engine developed by Nikolaus Otto, which produced 0.75 horse power and drop 10km per liter. The three-wheeled vehicle had a top speed of 16km/h, which was slow, but faster than the average walking speed of 4km/h. A rack steering system, which converted rotational motion into linear motion, was applied. It also was equipped with steel-spoke wheels, a chassis and an engine. The engine had many features found in model internal combustion engines, such as an electric ignition system and a cooling system. The vehicle weighed 265kg, with the engine weighing over 100kg.

Later, Émile Roger, a French engineer, received the diagram for the Patent Motorwagen and began selling them in France in1888. The world's first car was made by a German, but was first sold in France. France became the first market for motorized vehicles, because it had the world's most advanced transportation system at the time. In March 1893, the Frenchman Emile Levassor received the world's first driver's license after passing the test conducted by the Paris police. Test criteria were pulling out, driving and turns. The license was as big as a picture frame.

While Karl Benz invented the first motorized vehicle, Henry Ford was the first to popularize them. In 1908, 22 years after the Patent Motorwagen was introduced, Ford released Model T. Ford designed the Model T with a simple structure and shape to make assembly easy. In 1913, inspired by disassembly lines used in meat processing plants, Ford developed the conveyor belt system to accelerate mass production, leading to the birth of Fordism. The Model T was offered in only black because black paint required the shortest amount of time to dry – an indication of Ford's obsession with mass production.

The Model T was powered by a 2,900cc four-cylinder engine producing 20 horse powers and a top speed of 60km/h. The car was priced at 825 dollars, less than half of an average car (2,000 dollars) at the time. Thanks to the affordable price, Ford sold over 15 million Model Ts until it was discontinued in 1927.

This was the beginning of motorization, the phenomenon in which automobiles became a necessity in our everyday lives.

EMPIRE III

Toyota

CHAPTER 8

From Looms to Cars: Toyota's 90 Years of Innovation

In the fashion industry, the Louis Vuitton Monogrammed Speedy bags were known as the "3-second bag," meaning it was seen every three seconds on the street. In the auto industry, the cars of one company earned the nickname "3-second cars." That company was Toyota. Toyota sold 9.98 million cars in 2013, which translates to one car sold every three seconds. In 2013, Toyota sold the largest number of cars, beating Volkswagen AG (9.73 million) and GM (9.71 million) by more than 0.2 million units. Toyota's unit sales stood out among the heavily competing top three automakers in 2014, Toyota sold 10.23 million units and became the first automobile company to pass the 10 million mark. The company sold 10.15 million cars in 2015, defending its position as the leading car manufacturer against heavy competition from the VW Group and GM.

To fully grasp the significance of the "3-second car," it needs to be this way. Between its release in 1966 and July 2007, Toyota sold over 40 million units of its subcompact/compact sedan, Corolla, meaning that a Corolla was sold every 40 seconds for 46 years. The Corolla is listed in the Guinness Book of World Records as the bestselling nameplate in the world.

Despite having the capacity to produce 10 million units per year, Toyota has a relatively smaller number of brands than Volkswagen and GM, because it was not as eager to jump at M&A opportunities as the other two.

Toyota's current marque line-up consists of Toyota and Lexus at the forefront and Daihatsu, Hino and Scion filling the niches.

Toyota has yet to engage in any cross-border deals to acquire brands, but it did take over two local ones. It incorporated Hino Motors as a subsidiary in 1966. Daihatsu also became a subsidiary in September 1998, after Toyota purchased more than half of its shares via tender offers. In 1984, it joined hands with GM to build the NUMMI plant, an endeavor that ended as a joint-manufacturing factory for their respective vehicles. Aside from M&A deals to strengthen its weak commercial vehicle and small-sized vehicle line-ups, Toyota preferred to create new marques - Lexus and Scion – to wage its war against its multinational competitors. Eventually, it reached the top, becoming number one in output in 2007 and in units sold in 2008.

Toyota was founded as Toyoda Automatic Loom Works in 1926 and became Toyota Motor in 1937. Throughout its history, one word has remained a constant: innovation. *Kaizen* (improvement) and JIT (just in time) represent the company's unique production strategy, the Toyota Production System (TPS), which revolutionized the global automobile industry. The TPS is included in the text book used at Harvard Business School.

Toyota is recognized for its exceptional competence in marketing its products in foreign markets – a skill that has become a benchmark for numerous companies. The company has diversified its model line-up and reduced the burden of inventories by calculating market demand up to the point of actual production.

Toyota has undergone hardships, like the massive recall and the Great East Japan earthquake of 2011. Yet, it has established a sound foundation throughout its 90-year history, enabling it to solidify its position as the global leader.

From a loom company to an automobile company

With his dying breath, Sakichi Toyoda told his son, Kiichiro Toyoda, to make a Japan-made car. Sakichi Toyoda's last words had a major influence on the establishment of Toyota. It was the moment that caused the main business of the Toyoda clan to change from looms to automobiles. Sakichi Toyoda was born in 1876 as the son of a poor carpenter living in a small village in Sizuoka Prefecture, Japan. As the eldest son of four siblings, Sakichi had to inherit the family business. However, he was more interested in inventing machines. As a young man, Sakichi focused on the loom. At the time, looms were inconvenient to use, requiring both hands to operate. Looms also had low productivity. Determined to make a loom that was easy to use, Sakichi devoted his time to researching. In 1894, his venture was successful as he developed the Toyoda Wooden Hand Loom, which could be operated with one hand. Later, his design was improved to produce the power loom and the automatic loom. This was the foundation of *Kaizen*, using existing things to make something better. The root of Toyota's innovations can easily be traced to the inventor, Sakichi Toyoda.

Using his technology, Toyoda began a loom business sometime around 1915. Once Britain's textile exports began to decrease in the wake of WWI, the Japanese economy began to flourish and Sakichi's business with it. In 1926, he established Toyoda Automatic Loom Works, an automatic loom manufacturing company. Four years later, in 1930, Sakichi Toyoda died of a brain hemorrhage.

After numerous business trips to the US and Europe during the 1920, Toyoda realized that the automobile industry would emerge as a major industry. Before his death, he sold the patent for the Type G Automatic Loom to the British company, Platt Brothers & Company, for a million yen. He gave the money to his son Kiichiro Toyoda and asked that the money be used to develop cars.

Honoring his father's request, Kiichiro Toyoda visited the production lines of Ford and GM and returned to Japan to launch the automobile division at Toyoda Automatic Loom Works. The division was initially a task force team for the venture. Kiichiro Toyoda purchased a Chevrolet car and studied it to develop his own car. Being the son of an inventor, Kiichiro Toyoda was a mechanical engineer trained at the Tokyo Imperial University (currently, University of Tokyo). In May 1935, five years after his father passed away, Kiichiro managed to develop Toyota's first passenger car, the A1, and began selling it.

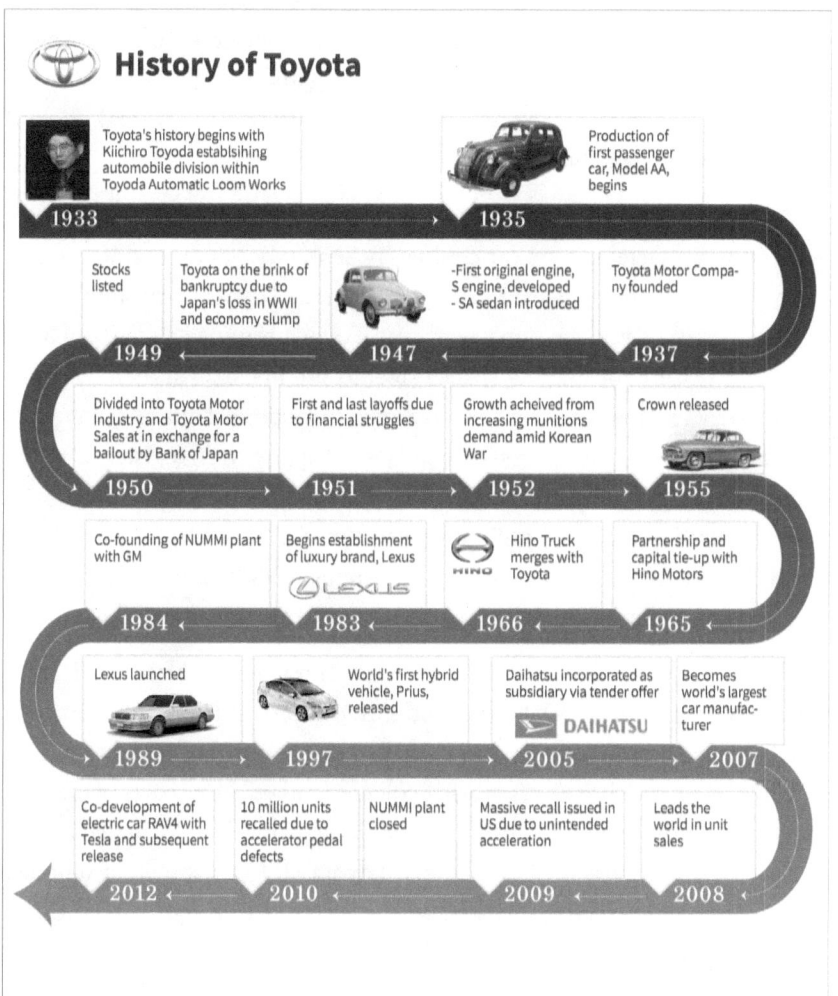

History of Toyota

1933 — Toyota's history begins with Kiichiro Toyoda establsihing automobile division within Toyoda Automatic Loom Works

1935 — Production of first passenger car, Model AA, begins

1937 — Toyota Motor Company founded

1947 — -First original engine, S engine, developed - SA sedan introduced

1949 — Stocks listed | Toyota on the brink of bankruptcy due to Japan's loss in WWII and economy slump

1950 — Divided into Toyota Motor Industry and Toyota Motor Sales at in exchange for a bailout by Bank of Japan

1951 — First and last layoffs due to financial struggles

1952 — Growth acheived from increasing munitions demand amid Korean War

1955 — Crown released

1965 — Partnership and capital tie-up with Hino Motors

1966 — Hino Truck merges with Toyota

1983 — Begins establishment of luxury brand, Lexus

1984 — Co-founding of NUMMI plant with GM

1989 — Lexus launched

1997 — World's first hybrid vehicle, Prius, released

2005 — Daihatsu incorporated as subsidiary via tender offer

2007 — Becomes world's largest car manufacturer

2008 — Leads the world in unit sales

2009 — Massive recall issued in US due to unintended acceleration

2010 — NUMMI plant closed | 10 million units recalled due to accelerator pedal defects

2012 — Co-development of electric car RAV4 with Tesla and subsequent release

Toyota founder engraves JIT in the company

While Sakichi Toyoda envisioned automobiles as the future of his company, his son, Kiichiro, was the man that realized the vision. In the eyes of Toyota Motor, the real founder of the company was Kiichiro Toyoda. When Kiichiro Toyoda began developing cars, many people inside and outside the company voiced their disapproval, because they felt the loom business might be damaged if Kiichiro failed to develop a car. However, Kiichiro did not give in to pressure and successfully launched the project. This is a good example of the importance of swift decision-making and boldness in business management.

After completing a factory to test produce cars in March 1934, Kiichiro Toyoda began developing a car engine. By September of that same year, he came up with a prototype of the Type A engine, Toyota's first automobile engine. It was also in the same year, that Toyoda founded a steel smelting research institute for making special steel to use in cars. He then began to develop trucks. The G1 truck entered mass production immediately after the prototype was completed. Once the company was registered as an approved car manufacturer under the automobile industry act of 1936, Toyoda purchased a 1.914 million square meter-plot of land in Koromo of Aichi Prefecture to build a factory. In August 1937, Toyota Motor was founded on the land. The village of Koromo is now the city of Toyota.

Toyoda was a marvelous entrepreneur. Immediately after the factory began production in 1937, he made continuous efforts to improve product quality and the production system. He had learned from his father. Thus, Toyota's *Kaizen* culture was born. Toyoda studied how parts would be moved along the assembly line and how many people would be needed for each process. This was the beginning of Toyota's JIT, a system that supplied parts in pertinent numbers at the appropriate time to prevent inventories from piling up. Once Toyota entered its heyday, the JIT system became a benchmark for automakers around the globe.

When the Japanese military attacked Pearl Harbor in December 1941, car production lines were dedicated to producing trucks and other military supplies. Following Japan's defeat in WWII in 1945, Toyoda began developing a small-sized car. By 1947, his efforts resulted in Toyota's first self-developed Type S engine and the SA sedan, the car the engine was used in.

However, Toyoda's outstanding management skills were not enough to overcome the difficulties that followed the war. Toyota began struggling as supply and demand were both disrupted by sharp inflation rates and labor disputes. In the end, the company's 7,000 workforce was cut by 2,000. Toyoda was also forced to resign in 1950 for neglecting his financial management duties. During this period, the Bank of Japan offered to provide a bailout loan to normalize the company's operations in exchange for Toyota being separated into Toyota Motor Industry and Toyota Motor Sales, citing production of cars that did not sell as the reason for the company's financial struggle. The company would remain separated until merging as Toyota in 1982.

Toyota enjoyed another growth spurt in1952, thanks to the Korean War, but Kiichiro Toyoda never returned to the company as the CEO, as he died of a brain hemorrhage in July 1952 at the age of 58, just before his reinstatement.

Toyota's growth

After Kiichiro Toyoda left the company, Toyota was at the hands of professional CEOs for 32 years, until Shoichiro Toyoda, Kiichiro Toyoda's eldest son, assumed the post in 1982. During their 32-year absence, the Toyoda family remained involved in the management of Toyota. After graduating from Nagoya University with a degree in mechanical engineering in 1952, Shoichiro Toyoda joined Toyota as a member of the board and was heavily involved in running the company. Toyota's rising prestige could be seen in its release of its flagship sedan, Crown, in 1955 and the city of Koromo changing its name to Toyota in 1959 to celebrate the completion of the Toyota Motomachi plant. In 1966, Toyota released its record-making model, the Corolla. In 1980, it rolled out the Camry, another one of its best sellers. Following the release of the Corolla, Toyota's annual output doubled from the 0.48 million units in 1965. Output exceeded the one million mark for the first time in 1968 (1.1 million units) and two million mark in 1972 (2.09 million units). Toyota went on to achieve economies of scale once again in 1980 (3.29 million units) with the release of the Camry. The Corolla and Camry proved that one well-made product could sustain a company.

While showing no eagerness for M&A opportunities, Toyota launched its own prestige brand and surprised the world. Toyota's new luxury brand performed better than expected in the North American market and gave Benz, BMW and Audi a run for their money. This brand was Lexus, which made its debut with its flagship LS400 in 1989.

CHAPTER 9

The Lexus Project:
The Final Piece of the Toyota Empire

It was an August day in 1983 executives were gathered in a conference room at Toyota's headquarters. Tension hung in the air. Chairman Eiji Toyoda, the nephew of Sakichi Toyoda and then CEO, entered the room. The agenda was the establishment of a prestige brand. The participants engaged in a heated discussion. Some acknowledged that a premium marque was necessary for the company's future, while others opposed the idea due to the massive amount of money needed and the low probability of success. Eiji Toyoda sat in silence, listening to the opinions exchanged. Then, he opened his mouth.

"Toyota is in need of a luxury brand, the likes of Mercedes-Benz, to advance further. There are bound to be many difficulties and numerous trials and errors, but we can succeed. Let's proceed with the premium brand project."

It was the moment that the F-1 (Flagship No. 1), the top secret project for establishing Toyota's prestige brand, was decided. After that day, Toyota would enter a new phase in its history, which was different from its previous 50-year history. Nonetheless, this is the story behind the conception of Lexus, which would eventually conquer the luxury car market in the US – which was at the time and continues to be the world's largest automobile market. The unexpected debut of Lexus placed Toyota, a company making cheap, quality cars, in a position to compete against Mercedes-Benz and BMW. As a result, the Toyota Empire grew in size as the Lexus marque added to Toyota's other brands - Hino, Daihatsu and Scion.

Toyota's M&As were fundamentally different from the deals Volkswagen AG and GM closed. Toyota spent years of careful planning to establish its subsidiary brands, Lexus and Scion. It considered the acquisition of Hino and Daihatsu only upon their request, not for its own needs. This is a clear indication of Toyota's unique conservative culture. Of course, Toyota was far from passive when it came to pioneering new markets and developing new technology. It was so aggressive in expanding its market that the company was revered for its sales strategy. It participated in Formula 1 and 24 Hours of Le Mans to test its technology against European automakers. Such bold ventures were all backed by Eiji Toyoda, who is considered one of the best CEOs in Toyota history. After Kiichiro Toyoda died, Eiji Toyoda successfully led Toyota Motor until Shoichiro Toyoda, Kiichiro's eldest son, gained control.

Lexus surprises Benz

It took six years after Eiji Toyoda's decision before Lexus was unveiled to the public. Being an unprecedented project, Toyota executives took extreme caution in planning every detail, from production of a single bolt to vehicle development and to distribution network establishment. The company spent three years in market research alone and a billion dollars until the brand was launched. The F-1 project was a success. The secret behind its success lay in offering cars with quality and performance that matched Benz, but at a far cheaper price. The 1989 LS400 was priced at $35,000, which was only 57.4% of the price of its competing model, the Benz 420SEL, which was priced at $61,000.

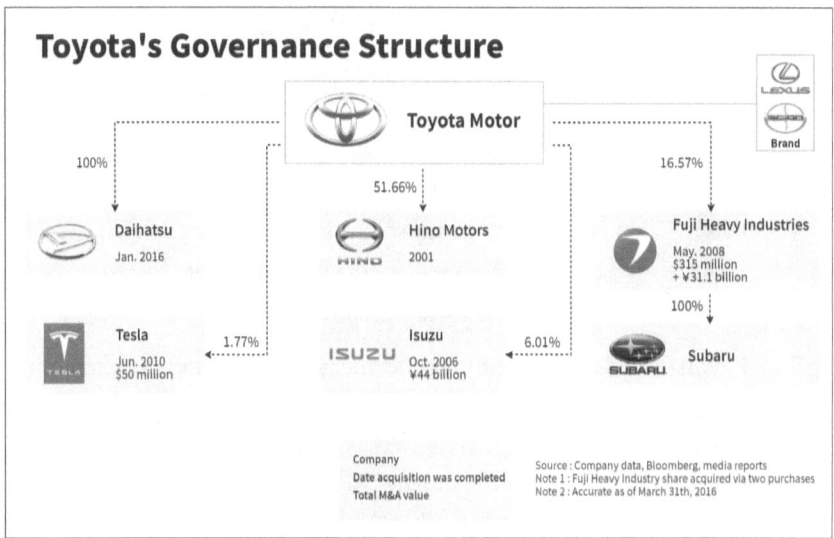

Toyota's Governance Structure

Toyota Motor

Brand

100%

51.66%

16.57%

Daihatsu
Jan. 2016

Hino Motors
2001

Fuji Heavy Industries
May. 2008
$315 million
+ ¥31.1 billion

100%

Tesla
Jun. 2010
$50 million

1.77%

Isuzu
Oct. 2006
¥44 billion

6.01%

Subaru

Company
Date acquisition was completed
Total M&A value

Source : Company data, Bloomberg, media reports
Note 1 : Fuji Heavy Industry share acquired via two purchases
Note 2 : Accurate as of March 31th, 2016

Consumers favored Lexus over Lincolns and Cadillacs, which were priced below $30,000, but had low quality. Lexus sold 42,806 units in 1990 and saw unit sales increase by 20-30 thousand each year. Eventually, the marque's share in the US luxury car market exceeded 10%. It accumulated the largest share in the prestige car market by 1999 and retained the title for 12 years until BMW claimed the throne.

The Lexus marque became such an icon in the US high-end vehicle market that New York Times columnist, Thomas Friedman, used Lexus to describe modern globalization systems in his book, *The Lexus and the Olive Tree*. When releasing the Genesis in the US market, the basis of Hyundai Motor's marketing strategy was the tagline: "performance of a BMW 5 Series, the price of a 3 series," which was inspired by Lexus' success.

Capital tie-up: Scheme to acquire the loss-stricken Hino

Before the establishment of Lexus, Toyota incorporated only two brands into the Toyota family in the form of alliances, not full incorporation. In October 1965, Toyota announced that it would be forming a business and capital tie-up with Hino Motors. At the time, Hino had a forged a technology partnership with Renault and was selling CKD (complete knock-down) versions of the Renault 4CV. Using the technology obtained from Renault, Hino developed and released the Contessa. However, poor sales pushed Hino into financial difficulties. Mitsui Bank, Hino's main bank, was aware of the situation. Since Mitsui Bank was Toyota's main bank as well, Chairman Kiichiro Sato of Mitsui Bank was close friends with then Toyota CEO, Taizo Ishida. Sato proposed to Ishida the acquisition of Hino Motors. Ishida assigned Eiji Toyoda, then vice president, to oversee the negotiations for the Hino acquisition.

Eiji Toyoda was skeptical about the acquisition of the loss-stricken Hino Motors. Moreover, the Hino Contessa was competing in the same segment as the Corolla. Eiji Toyoda feared that the acquisition of Hino might cannibalize Corolla sales. Being aware of this, Hino CEO Mitsunobu Mitsukata made a surprising offer to Eiji Toyoda in the spring of 1965: Hino would stop manufacturing Contessas. Determined to save the company, Mitsukata had made an offer that Toyoda "could not refuse." However, Toyoda did not give his approval as the acquisition would only hurt Toyota financially. Moreover, anti-trust laws were likely to prevent the government from authorizing the acquisition. So, Toyoda came up with a plan to protect Toyota, while satisfying Hino at the same time: a business and capital partnership. According to Toyoda's plan, Toyota's stake in Hino would be limited to 5%, and Toyota would consign small-sized truck production to Hino. Toyoda also had demands of his own.

"Toyota is the largest company in Japan. As our partner, Hino must become the best truck company. Hino may not have a future if it is complacent as second or third."

Mitsukata knew very well what that meant. He fully committed Hino to manufacturing trucks and efforts were rewarded by increase in sales. Afterwards, Toyota slowly increased its stake in Hino. Toyota increased its ownership in Hino to a solid 20.1% in March 2000 to solidify its management rights and to 50.1% in 2001.

The raw diamond Daihatsu sends out a distress signal

Toyota's partnership with Hino was a catalyst for another partnership. The then President of Sanwa Bank (currently Mitsumishi Tokyo UFJ), Tadao Watanabe, heard the news of the Toyota-Hino alliance and proposed a partnership with Daihatsu to Eiji Toyoda. Sanwa Bank was the main bank for Daihatsu. Toyoda was taken aback because unlike Hino, Daihatsu was performing well. The dominant explanation for the proposal is that it was made because Daihatsu was feeling threatened because of the Japanese automobile industry's reform, during which companies were actively increasing their size through M&As. Nissan had merged with Prince Motor prior to Toyota's partnership with Hino. Another underlying factor might have been Watanabe's desire that Sanwa Bank open business ties with Toyota, the leading auto company in Japan at the time.

Daihatsu was also manufacturing passenger cars that were competing with Toyota's. Just as he did with Hino, Eiji Toyoda requested that Daihatsu focus on building city (subcompact) cars, a segment Toyota had no presence in. However, the then-Daihatsu President Yuji Koish declined. Ultimately, both sides each took a step back: Daihatsu would focus on manufacturing subcompact cars, but continue to produce and sell compact cars, and in exchange, Toyota would buy 6% of Daihatsu's shares. The Toyota-Daihatsu partnership was formed in January 1967, only three months after Toyota announced its alliance with Hino. As a result of the alliance, Sanwa Bank received a hefty sum in brokerage fees and became one of Toyota's main banks.

In 1998, Daihatsu became a subsidiary of Toyota when the later secured a 51.2% stake via a tender offer. Since then, Daihatsu has been manufacturing compact cars for Toyota. In January 2016, Toyota exchanged one Daihatsu share for 0.26 Toyota shares to gain full ownership of its subsidiary and had it delisted to push forward with its plans to venture into Southeast Asia and other new markets.

Toyota targets US youths with Scion

Toyota has a culture of maintaining "purity," which is reflected in the fact that the CEO position has been kept within the Toyoda clan. The company has placed emphasis on homogeneity and has avoided growth via M&As, unlike other competing companies. If needed, Toyota would establish a fully owned subsidiary. Despite having a dominating influence, Toyota significantly increased its stake in Hino and Daihatsu in the late 1990s, not because it wanted to strengthen the partnerships, but to prevent other companies gaining influence by buying shares while either of the companies were performing poorly.

Against this backdrop, Toyota's establishment of Scion in 2003 has significance. Scion was a cheap and fun marque established to target the younger generations in the US. In 2005, Toyota had sold 7.09 cars worldwide, passing Ford and coming in as the second largest automaker after GM. Even so, Toyota was troubled, because the people buying its cars were getting older. At the time, the largest consumer class in the US was the baby boomers, born in the 1940s and 1950s. The baby boomers accounted for 29% (82 million) of the US population, but they were in their 40s and 50s. Toyota realized that once the baby boomers began retiring, they would stop buying cars, causing Toyota's sales to drop. So Toyota turned its focus to the Generation Y, people born between the 1970s and 1990s. This generation formed 26% (73 million) of the US population and was also called the echo boomers. The echo boomers were likely to become the largest consumer class after baby boomers in a decade or so. Hence, the Scion brand was born. Scion cars were priced at around $15,000, neatly designed and offered the "joy of driving (manual transmission)." In 2003, Scion released the subcompact car xA and the box-car xB. The marque sold 10,898 units in its first year, beating its initial target of 10,000. The compact sedan tC was added to Scion's line-up and the brand sold over 100,000 cars. However, unit sales dropped to 4,323 units in 2013. It seems that even with Toyota's outstanding marketing skills on its back, Scion was unable to gain traction in the US market, where cheap and quality cars were fiercely competing to maintain a presence. Realizing that Scion's unit sales were suffering because the marque's target customer group preferred the Toyota brand, the company decided to discontinue the Scion brand in February 2016.

However, the Toyota Empire seemed impervious to the poor performance of Scion.

The empire continued to grow. Toyota branched out to various markets with a variety of brands and increased its market presence, while secretly launching an eco-friendly car project. In 1997, Toyota unveiled a car that changed the automobile history: the Prius, the world's first hybrid car.

The Prius Miracle: Overcoming the mass recall and the great earthquake

In October 1997, a strange car caught the eyes of reporters and automobile industry people present at the Tokyo Motor Show. This particular vehicle was a hybrid, powered by both a gasoline engine and an electric motor. Classifying itself as an eco-friendly car, it boasted a mileage of 25.5km/l (based on Japan's standards), which was nearly twice as high as average cars of its era. It was the world's first mass-produced hybrid car, the Toyota Prius. While being surprised, people showed a lukewarm response, because they did not trust hybrid technology and the Prius was not aesthetically appealing. The larger problem was it was priced at 2.5 million yen, which was nearly enough to buy two internal combustion engine cars of the same segment. The Prius was smaller than Toyota's compact car, Corolla, but was almost as expensive as the Camry, a mid-sized sedan.

A decade later, in July 2007, the New York Times published an article, titled "Say 'Hybrid' and Many People Will Hear 'Prius,'" which addressed the mystery behind the success of the Prius. At the time, over 400 thousand Priuses were sold in the US and a little less than a million worldwide (Prius' worldwide unit sales surpassed the one million mark in April 2008. Even while other hybrids were struggling to establish a market presence, the Prius continued to sell well because it was so well recognized as the leading hybrid vehicle that its nameplate had become synonymous with hybrid.

After conquering the luxury car market with Lexus, Toyota, a company known offer quality cars at affordable prices, had emerged as the world's leading company in the cutting-edge, eco-friendly car market through the Prius.

In 2008, Toyota beat GM to become the number one automobile manufacturer in the world. Despite the fatal hits from the mass recall, the Great East Japan Earthquake and the flood in Thailand, the company refused to fall. In fact, the company used such setbacks as opportunities to improve. Thanks to such efforts, Toyota was in position to become the first automaker to record annual unit sales of 10 million in 2015.

Dominant leader in the eco-friendly car market

Hybrids were not first conceived by Toyota. At the Paris Exposition of 1900, Porsche founder, Dr. Ferdinand Porsche, entered the Lohner Porsche, which used a combination of a gasoline engine and an electric motor, making it the first hybrid vehicle. Toyota was the first to commercialize the technology.

While Toyota benchmarked Porsche's technology concept, Porsche adopted the TPS. In 1990, Porsche recruited Toyota retirees and implemented the TPS in all of its plants. The TPS, which encourages onsite workers to voluntarily improve productivity, contributed greatly to the increase of Porsche's productivity. The two companies had exchanged one for one.

Eiji Toyoda was the mastermind behind the release of the Prius. Toyoda had set a goal of "doubling gas mileage." He also urged employees to develop a technology that would either be essential in the 21st century or remain valid for the next 100 years. This was the Globe 21 project that resulted in the Prius. By July 2013, Toyota had sold over 3 million units under the nameplate. The first generation Prius was disappointing, selling only 123 thousand units, but the second (2003) and third (2009) generations were successful, each selling 1,992,000 and 1,688,000 units. Through the Prius,

Toyota emerged as the hybrid car master and sold over a total of 6 million hybrid vehicles until 2013.

Stint with GM

M&As is an abbreviation for mergers and acquisitions between companies. When the definition is stretched, strategic alliances between companies may be considered a type of M&A. Showing a preference for strategic alliances, Toyota had close ties with only GM until the financial crisis.

The first Toyota-GM partnership resulted in the establishment of the NUMMI (New United Motor Manufacturing Incorporation) plant, which was named after United Motors, the company former GM Chairman Alfred Sloan worked at as a CEO. United Motors acquired Hyatt Roller Bearing Company, before becoming a member of the GM family.

In the late 1970s, advances of Japanese automobiles had begun to cause trouble for US car companies. While US companies were struggling, Japanese companies were considering building factories in the US. In order to minimize trade friction, Toyota decided to establish a production base in the US through a partnership. It began negotiating with Ford, but was unable to come to an agreement, as many of the two companies' cars were competing in the same segments. As a result, Toyota decided to join hands with GM. Toyota and GM decided to use GM's Fremont Plant, which was built in 1962 and closed in 1982. In the seven years since it began operating, the NUMMI plant boasted the best quality and productivity among GM's production facilities in the US. The time required to assemble a car at the NUMMI plant was reduced to 21 hours, down from 43 hours in 1978, when GM was operating the plant alone.

Struggling in the wake of the financial crisis, GM notified Toyota in June 2009 that it would withdraw from the NUMMI plant. With the NUMMI plant's productivity lower than its other US plants, Toyota concluded it would not be able to operate the plant alone and decided to shut it down in April 2010. A month later, Toyota President Akio Toyoda met with Tesla CEO Elon Musk at Tesla's headquarter in California. In a meeting with Governor Arnold Schwarzenegger participating, Toyota announced that the NUMMI plant site and its facilities would be sold to Tesla for $57 million. As a result, all conveyor belts were removed from the NUMMI plant, and it was reborn as Tesla's state-of-the-art factory.

Toyota had another joint endeavor with GM: the Subaru-owned Fuji Heavy Industries. GM owned 20.1% of Fuji Heavy Industries, which failed to provide any benefits for GM. Struggling financially, GM decided to sell its stake in Fuji Heavy Industries. In October 2005, Toyota purchased an 8.7% stake (68 million shares) directly from GM and GM sold the remaining 11.4% on the stock exchange. Toyota had provided side support to GM. Toyota increased its stake to 16.66% in 2008 by purchasing 61 million of Fuji Heavy Industries' treasury shares. Subaru is currently generating synergy with Toyota placing OEM orders for subcompact cars with Daihatsu and joint-developing hybrids with Toyota. Toyota obtained a 5.9% stake in the Japanese truck company Isuzu by purchasing a portion of shares GM sold in 2006. GM had acquired a 7.9% stake in Isuzu to develop diesel engines, but financial troubles forced it to sell the shares to Toyota and Mitsubishi. In short, Toyota seemed to be opening its wallet every time GM was in trouble. Although this is only a guess, it's possible the US government might have indirectly pressured Toyota to do so.

Winter comes

On February 24, 2010, Toyota President Akio Toyoda was called as a witness for a hearing at the US House of Representatives. Toyoda bowed his head and apologized. At the time, Toyota had recalled a staggering 10 million units due to defective gas pedals. After three hours of intense questioning by representatives, Toyoda met with local employees at the National Press Club in Washington D.C. and burst into tears. This moment was identical to the moment his grandfather and Toyota founder, Kiichiro Toyoda, shed tears when resigning for pushing the company to the brink of bankruptcy.

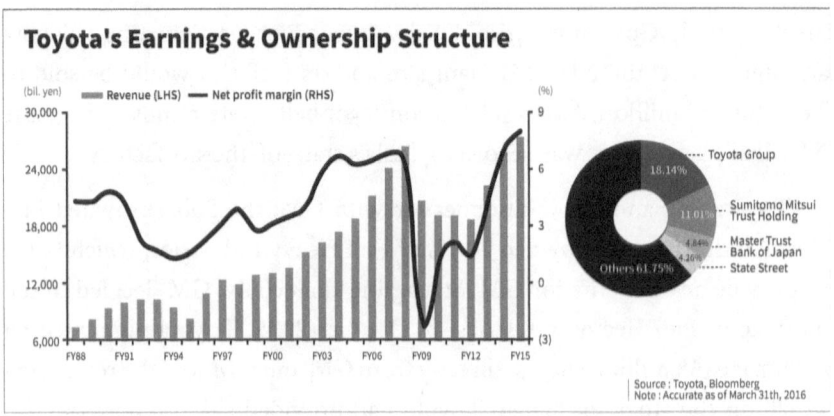

Toyota's Earnings & Ownership Structure

Source : Toyota, Bloomberg
Note : Accurate as of March 31th, 2016

In 2008, Toyota sold 8.42 million cars worldwide, topped the 8.36million sold by GM, which had been the reigning leader in unit sales for the previous 77 years (1931-2007). Based on output, Toyota had become the leader in 2007. The Toyota Group had turned in sales of 26.518 trillion yen and an operating profit of 24 trillion yen (9.4% margin) in 2007. Toyota was ranked at an all-time high: fifth on the Fortune 500, coming in behind Wal-Mart, ExxonMobil, Royal Dutch Shell and BP. It seemed like no one could put a stop to Toyota's run.

However, a series of setbacks began in 2009 and shook the very foundation of Toyota. That year, Toyota was hit hard by the financial crisis resulting from the collapse of Lehman Brothers, causing unit sales to plunge 21% year-on-year to 6.67mn units. The company suffered a 630.3 billion-yen loss (461.0 billion from April 2008 to March 2009, the Japanese fiscal year of 2009). It was its first subpar earnings in 71 years. In the following year, Toyota suffered a devastating blow from the recall of unprecedented proportions, causing irreversible damage to its identity defined by quality and *monozukuri* (craftsmanship).

Some conspiracy theorists claimed that the recall was issued to appease disarray caused by the fall of GM, Ford and Chrysler. In reality, Toyota could have easily been the subject of envy, because as a result of concentrating efforts on its "secondary market," it had earned over half of its total 1990-2008 operating profits from the US.

The recall was only the beginning. In March 2011, the largest earthquake since Japan began keeping records (9.0 on the Richter scale) struck Japan and the ensuing tsunamis left the southeastern region of Japan in ruins. The tsunami also claimed Toyota's plant. Not having a sufficient stockpile, since Toyota did not stock its inventories sufficiently, output in April-September of 2011 was less than 70% of the output during the same period in 2014. This exposed the weakness of Toyota's JIT system. In October of the same year, production was disrupted once again by the flood in Thailand. Toyota had become a candle in the wind.

Toyota gets back up: Expanding the eco-friendly car line-up

Even after the Lehman shock, the unprecedented recall, yen appreciation, the Great East Japan Earthquake and the Thailand flood, Toyota refused to go down. In fact, adversity had only made it stronger. The industry speculated it would take decades for Toyota to recover. However, Toyota defied all expectations and reclaimed the throne in 2012 thanks to the restructuring initiated by Akio Toyoda, who was appointed CEO in 2009, when Toyota was struggling from the fallout of the Lehman crisis. The company managed to complete the recall in six months, preventing it from losing consumer confidence. It also localized parts procurements to ensure stable production. It perfected its model portfolio by adding cars with innovative designs and cars that were fun to drive, allowing Toyotas to appeal to consumers of all ages. Thanks to its efforts, Toyota's unit sales came in at 9.98 million in 2013 and surpassed to 10 million-milestone in 2014. Thanks to its efforts, Toyota's unit sales stopped at 9.98 million in 2013 and surpassed the 10 million mark in 2014 and 2015.

The crisis also brought a change to the company's conservative corporate culture. Toyota discarded its reluctance toward M&As and began forging a number of partnerships. During Tesla's initial public offering, Toyota acquired a 3.2% share for $50 million. The Toyota-Tesla alliance led to the co-development of the electric car, LAV4, in May 2012. In August 2012, Toyota also agreed to the joint development of hybrid technology for pickups and SUVs with Ford. Four months later, it partnered with BMW to procure diesel engines and develop hybrid technology. The cooperative tie with BMW has become particularly strong. In January 2013, the two announced a joint effort to develop eco-friendly car technology–namely, fuel cells which produce electricity from the chemical reaction between hydrogen and oxygen - and attempt to roll out a fuel cell vehicle by 2020.

Although Volkswagen and GM are at its heels, Toyota seems to be capable of defending the crown for the time being. In addition to fending off competition, the company is expanding its eco-friendly vehicle line-up though partnerships and alliances.

Toyota unveiled the 4th generation Prius in 2015, which will make the "Prius effect" to continue to grow with time.

Industry-Altering Event #2

World War II

After WWI, the automobile industry blossomed using the technological advances made during the war. The affluent life styles of the upper classes allowed Rolls-Royce, Lincoln, Bugatti and other luxury car companies to stand out from the flock. Motorsports events, such as Italy's Mille Miglia and France's 24 Hours of Le Mans, gained massive popularity. In Germany, Auto Union (Audi), Daimler-Benz and Porsche made great technological advances with support from Adolf Hitler, who was a motorsports enthusiast. Hitler had a keen interest in the automobile industry. In 1933, six months after since rising to power, Hitler ordered the construction of the Autobahn. In Italy, the Mussolini Administration provided support to Alfa Romeo, which was headed by Enzo Ferrari, allowing it to claim its first title in a motorsports event.

Economies were booming in the aftermath of WWI. However, the resulting excessive production and the US stock market collapse triggered the Great Depression in 1929, pushing the global economy into a slump. In efforts to overcome the depression, Britain and France transferred local production facilities to their colonies. On the other hand, Germany, Italy and Japan did not have enough colonies to do so. As a result, an increasing number of people believed that invading and colonizing other countries was the only way to survive the Great Depression. Ultimately, Germany invaded Poland on September 1, 1939, causing the UK and France to declare war on Germany. Thus began World War II.

As soon as war broke out, automobile manufacturers around the world shifted to wartime operations. At the orders of Hitler, Daimler-Benz began manufacturing aircrafts and tanks, BMW fighter engines and Opel aircraft parts and tanks. Porsche designed tanks and, at the order of the German government, Dr. Ferdinand Porsche began producing the Beetle for the military. Just as it did during WWI, Fiat began producing tanks and aircrafts.

Toyota, which entered the automobile industry in 1933, began supplying military trucks and began opening Toyota Steel (currently, Aichi Steel), Tokai Air Industry (currently, Aisin Seiki) and other military equipment companies. Nakajima Aircraft, which became Fuji Heavy Industries, manufactured engines for Japan's Zero-sen fighters from 1936 to the end of the war. After the war, Fuji Heavy Industries founded Subaru, which gained fame for its flat engine. Tachikawa Aircraft, which had a technology alliance with Nakajima Aircraft, became Tama Electric Car Company and then Prince Motor, before merging with Nissan. The chief engineer of Tachikawa Aircraft went on to join Toyota and made significant contributions to the development of the Corolla. After the War, Jeep was founded in the US.

Because Germany had lost the war, German automakers went through extreme difficulties. Unable to manufacture engines, BMW produced bicycles and kitchenware until 1952. Daimler-Benz was, at one point, owned by the steel tycoon Friedrich Flick and was almost sold to one of the oil-producing Middle Eastern countries. Volkswagen fell into the hands of the Allied Forces –US and UK – before it was transferred back to the German government in 1949.

Because Renault produced military supplies for the German army during the war, founder Louis Renault was imprisoned and died a month later. Ferdinand Porsche and his son-in-law, Anton Piëch, also suffered in prison for collaborating with the Third Reich.

EMPIRE IV

Renault Nissan

CHAPTER 11

Renault: Misfortune of War

On September 5, 1956, a group of people were gathered around a strange blue car at the Bonneville Salt Flats in Utah. The car was unlike any seen at the time – it had a curved chassis and a low ground clearance. This was a supercar built by Renault called the Etoile Filante, which means 'Shooting Star'. The car roared and raced across a distance. The people watch cheered with joy. The car had reached a speed of 308.85km/h, which is fast by today's standards, but it was a new world record at the time. Thanks to the Etoile Filante, Renault, which was only a manufacturer of mass-produced cars, received the spotlight of the automobile industry.

Despite its focus on subcompact cars for working-class people, Renault never hid its passion for new and better technology. Thanks to such passion, Renault became, and remains to this day, a prominent manufacturer of high performance engines used in F1 machines. Renault began supplying engines for F1 machines in 1977. As of 2013, it had been providing engines for Red Bull Racing, which won four championships in a row, as well as Lotus F1, Caterham F1 and a number of other F1 teams. Renault, which had been an engine supplier for F1 teams, acquired the Lotus F1 team in 2011 from Genii Capital, which had been struggling because of overdue taxes, and returned as a contender in 2016.

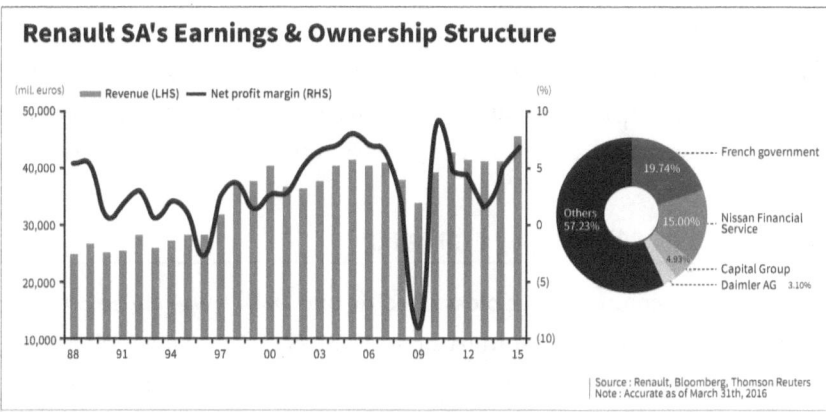

Renault SA's Earnings & Ownership Structure

Boasting a 115-year history, Renault is the leading automobile company in France and possesses the fourth largest production capacity (Renault-Nissan Alliance) in the world. Renault had a bumpy history. It was a major contributor to France's campaign during WWI, but was convicted for assisting Nazi Germany in WWII. After nationalization, privatization and a number of historical M&As, Renault developed into one of the world's most prominent automobile marques.

3 Renault brothers build a car

Renault was founded by Louis Renault (1877-1944). Coming from a wealthy family, Louis was an engineer with a love of cars. In 1898, the 21-year-old Louis Renault built the first motorized car for De Dion–Bouton. He named the car Voiturette, which means small car. The vehicle was also called 1CV. The Voiturette was a small two-seater, but it performed as well as any other car. Confident in its potential, Louis and his brothers, Marcel and Ferdinand, founded an automobile company bearing their family name. Thus, in 1899, the history of Renault cars began. The company began to grow when the AG1 released in 1905 was well-received by people as a taxi.

Renault emerged as the largest company in France after WWI broke out in 1914. The company had just begun to manufacture buses and truck and the war had caused demand to skyrocket. The company also manufactured FT-17 tanks, playing a strong role as a munitions manufacturer in France. In light of the agriculture boom that began in 1918, Renault expanded its business to agricultural machinery. Timely expansions to new business areas added more sails to the already cruising business. It seemed that the company was on the highway to success

Nationalized for collaborating with Nazis

Ironically, the company that blossomed during WWI was endangered by WWII. After the French capitulation in 1940, Nazi Germany took control of Renault. The Nazis brought in workers from their own automobile companies, Daimler and Benz, to produce military supplies at Renault's factory. Renault, which manufactured tanks for France, was forced to build tanks for the German military. Naturally, the Allied Forces targeted the Renault factory and destroyed it in an airstrike in March 1942. It was the moment everything Louis Renault spent 40 years building crumbled into dust.

Louis Renault was shocked, but another ordeal had yet to come. Once France was liberated in 1944, trials for Nazi collaborators began. Louis Renault was among the people incarcerated. Louis Renault could not stand his situation and met his tragic death a month after being imprisoned. The French government seized all of Renault's assets, and Renault became a state-run company.

4CV and Renault 4 make Renault the leading corporation in France

It is almost hilarious to know that the French government, which incarcerated Louis Renault and confiscated all his assets for collaborating with Nazi Germany, received help from another Nazi collaborator to build the most popular car in France: the subcompact car 4CV released in 1947. Among the group of engineers that developed the 4CV was Porsche founder, Ferdinand Porsche, who headed the development of the Beetle to fulfill Hitler's vision of filling Germany's roads with cheap, simple cars. Ferdinand Porsche also paid dearly for his contributions to the Third Reich.

Regardless of its back story, the Porsche-developed 4CV was an immediate success. Even as France struggled to recover from war damages, 4CV sales continued to rise. By the 1950s, the 4CV was the most common car in France. The reputation of the 4CV was inherited by Renault 4, released in 1961. Recognized for being an affordable, practical and durable car, the Renault 4 quickly established a market presence. By 1966, Renault had sold over a million Renault 4s. By the time the Renault 4 was discontinued in 1994, a total of 8,135,424 units had been sold over a 33-year span. Thanks to the Renault 4, Renault was able to become the largest automobile company in France and Europe in the 1970s.

Internal discord escalates as size increases

The French government gave Renault its full support, because it knew that the only way to reinvigorate the economy was to revive the manufacturing industry. As a result, Renault enjoyed abundant funding and supportive policies between the 1950s and 1970s, allowing it to establish production facilities and pursue M&A deals with automobile-related corporations.

In the 1950s, Renault absorbed Somua and Latil, small-sized manufacturers of medium and large-size commercial vehicles, and merged with the truck/bus company, Saviem, in 1955 to complete its first inorganic growth. In 1978, Saviem merged with Automobiles M.Berliet, a subsidiary of Citroen, and became RVI (Renault Véhicules Industriels or Renault Industrial Vehicles in English), which manufactured and sold commercial vehicles. Because Automobiles M.Berliet was struggling at the time, The French government provided 2.2 billion francs for the acquisition of Automobiles M.Berliet and its merger with Saviem. Based on the average exchange rate in 2013, the 2.2 billion francs equaled around 335.4 million euros.

In an effort to improve its competence, Renault formed technological partnerships with Peugeot and Volvo to joint-develop an engine, which was used in the cars of all three companies. Renault had established a foundation in France and in Europe, so it turned its attention to the US. In

1979, Renault acquired a 22.5% stake in AMC (American Motors) and a 20% stake in Mack Trucks to obtain a distribution network in North America. This was a bold step for Renault. Later, when AMC was on the verge of bankruptcy, Renault spent massive amounts of money to increase its ownership in AMC to 47.5%. In 1983, it increased its Mack Truck stake to 44.6%.

Louis Schweitzer engages in privatization project

Renault's foray into the US market was a failure, because the small French cars did not appeal to Americans, who preferred big cars. Due to such adversity, Renault entered a slump in the 1980s, suffering losses for three straight years starting in 1984. The subpar earnings were attributable to rising labor costs, unstable labor-management relations and the poor performance of RVI. The passenger car division was also a problem. The Renault 4 continued to sell well, but Renault did not have a follow-up. Renault cars failed to gain distinction in other segments as well. As a result, sales began to nosedive. Renault was force to restructure. It sold AMC to Chrysler in 1987 and AMC became Jeep. Renault downsized its workforce and discontinued unnecessary businesses. The French government supplied 12.0 billion francs for the restructuring and in September 1991, the decision was made to privatize Renault along with 20 other state-run corporations. After becoming a private corporation, Renault exchanged stocks with Volvo to initiate a merger.

It was at this point in time that the government dispatched a savior to Renault. This individual was tasked to supervise the restructuring and privatization of Renault. This person was Louis Schweitzer. Schweitzer was the great grandson of the medical missionary in Africa, Albert Schweitzer, and came from a prominent family of elite administrative officials. Louis Schweitzer's father was a former President of the International Monetary Fund and the nephew of existentialist Jean-Paul Sartre. True to his heritage, Louis Schweitzer was an ENA (École nationale d'administration) graduate and worked at the French finance ministry for a long time. After spending time as a special assistant to Laurent Fabius, then Prime Minister and current Foreign Minister, Schweitzer was inaugurated as the vice president of the Renault Group in 1986. Many opposed Schweitzer's appointment and concerns escalated throughout the industry. It may have been because Schweitzer, who was in his mid 40s, tall and wore horn-rimmed glasses, seemed like the stereotypical scholar. Whatever the reason, Schweitzer ignored the disapproval and carried out his vision, step by step.

By 1996, the French government's ownership of Renault had dropped to 46% from 79% in 1993. The stocks were sold to individual and institutional investors – and even Renault employees. The French government took Renault's slump as an opportunity for selling its stake in Renault to increase its financial resources and met the requirements for joining the EU. As a result, Renault became a private company for the first time in 51 years and all decision-making authority was given to the company. As a result of the privatization, Renault slimmed down its 100,000-employee workforce.

Schweitzer concluded that European demand alone was not enough to fuel Renault's growth. So, he had the company branch out to Brazil in August 1995. In June 1996, Renault partnered with GM Europe to collaborate in small-sized commercial vehicle. Believing it was unnecessary, Schweitzer closed Renault's Portuguese plant. Schweitzer also had an eye for talent. He would develop a deep trust in Carlos Ghosn, who took hold of the reins and rebuilt Renault.

CHAPTER 12

Embracing Nissan:
Rise to 4th in the World

"If we continue this path, Renault will have no future."

One day in March 1999, Renault Chairman Louis Schweitzer was in his office at Renault headquarters in Boulogne-Billancourt, just outside Paris. Schweitzer was sitting at his desk in silence, staring out the window. His mind was in turmoil. Renault had to increase in size to compete in the global market, and the Daimler-Chrysler merger of May 1985 had only increased his anxiety. Joining hands with another company was not easy. From 1992, Renault had worked hard for two years to merge with Volvo, but dissent from Volvo shareholders forced Renault to abandon its plans at the last minute. Renault got stuck in a hole for the next five years. A dark cloud seemed to be blocking the company's future. Renault reached out to Nissan, Mitsubishi and other Japanese automobile companies, but failed to reach any conclusion.

Then, the phone rang. The call was from Yoshihito Hanawa, the Chairman and CEO of Nissan. Hanawa kept things short, simple and to the point. He desperately said, "We need your help."

At the time, Nissan had been pursuing an alliance with Daimler-Chrysler. The two had failed to reach an agreement after a year of negotiations. Having suffered losses for a long period, Nissan was on the brink of collapsing.

Hanawa set up a meeting with Schweitzer and flew to France from Germany.

The two men met in the chairman's office at Renault headquarters – Schweitzer, who desired to achieve economy of scale, and Hanawa, who was on a mission to save his company. Desperation enabled the two to reach a swift agreement. In just six hours, the two CEOs agreed to form a joint front. The signing ceremony for the alliance was held on March 27, 1999. Everything was completed in a blink of an eye.

The resulting Renault-Nissan Alliance was the fourth largest automaker after Toyota, Volkswagen and GM. The Hyundai-Kia Automotive Group is at its heels, but the Alliance has been successful in defending its position by constantly increasing its size.

The companies of the two countries that were enemies during WWII merged under one roof, manufacturing and selling cars and aspiring to prosper together. This is a good example that shows that today's enemy can be tomorrow's best friend. At a glance, it may seem a heterogeneous union between western and oriental corporations, but the Alliance was able to produce maximum results thanks to its outstanding leader, Carlos Ghosn.

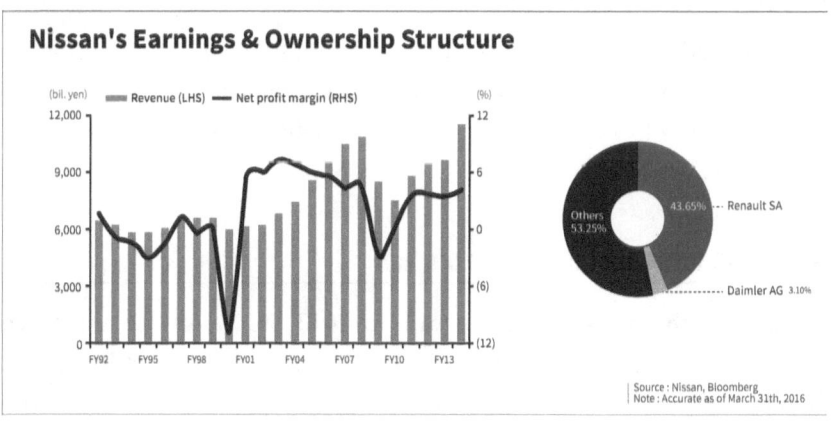

Nissan's Earnings & Ownership Structure

Source : Nissan, Bloomberg
Note : Accurate as of March 31th, 2016

Nissan embraces the smaller Renault

The shock of the Renault-Nissan Alliance rippled throughout the industry as well as the world, because Renault was a smaller company than Nissan. In 1999, Renault's output was 2.19 million units, whereas Nissan had manufactured 2.45 million units. As the French government reduced its stake in Renault from 79% in 1993 to 46% in 1999, Renault bought 36.8% of Nissan stocks for 33 billion francs (or 5.4 billion dollars or 643.0 billion yen) and became the majority shareholder. Renault had managed to become a private company and increase its size in the same year. After utilizing its cash reserves accumulated over the years to become the majority shareholder of its larger partner, Renault was immediately able to expand its "Eurocentric" operations to North America and beyond. In 1999, the two enterprises, manufactured a combined total of 4.47 million cars, ranking it fifth after GM, Ford, Daimler-Chrysler and Toyota. Individually, the companies were each ranked somewhere around tenth.

Renault did not acquire Nissan. As seen in its name, the Renault-Nissan Alliance strives to facilitate the independent growth of each company under a single roof. At the same time, they attempt to achieve economy of scale and generate synergy via collaboration of research and development, establishment of RNPO (Renault Nissan Purchase Organization) for bulk purchase of parts and sharing of sales networks.

The relationship between the two companies got strong over time. In 2011, Nissan purchased 15% of Renault's stocks, while Renault increased its Nissan stake to 43.4% to fortify their defense against hostile takeovers from third parties.

Substitute turns out better than original

Nissan, which sold 4.93 million cars in 2013, is one of the top three automobile companies in Japan along with Toyota (9.98 million) and Honda (3.93 million). Founded in 1914 following the establishment of the Kaishinsha Motorcar Works in Tokyo, Nissan recently celebrated its 100th anniversary. Today, the company has achieved numerous milestones, which are a testament to its solid foundation. For instance, its determination to beat Porsche resulted in the supercar GT-R, which surprised the world. Its prestige marque, Infiniti, is a major rival to German luxury car makers. Back in 1999, Nissan was nothing like its present self. For the fiscal year of 1999 (April 1999 to March 2000), the company recorded a net loss of 684.3 billion yen. The larger issue was that during the eight years between 1993 and 2000 (based on Japanese fiscal years), the company failed to break even every year – except for in 1997. Its global market share plunged from 6.6% in 1991 to below 5% in 1999. There were rumors that company was going under among employees. Hence, Nissan had no choice but to reach out to Renault.

Before the 1980s, Nissan's profits were soaring. Nissan was first born as DAT Motorcar. DAT was an acronym of the surnames of the company's founders, Kenjiro Den, Rokuro Aoyama and Meitaro Takeuchi. DAT was mainly a manufacturer of military trucks, until in 1931, it made its way into the passenger car market with the small-sized car, Datson (name changed to Datsun in 1933), which is Japan's first domestically manufactured car. In 1933, DAT was acquired by the Nissan Group, along with a number of automobile parts companies, and was later renamed Nissan Motor.

Until the end of the 1950s, the Datsun was manufactured and exported to the US in its sedan and small-size pickup truck variants. In 1959, the company forged a technology alliance with Austin Motor in England and released the popular Bluebird. The Bluebird was imported into Korea in 1962 by Saenara Motor Company, which assembled CKD parts and sold them in Korea. In addition to the release of the Bluebird, Nissan opened a subsidiary in the US and continued on the fast track to success. In 1966, Nissan took over Prince Motor, which developed the legendary Skyline. The Skyline is the ancestor of today's GT-Rs.

Following the surge of small-sized car demand in the aftermath of the 1973 oil shock, Nissan established production bases in Mexico, Australia, Taiwan and the Republic of South Africa. In 1975, Nissan was the best-selling imported brand – ahead of Toyota - in the US. In the 1980s, it built factories in the US and England.

Nissan's situation took a turn for the worse in the 1980s. Honda achieved moderate success with the Acura, while Toyota's Lexus brand was a major hit. So, Nissan responded with hasty launch of its luxury brand Infiniti in 1989. The company had spent a massive amount of money in the Infiniti project, but the brand was a failure. The marketing strategy for Infiniti was based on the image of meditation, emphasizing the tranquility of gardens, trees and stones. However, this did not appeal to Americans, who were unfamiliar with the concept. With the marketing campaign failing to provide anything solid except for some images of random objects, consumers did not warm up to the new brand. Infiniti devastated the company. To make matters worse, Japan was beginning to slip into an extended economic slump: the so-called Lost 20 Years (1991-2011). The complacent working system of Nissan's bureaucratic organization was unable to pull the company out of its downfall.

Thus, in 1999, Nissan President and CEO Yoshihito Hanawa began to search for an alliance partner. Hanawa got Ford, Daimler-Chrysler and Renault to the negotiation table. Ultimately, Nissan allied with Renault and Renault sent Carlos Ghosn to become the president and COO of Nissan. Ghosn turned Nissan's earnings positive in a year. With Ghosn at the helm, Nissan underwent radical restructurings and corporate culture reforms, while engaging in the development of new models. Once everything fell into place, the company's profits started moving up. For Nissan, Renault was its savior. Nissan was equally important to Renault because the alliance, which was formed after the deal with Volvo fell through, produced better results than expected.

The exploits of Le Cost Killer

After the alliance with Nissan, Schweitzer decided to gamble again – this time with a person. He had his eye on Carlos Ghosn, President and COO of Michelin North America. After one interview, Schweitzer offered Ghosn the position of vice president and COO at Nissan. Schweitzer's surprising move astonished the world.

Ghosn is one of the success stories, in which an ordinary employee works his/her way to the top. Ghosn was born in 1954 in Brazil to a Lebanese father and a French mother, who was a third-generation Lebanese immigrant. He graduated from École des mines, one of the most prominent engineering schools in France, and joined Michelin.

In 1985, at the age of 32, Ghosn was appointed COO of Michelin Brazil and subsequently saved it from hyperinflation. Because of his achievements in Brazil, Ghosn was appointed to CEO of Michelin North America in 1989. The Brazil-born man had received an education in France, got hired by a company and became the CEO of organization doing business in one of the largest markets in the world. Being an engineer with a knack for running a company, Ghosn had the perfect résumé for an automobile company —It is no wonder why Schweitzer chose Ghosn as the vice president of Renault

Upon arriving at Renault, Ghosn was met with concerns, but he was quick, decisive and indifferent to the skepticism. In just five months, he set forth the NRP (Nissan Revival Plan), reducing costs by 20 billion dollars and initiating reforms. Soon, Ghosn was sarcastically nicknamed "Le Cost Killer." In the following year, Nissan's earnings made a literal U-turn and swung positive. People's opinions of him also changed, and he was re-nicknamed "the Ice Breaker" for pulling the company "out of its frozen prison."

CHAPTER 13

Ghosn's Magic Takes Renault Global

"As requested, we will pay the incentives for the 5.2 months."

Heads shot up at the interpreter's translation of Ghosn's words. It was in 2001, the labor union representatives had demanded a raise and gathered in the auditorium at Nissan headquarters in Tokyo to hear Ghosn's counterproposal. To their surprise, their COO had accepted their terms. Ghosn smiled and continued to say, "Wages will be raised from last year's 6,500 yen to 7,000 yen in return for all your hard work."

The labor union had no reason to continue negotiating. When the labor union stated their demands, Nissan management would generally drag negotiations on until the spring labor offensives and would seek to reach an agreement after observing what Toyota did. So, Nissan employees were taken aback by Ghosn's answer and the fact that the answer came immediately after the demands were made.

In September 1996, Ghosn arrived at Nissan as the third highest ranked executive. He immediately made bold decisions to cut costs and improved the company's financial health, swiftly transforming the loss-stricken Nissan into a profit-generating company. Under Ghosn's leadership, the Renault-Nissan Alliance pursued M&A opportunities in Europe and Asia, leading to the acquisition of Dacia, Samsung Motors and AvtoVAZ. As a result, the Alliance was able to hold its position as the fourth largest automobile manufacturer in the world.

Carlos "Mr. V" Ghosn

Upon recruiting him in 1996, Schweitzer gave Ghosn complete control over technology, development, manufacturing and purchasing. Due to his experience in the region, Ghosn was also given control over South American operations. Despite being tasked with a crucial mission for France's leading car company, he was far from hesitant. CEOs generally spend the first five months at a new company struggling to get a grip on their jobs. In his first five months at Nissan, he had devised a plan to cut costs by 20 billion dollars.

One of Ghosn's finer attribute was his initiative. For instance, in February 1997, Ghosn announced that the Vilvoorde plant in Belgium would close. The 300 employees working there strongly voiced their dissent, but he did not change his plans. The plant was closed that year.

For 1996, its first year as a private company, Renault recorded a 5.25 billion-franc (105 billion yen) loss. The following year the company made a U-turn and recorded a 5.43 billion-franc (118.5 billion yen profit). In an interview with the French newspaper, Le Figaro, in September 1997, Ghosn said, "Strong countermeasures must be implemented when the company is suffering losses under difficult circumstances. Excessive costs were the problem for Renault. Enterprises must grow."

Feeding on the momentum of its successful turnaround, Renault established further plans for growth. In November 1997, Renault announced that it would reduce costs by 20 billion francs (400 billion yen) between 1998 and 2000. The company also began to streamline its parts vendors. Ghosn reduced the number of parts vendors and requested lower prices in exchange for a guarantee of long-term business ties. This was the so-called optima system, which earned Ghosn the nickname Le Cost Killer.

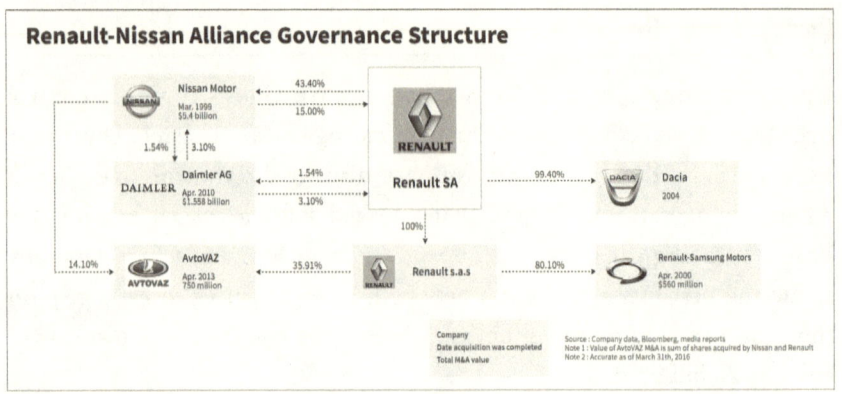

Renault-Nissan Alliance Governance Structure

Nissan falters

Born from a secret project code-named, Pacific, the Renault-Nissan Alliance provided the opportunity for growth, but also a risky endeavor. If Nissan was unable to solve its financial troubles, both companies would be endangered.

On April 2, 1999, Ghosn took office as Nissan's COO and immediately began restructuring processes under a set of plans titled the Nissan Revival Plan (NRP). The most urgent task was the unifying platforms (chassis and power train) and sharing parts. Together, Nissan and Renault had 34 platforms, which Ghosn decided to reduce to 10. Overlapping production facilities and sales networks needed to be reduced and more efficient. He also began implementing a system that would allow Renault and Nissan to share their production facilities and distribution networks around the world. For example, Nissan would access Renault's factories and dealership networks in Brazil and Argentina, while Renault would utilize Nissan's plant in Mexico. Ghosn's vision reduced the two companies' combined costs by 390 billion yen during the three years since 2000.

Assembly systems were reorganized. Ghosn announced his plan to shut down five plants in Japan and reduce the workforce by 21,000, which represented 14% of Nissan Group's employees around the world. His decision to close the Murayama plant, which had 2,300 employees, came as a shock to people inside and outside Nissan. This was because the plant, which Nissan obtained through the acquisition of Prince Motor in 1966, had a long history and a number of long-serving employees. Ghosn said that people being forced to leave factories was the most difficult part of implementing the NRP. As heart-broken as he was, Ghosn showed no hesitation in executing his plans, because his goal was to revive the company.

Nissan owned stocks in 1,394 companies. With the exception of the stakes in four, all were sold off by Ghosn. He also reduced the number of Nissan's parts vendors from 1,145 to less than 600 by 2002. This was the Nissan disaffiliation that upset the Japanese business world. People expressed disdain toward Ghosn's method of digging into Nissan's problems and amputating the cause.

The effectiveness of the NRP was proven as Nissan turned around from a 684.3 billion-yen loss for the 1999 fiscal year (April 1999 to March 2000) to a 331.1 billion profit in 2000 fiscal year (April 2000 to March 2001). Nissan sold 2.6 million cars in 2000 alone, becoming the second largest automaker in Japan after Toyota in just two years. On June 1, 2005, Ghosn succeeded Schweitzer as the Chairman of the Renault Group and was appointed CEO of Nissan.

Troublesome Nissan Diesel goes to Volvo

One of the reasons Nissan sought a financial alliance was the massive debts of its truck manufacturing affiliate, Nissan Diesel. At the time, Nissan Diesel had 500 billion yen in outstanding debts. The company was unable to get further loans, because banks had turned their backs on Nissan Diesel. Due to sluggish sales, Nissan Diesel suffered a 44 billion loss for the fiscal year of 2000. When acquiring the 36.8% stake in Nissan, Renault had also bought a 23.5% stake in Nissan Diesel. Preoccupied with Nissan, Ghosn and other Renault executives did not have any detailed plans for Nissan Diesel.

In April 2000, Ghosn finally visited Nissan Diesel. On the 25th of the same month, Renault announced a merger between its truck manufacturing wing and Volvo's truck division. According to the announcement, Renault would sell its truck units – the subsidiary Renault NI and Mack, which was acquired to assist Renault's foray into the US – to Volvo, while becoming Volvo's majority shareholder by buying a 21.4% stake. Volvo had decided to fully commit to its truck business and sold off its passenger car business to Ford, which made Volvo the second largest truck manufacturer in the world. This was a major landscape change for the truck industry. Nissan Diesel naturally found its way into Volvo's arms and was later renamed UD Truck. Sometime after, Renault decided to sell its Volvo shares to improve its financial health and secure funds for future M&A endeavors. So, Renault sold a 14.9% stake for 3 billion euros in 2010 and the remaining share for 1.5 billion euros in 2012.

Putting down roots in Korea

Renault also has close ties in Korea. On April 27, 2000, Renault took over Samsung Motors. It bought all of Samsung Motors' assets –the Busan factory and its land, the research facility and so on– for 560 million dollars. Renault owned 80.1% of Samsung Motors, while the remaining 19.9% was owned by Samsung Card. The Samsung Group has forfeited automobile manufacturing, but the 19.9% stake suggests that it still has its eyes on the automobile industry. Samsung is also in the process of expanding its business in electric vehicle batteries and other automotive parts through Samsung SDI and other subsidiaries. Therefore, it would be worth watching how Samsung advances its automobile-related operations.

From the start, the Samsung Motors (renamed Renault-Samsung after the acquisition) deal acquisition caused noise. The Samsung Group was criticized for selling the company "dirt cheap." After the acquisition, the company began losing its competitiveness and struggled with poor sales because development of new models were delayed and it had a product line of only four models – the SM3, SM5, SM7 and QM5. The company also downsized its workforce, accepting voluntary retirement. This created rumors that Renault was pulling out of Korea or Renault would sell Renault-Samsung. However, Renault-Samsung is improving its fundamentals. It released the popular QM3 in late 2013. In September 2014, it was tasked with the production of Nissan's the through the QM3 released in late 2013 and the production of Nissan Rogues that were intended to be exported to North America.

Continuing growth

Renault's aspiration to become a bigger corporation continued to burn. Aggressive M&As and financial alliances were the cornerstone of Renault's rise to the fourth largest name in the automobile industry a few years after its privatization in 1996.

While Renault and Nissan were forming their alliance in 1999, Renault was pursuing another takeover – this time, in Romania. Late in the year, Renault dropped yet another bombshell by purchasing a 51% stake in Dacia, the largest state-run automobile manufacturer in Romania, and gaining management rights. This deal is considered one of the most successful instances of brand diversification strategy. Dacia had taken advantage of Romania's low labor costs to make affordable durable cars; attracting consumers had no choice but to rely on used cars.

Dacia's output reached an all-time high 340 thousand units in 2013, increasing 16% from the previous year. That year, it sold 430 thousand cars, which was 19.3% more than in 2012. Dacia was achieving the fastest growth among automakers based in EU countries.

Dacia is the ancient Roman name for the area that became Romania. Dacia, which is the most popular marque in the country, display signs of Renault's DNA. Dacia was founded in 1968 importing, assembling and selling the subcompact Renault 8. Romania's per hour income of 3.75 euros was among the lowest in Europe. Dacia took advantage of the low wages to build neatly designed, durable sedans and SUVs that appealed to consumers in both Eastern and Western Europe. By 2004, Renault had increased its ownership of Dacia to 99.3% and gained full control.

Savoring the taste of success from Dacia, Renault-Nissan reached out to Russia. The Alliance secured a 25% stake in Russia's state-owned car manufacturer, AvtoVAZ, for 1.17 billion euros in 2008. Three years later, Renault-Nissan acquired another 25% stake and gained management rights. In 2014, Renault-Nissan changed its plans for AvtoVAZ and decided to establish a joint venture: it would establish a joint company with Russian Technology, which holds a 29% stake in AvtoVAZ, and hold a 67.13% stake. The joint venture would own 74.5% of AvtoVAZ, and by extension Renault-Nissan would possess 50.01% of AvtoVAZ shares. The Alliance invested 750 million dollars in the venture, with Renault contributing 300 million and Nissan 450 million.

AvtoVAZ was founded in 1966 through a technology collaboration agreement with Fiat. In 1970, AvtoVAZ released the sedan, Zhiguli, which was based on the Fiat 124. The Zhiguli was exported under the nameplate, Lada. AvtoVAZ manufactured and sold the Zhiguli without any major changes until 1991. It also released the Fiat 124.

In 2013, Renault-Nissan forayed into the Chinese market by launching a joint venture with Dongfeng Motor. It was a latecomer in China, which had become one of the world's largest automobile markets, but late was better than never. Nissan already had strong footing in North America, but was unable to establish a solid presence in China, making Renault's support crucial. The decision was made by Ghosn after analyzing the global automobile market landscape.

Having established itself in the mass production and affordable automobile market, the company decided to revive its high-end Alpine nameplate. Founded by Jean Rédélé in 1955, Alpine originally used Renault engines and chassis to build racing cars. The company was acquired by Renault after winning the World Rally Championship in 1973. The marque was discontinued in 1995 due to poor sales. Renault-Nissan decided to separate Alpine from its existing mass-production prestige Infiniti marque and position it as an independent premium, high-performance sports car brand utilizing the Renault F1 team's technology.

French government reduces influence over Renault-Nissan

After the two struggling companies joined hands to become the fourth largest presence in the automobile industry, the Alliance stumbled into trouble in March 2014. The Hollande administration enforced the " Florange Act," which stipulated that the voting rights attached to stocks held by the French government for two or more years be doubled. The law was established to protect French corporations against speculative foreign investment and ensure sustainable growth of French companies and job security. The law would not apply to companies if two thirds of shareholders voted against it. After the law took effect, the French government purchased an additional 14 million Renault-Nissan shares in April 2015, increasing its stake to 19.7% and effectively increasing its voting rights to 39.4%. The change had the potential of affecting Nissan, 43.4% of which was owned by Renault.

In December 2015, the Renault board of directors voted to limit the voting rights of the French government, its majority shareholder, and guarantee the operational independence of Nissan. Renault limited the voting right increase resulting from the Florange Act to strategic decisions and special projects conducted in France. Nissan would remain free of any interference from Renault and was given the right to sell off its Renault stake if the independence of its management was violated. Crisis had befallen the strong alliance, but the companies overcame it through wise decisions. In fact, the crisis had only made the partnership stronger as the two companies decided to merge operations in new areas, adding to pre-existing joint efforts in R&D, production, purchase and logistics.

Even now, the Renault-Nissan Alliance is going full speed ahead with Ghosn at the helm.

Groundbreaking Classics #2

Jeep, the Original SUV

There is no doubt that war is a tragedy. At times, war brings significant changes. The automobile industry is no exception. War was instrumental to the birth of some of the most famous vehicles in history. A good example is the Jeep, the original SUV.

When talking about Jeeps, it is impossible not to mention Germany's G-5. The G-5 is the ancestor of Mercedes-Benz's off-roader vehicle G-Wagen. Having lost WWI, Germany was prohibited from developing tanks. So, it decided to develop a 4-wheel drive vehicle to replace tanks. The result was the G-5, unveiled in 1937. Thanks to its outstanding mobility, the strong, powerful 4-wheel drive vehicle was instrumental to successful military operations. Early during WWII, the Allied Forces were defenseless against the G-5. They were in desperate need of a counter measure.

So, the US stepped up. In July 1940, the Pentagon contacted automobile companies for a vehicle that has a 4-wheel drive system, a folding windshield, a wheel base of 2,032mm and a top speed of 80km/h, while weighing 1,300 pounds (589kg) or less, has a load capacity of 0.25 tons or less and carries three people. Since the country was at war, the Pentagon demanded that 40 prototypes be supplied in 49 days and 70 in 75 days.

Only American Bantam Car Company and Willys-Overland responded to the request with Ford applying later. Ultimately, Willys-Overland's vehicle was selected. *The Willys Quad showed the best road test results. The vehicle was related Willys MA and then Willys MB. A total of 600 thousand units were manufactured during WWII.*

So, how did the name of this vehicle become Jeep? One theory is that Jeep comes from GP (General Purpose). Another explanation is that GPW (Government-P-Wheelbase Willy's) was slurred into Jeep. There is also the opinion that the name comes from Eugene the Jeep, a magic puppy in the comic series Popeye. Regardless of its origin, Willys-Overland registered Jeep as a trademark.

After the war, the multipurpose vehicle found its way to the general public. The Jeeps were used as everyday vehicles, cargo transports, agricultural vehicles and more. As a result, Willys-Overland released the CJ-1A, which means "civilian Jeep first model of the Army," in 1944. In August 1945, the CJ-2A was announced. In Korea, Shinjin Motors manufactured CJs from 1969. Shinjin Motors was renamed Geohwa Motor, and the CJ nameplate was changed to Korando. Production of the Korando continued after Geowha was acquired by Dong-A Motors and subsequently, by SsangYong Motor. The model resembling Jeeps have been discontinued, but the Korando nameplate lives on.

EMPIRE V

Hyundai Motor Group

CHAPTER 14

The Pony Miracle: Parting with Ford

"Hyundai becomes tenth largest automobile company with acquisition of Kia."

On October 19, 1998, world media rushed to report news of Hyundai Motor's acquisition of Kia Motors. In 1997, Hyundai Motor was producing around 1.8 million cars per year, which was around one seventh of the global leader, GM. But then, it acquired Kia Motors, which had a production capacity of 0.83 million units, and emerged as the tenth largest automaker in the world.

During the 1990s, automobile companies around the world were competing to increase their size in an effort to achieve economies of scale. People were accepting Jürgen E. Schrempp's prophecy - only five companies with an annual production capacity of over 5 million would make it into the 21st century - as the truth. Schrempp was preoccupied with the Daimler-Chrysler merger in an effort to become one of the five that survive in the 21st century.

Hyundai was pushing forward to produce 2 million cars by 2000. It needed Kia to boost its production capacity. Taking over an established company would be much easier than increasing factories.

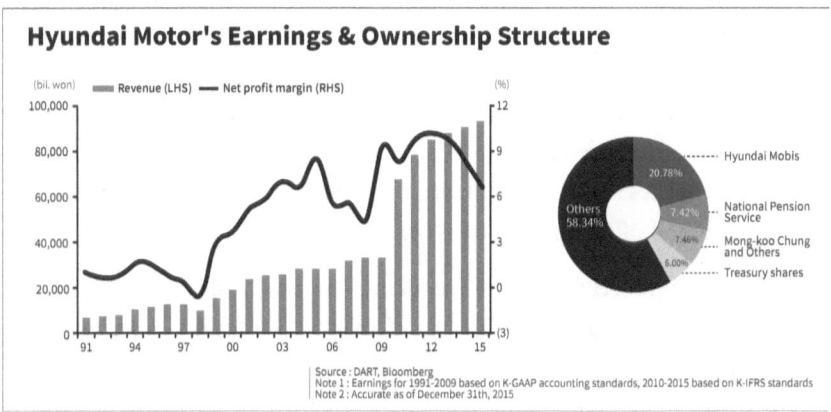

Hyundai Motor's Earnings & Ownership Structure

Source : DART, Bloomberg
Note 1 : Earnings for 1991-2009 based on K-GAAP accounting standards, 2010-2015 based on K-IFRS standards
Note 2 : Accurate as of December 31th, 2015

The Kia acquisition was no cruise. Having failed to withstand the onslaught of the financial crisis that hit Korea in 1997, Kia had filed for bankruptcy and was placed under court receivership. Ford and Samsung Motors were competing against Hyundai to become the new owner of Kia. The acquisition was particularly crucial for Samsung Motors, because it would become the subject of restructuring should it fail.

However, fortune favored Hyundai and 15 years later, in 2013, the Hyundai-Kia Automotive Group established itself as the fifth largest automobile manufacturer with a combined annual output of 7.56 million units.

From its days under founder Ju-yung Chung to his brother Se-yung Chung and to HMC (Hyundai Motor Company) Group Chairman Mong-koo Chung, Hyundai's half-century history is the focus of the global auto industry and a representation of the advances of the Korean auto industry.

Cars blossom in the ruins of the Korea War

Hyundai Motor was founded in 1967, but its history goes back 27 years to 1940, when Art Service was established during the Japanese Empire's colonial rule of Korea. Hyundai Group founder Ju-yung Chung bought Art Service, an automobile maintenance plant, for 3,500 won. Business flourished, but it was forcefully merged with the Japanese company, Nishin Factory, two years later. Once car demand began to grow after Korea gained independence in 1945, Chung made another attempt in the automobile business. He bought a 660 square meter lot near Myeongbo Theater in Cho-dong, Jung-gu, Seoul, and founded an automobile repair shop under the Hyundai name. The repair shop was contracted by the US forces in Korea to replace engines and repair outdated Japanese vehicles. During this time, Chung dreamed of making his own car.

One day, opportunity came knocking. In 1950, the repair shop was merged with Hyundai Engineering & Construction and Chung began to save up money. In December 1967, he founded Hyundai Motor with 100 million won in capital. Chung appointed his brother, Se-yung Chung, as the first president of Hyundai Motor.

Asia Motors, which opened two years earlier (Gwangju plant approved in December 1966), already had established a presence in the Korean automobile industry. Shinjin Motors, which acquired Saenara Motors (established in 1962), was manufacturing Toyota Coronas; Shinjin Motors would later become Daewoo Motors. In 1967, the Korean government announced the automaker tri-polarization plant and selected Hyundai Motor as the third company.

Hyundai Motor kicked off with a technological alliance with Ford. Since it had no technology related to automobiles, Hyundai had to settle for assembling SKD (semi knockdown) parts of Ford vehicles. Ford headquarters designated Ford Europe as Hyundai's partner and selected the Cortina (1,598cc), the 20M (1,985cc mid-sized sedan), the D750 (truck) and buses as models to be produced by its Korean partner. The Cortina was developed in the UK in 1966 and was the second best-selling car in the country from the beginning of 1967.

In May 1968, Hyundai Motor secured a 660 thousand square meter lot in the city of Ulsan and began building a factory capable of churning out 3,500 vehicles per year. Korea's Automobile Industry Protection Act of 1962 stipulated that 21% of vehicle parts used to assemble cars must come from domestic sources. So, Hyundai and Ford compiled a list of some 50 Korean companies that would supply batteries, electric wires, cooling system components, springs, glass, seats and other parts. Ford predicted that Hyundai would need three years to begin production, but the Chung brothers were determined to shorten the preparation period. By November 1968, less than a year later, Hyundai began assembling its first Cortina. Hyundai sold 533 Cortinas in 1968 and 5,567 in the following year.

Soon, the Cortina's performance came into question as it broke down often. Hyundai's low assembly proficiency was a problem, but parts wore down quickly because the cars, which were designed for asphalt streets, were being driven on unpaved roads. Chung blamed "Ford's stingy technology transfer" as the main reason for the failure. Thus, Chung reiterated the importance of making "a car built with our own technology" to his brother.

The D750 was criticized heavily at first. Cargo trucks operated at the time were modified US military vehicles, which made them capable of transporting cargo that exceeded their load capacity. Cargo truck owners were having trucks move twice their load capacity. Unless owners acknowledged the fact that military vehicles were different from commercial vehicles, commercial vehicles would break down more often because they were constantly overloaded. Moreover, repairs took long because parts needed to be imported. Due to these problems, Chung separated the car repair division from the manufacturing division in 1973.

A "Pony" surprises the world

"Do not accept even a bowl of soup from suppliers. Never do anything that places you at a disadvantage"

Hyundai Motor was being run by Ju-yung Chung's fourth brother, Se-yung Chung. He was a person who lived by the book. For instance, Se-yung Chung refused even the smallest generosity from suppliers, believing the acceptance of any gift may result in defective products. Having a Master's degree from the University of Miami, he was one of the few people in Korea with overseas at the time.

Once automobile production got on track, Se-yung Chung established plans to export Hyundai cars using Ford's global sales network. However, Ford was against Hyundai exporting cars to any market Ford was operating in.

Having developed Hyundai Motor into the third largest automaker in the country, Ju-yung Chung told his sibling that Hyundai Motor would remain a backwater company unless it manufactured and exported cars independently.

With the government voiding the approval of the alliance, Hyundai severed ties with Ford in 1973. In March of the same year, Hyundai Group Chairman Ju-yung Chung instructed Hyundai Motor President Se-yung Chung to "build a car using our own technology" and that "failure was not an option."

The Chairman's decision was met with opposition from the inside as CKD assembly of cars like the Cortina was a lucrative business that did not require high cost. There was also dissent externally. Since local car demand was under 10 thousand, there was no reason to roll out 56 thousand cars per year. However, market studies revealed that automobile demand would increase from 46 thousand in 1976 to 198 thousand by 1980. Hyundai concluded that it could manufacture its own cars for USD 1,932 per unit, which was below the government's USD 2,000-target. Hence, Chung gained enough support to push the plan forward. Hyundai secured funding through a loan with the Korean government providing surety.

The biggest obstacle was the engine as it was impossible to secure the necessary technology in a short period of time. But, Hyundai was able to shorten the development period by receiving assistance from established countries. So, Se-yung Chung traveled to Japan in May 1973 and went to Mitsubishi to obtain technology for a 1,238cc, water-cooled gasoline engine. Upon returning, he made plans to develop Hyundai's first car based on the Mitsubishi Lancer and the Ford Cortina. The design was contracted to Giorgetto Giugiaro's Italdesign and the diesel engine technology was obtained from the British company, Perkins Engines.

After a nationwide naming contest, Hyundai settled for "Pony" as the name of its car. But, this was also a problem because Ford had trademarked Pony in various countries. So, Hyundai purchased the trademark from Ford, but failed to acquire the trademark in the US because Ford refused to relinquish it.

After the eventful journey, the Pony was presented at the Turin Auto Show in October 1974. The industry was amazed by the neat car made by an unknown company in a country people had never heard of. The Pony received the media's spotlight. Mass production of the Pony began at the Ulsan plant 15 months later. As a result, Korea became the 16th country in the world and the second in Asia, after Japan, to produce a vehicle with its own technology.

During its first year, Hyundai sold 10,726 Pony's and secured a 43.6% market share. Sales benefitted significantly from the government campaign urging people to consume domestic goods. Hyundai's first overseas venture came in 1976 – a deal for exporting five Pony's and one bus to Ecuador. Prior to this, Hyundai exported 15 Pony's to Saudi Arabia, but this is not considered an overseas foray as the cars were purchased by Hyundai Engineering & Construction for its operations in the area.

The Pony was a success; it held a 60% market share in Korea and by 1985, it became the first nameplate to sell over 280 thousand units in Korea. The success of the Pony gave Hyundai enough confidence to release more original models – the Excel in 1985, the Grandeur in 1987, Sonata in 1988 and more.

As Hyundai Motor was developing into an empire, a young man was silently working in one corner. He was Mong-koo Chung, who got a job at the Seoul branch of Hyundai Motor Service in 1970 with the help of his mother, Joong-seok Byun, Ju-yung Chung's wife. As the first lesson in business management, Mong-koo Chung was a lowly manager traveling around the nation, driving a truck full of automobile parts. Despite being the son of the Chairman, he received no privileges. In 21 years, he would surprise the Korean automobile industry with the release of the successful

Galloper at Hyundai Precision & Industries (currently, Hyundai Mobis). After the acquisition of Kia Motors in 1998, Mong-koo Chung would be promoted to Chairman and head the Hyundai-Kia Automotive Group. The acquisition would be both an opportunity and a threat and he would stand at the crossroads of success and failure.

CHAPTER 15

Growth Pains:
Bromont Disaster and the 1st & 2nd Oil Shocks

"I realized how foolish the decision was."

In his autobiography released in 2000, Se-yung Chung expresses a particularly poignant regret about one incident – the nightmarish failure of the Hyundai Motor's Bromont plant. He reminisces, "It was a devastating mistake to build a factory without sufficient market research."

In July 1989, the Korean automobile industry witnessed the completion of its first overseas production facility in Bromont, Quebec, Canada. Construction began in September 1986 on a 1,696,200 square meter lot. Hyundai Motor spent 325 million Canadian dollars to build the plant, which included chassis production facilities, steel presses, painting facilities, assembly lines, a research center and test track. Confident after the success of the Pony and the Excel in Canada, Hyundai decided to build a factory to lower export tariffs on cars and facilitate its foray into the US market. The Canadian government provided the property for one Canadian dollar and a 100 million discount on interest and utilities costs. The government sweetened the pot by adding 9.4 million Canadian dollars for training engineers. At this moment, the future was all roses and rainbows.

The venture was a disaster. The plant, which had an annual production capacity of 100 thousand units, began production with 15 thousand in 1989.

Output came in at 27 thousand in 1990, 28 thousand in 1991 and 15 thousand in 1992, failing to come anywhere close to the break-even point of 60 thousand units. Hyundai was struggling because the US market began to slump in 1989, while competition was escalating with Japanese automakers increasing their North American output. Moreover, the Bromont plant was dedicated to manufacturing Sonatas, which was critically panned in the US because its quality was inferior to competing models, such as the Toyota Camry and the Honda Accord. In a desperate move to salvage the failing foray, Hyundai attempted to sell 30,000 Sonatas per year in the US through Chrysler. However, Hyundai failed to seal the deal due to adverse market conditions.

After the Bromont plant accumulated 500 million Canadian dollars in losses, Hyundai decided to shut down the plant in October 1993. The Canadian government attempted to save it, offering an additional 64 million in assistance. So, Hyundai began seeking ways to make operating the plant worthwhile, such as changing the production model to the Elantra. Failing to find a solution, Hyundai sought to sell the factory to GM and Ford. Ultimately, Hyundai returned the 30 million Canadian dollars it received in funding from the Canadian government and closed the plant. Hyundai's first step into North America ended in utter failure – one Hyundai would be eager to forget.

Growth pains

Like other companies, Hyundai Motor also suffered growth pains. As history shows, company that overcomes growing pains achieves greatness, but those that succumb, collapse into ruin.

Even before the Bromont plant, Hyundai faced many incidents that threatened to upset its foundations. Among the most impactful incidents was the first oil shock in 1973 and the second oil shock in 1979. Like other automakers, Hyundai was unable to shield itself from the impact. The price of gasoline in Korea shot up from 198.5 won/liter at the beginning of 1979 to 740 won/liter at the end of 1981, jumping four fold in three years.

The government made the situation worse. Concerned about fuel consumption, the government implemented measures to curb automobile demand - automobile tax was raised by 50% and car registration was limited. This caused the utilization rate of Hyundai Motor's plant to plunge. Work became so scarce that a third of Hyundai Motor's 12 thousand employees weeded the company's lawns. Hyundai Motor even transferred 300 employees to Hyundai Heavy Industries, which was booming at the time. In the end, the situation deteriorated to a point where Hyundai Motor had no choice but to lay off four thousand employees.

Despite the difficulties, Hyundai Motor could not stop developing new models, which are critical for the survival of any automobile manufacturer. In July 1978, Hyundai began preparing a facelift for the Pony. Once again, designing duties were outsourced to Giorgetto Giugiaro's firm and over half of the components were replaced to upgrade the model. The resulting Pony 2 was released in March 1982. The car sustained Hyundai, selling 39,344 units in 1982 and 49,226 units in 1984.

The political turmoil that followed the oil shocks hit the Korean automobile industry hard. The distress was caused by the theory of comparative advantage spotlighted by the Legislative Council for National Security that emerged after the collapse of the Yushin Dictatorship in 1978. The theory of comparative advantage states that even if a country produces two commodities, it stands to gain by producing the item in which it has a comparative advantage (requires less opportunity cost) and importing the other from a country with a comparative advantage in the second commodity. The Council considered placing the Korean automobile industry, which was not advanced, under the control of GM. From today's perspectives, the logic borders on stupidity, but at the time, Hyundai Motors was almost forced to close. In the end, the government decided against having one company running a single industry and settled for a "single segment production" mandate, which stipulates that a company should exclusively manufacture one type of car to maximize its competitive edge. Under the unification mandate, Hyundai Motor and Saehan Motor (50% owned by GM) manufactured passenger cars, while Kia Motors produced only 5-ton or smaller trucks and buses. This forced Hyundai to cease production of the popular Porter and other trucks. The mandate remained in force for six years, until it was abolished in 1986.

While the Pony won Hyundai its first export deal, the Excel is significant because it enabled Hyundai to penetrate the US market. The US was the largest automobile market in the world at the time and had no equal. Today, China has emerged as the biggest market. Nonetheless, Hyundai Motor aspired to establish a presence in the US market. It knocked at the door of the North American market in November 1983 when it shipped 1,500 Pony 2s to Canada, but was unable to sell them as they did not meet the US's exhaust emission standards. Ford's trademark of the Pony nameplate also discouraged the attempt. Despite repeated requests, Ford refused to relinquish the trademark.

Hyundai decided to enter the US market with a different model. The company conducted a market study through Temple, Barker & Sloane/Strategic Planning Associates (currently, Mercer Management Consulting), which helped Mitsubishi establish its US sales network in its initial foray. Hyundai also launched the "X Car Project." After two years of thorough market studies for its foray into the US, Hyundai released the Excel in February 1986. Hyundai sold 10,432 Excels in the US in March 1986 and exported a total 92,609 units in 1986.

The Excel was initially a success. The car was voted one of top 10 products of 1986 by Fortune magazine. However, the Excel soon became the subject of jokes. Consumers bought the Excel for its cheap price and became disappointed by its poor quality. People called the Excel a "disposable car" and joked that "anything stuck to it will fall off." It was a painful rite of passage for Hyundai as it entered the world's largest and hugely competitive market.

Mong-koo Chung steps forward after the Galloper miracle

While Ju-yung and Se-yung Chung are credited with the establishment of Hyundai Motor and making their mark in the global market with the Pony and Excel, it was Hyundai Motor Group Chairman Mong-koo "MK" Chung who catapulted the company into the world's fifth largest car company. MK was born in 1938 as the second child of eight siblings. After receiving an engineering degree, he spent two years studying at the University of Connecticut. He took his first step into the automobile industry when he found a part-time job at an automobile press factory in the US. In February 1970, he was hired as the parts department manager at Hyundai Motor's Seoul office, where he busied himself repairing cars. No car company CEO in the world has worked as a mechanic as long as MK. Due to his career background, Chung still puts on gloves to personally inspect every new model developed at Hyundai and gives specific instructions.

In 1973, MK had a stint as the head of the procurement department and Hyundai Heavy Industry's shipbuilding unit, but was promoted by his father a year later as the head of Hyundai Motor's spun off repair division, Hyundai Motor Service. Hyundai Motor Service ventured into the filter manufacturing sector by acquiring Hyundai's filter supplier, Taeshin, in 1975, following the latter's bankruptcy. The company expanded to valve and container businesses. Believing that the container business did not comply with automotive parts manufacturing and car repairs, the container business was separated into an independent entity in 1977 and became Hyundai Precision & Industries (later, Hyundai Mobis). Hyundai Motor Service continued to grow at a fast pace until the late 1970s. However, the second oil shock in 1978 and the assassination of President Chung-hee Park on October 26, 1979, left the country in chaos; meanwhile, wages surged. This caused trouble for Hyundai Motor Service's operations, in which the employees were the company's main assets. MK told his father that Hyundai Motor Service needed to expand to car sales to continue growing and that Hyundai Motor Company needed to separate production and sales, while integrating sales and maintenance. The Chairman accepted MK's proposal and in 1982, Hyundai Motor Service obtained dealership rights around the nation, except in some areas of Incheon and Gyeonggi Province and the Yeongnam Region.

MK had proven his entrepreneurship to his father by getting Hyundai Motor Service and Hyundai Precision & Industries on track. MK demonstrated his business skills once again through the Galloper Project. Once wages began surging from 1987, Hyundai Precision & Industries' container business hit a reef. Up until this point, MK's achievements in the automobile business were limited to repair, maintenance and sales. So, he decided to make a car.

MK started with golf carts. With the help of Deere & Company, MK successfully began producing golf carts. Having gained confidence from the endeavor, he ordered the development of a 4WD (four-wheel drive) vehicle in July 1988. At the time, SsangYong Motor had monopolized the 4WD vehicle market with the Korando. Hyundai did not have the money to develop a 4WD car because of the Bromont plant construction. But, MK found an opening. Hyundai Precision & Industries contacted Mitsubishi, which owned 15% of Hyundai Motor, to strike a deal, in which Mitsubishi would provide technology related to engines, transmissions and chassis in exchange for royalties. Initially, MK wanted to have the company develop its own technology, but revised his plans due to time and costs involved. Instead, he settled for domestically producing Mitsubishi Pajeros. It was close to CKD production, but since the company's future was at stake, there was no time to spare.

MK was also passionate about the project. Once a prototype was built, he personally test drove the car and ordered instructions. For example, MK found that the Scoupe steering wheel did not provide any stability and ordered that a large-sized handle be made.

The Hyundai Galloper was released in October 1991 and beat the Korando as the leading seller in just four months. Astonished, the industry praised the Galloper saying that the surprise vehicle had created a miracle. The Galloper sold 16 thousand units in the first year and 25 thousand in 1992. When the 7-seat minivan, Santamo, was released in 1995 and proved to be just as successful, Ju-yung Chung was confident about his son's abilities. Being the first son and having proven his business prowess, MK was appointed Chairman of the Hyundai Group on December 28, 1995. Se-yung Chung became Honorary Chairman of Hyundai Motors and removed himself from management. MK's time had come.

CHAPTER 16

Kia Motors:
Dream of Technological Independence

"This is the true beginning of Kia Motors."

These were words spoken by Kia Motors Chairman Sun-hong Kim at the 1991 Tokyo Motor Show. At the time, Kia unveiled three models – the Sportage, Sephia and Sephia Convertible – developed by using its own technology. But the spotlight was shining on the Sportage. The Sportage was the world's first compact SUV, establishing a new segment of cars that was both a passenger car and an SUV. The unprecedented vehicle caused murmurs throughout the auditorium. Engineers from prominent Japanese automobile companies flocked around the car presented by an unknown automaker from a little-known country. The Sportage was invited to return to the Tokyo Motor Show for four straight years until 1995. A few years later, Toyota benchmarked the Sportage and released RAV4 in 1994 and Honda the CR-V in 1995.

Underlying the Sportage is Kia Motors' struggle to stand on its own. After the single segment production mandate was abolished in 1986, Kia partnered with Mazda and released the successful Pride (sold in the US as the Ford Festiva). Mazda's partner, Ford (25% stake in Mazda acquired in 1978), wanted to develop a subcompact car to sell in the US, but found Japan's wages to be burdensome. Mazda also did not have the funds to build a new factory. Hence, Ford took an interest in Mazda's other partner, Kia.

Since Kia was faithfully fulfilling a role as a quality production base, Ford proposed the joint development of a small-size SUV – the UW-52 project. At the time, Kia was only capable of churning out 20 thousand cars per year. For Kia, the UW-52 project was a massive undertaking that required Kia to produce 15 thousand units of one model.

The project created friction immediately as Ford demanded a 50% stake in Kia, which the Chairman and Kia management thought to be ridiculous. Ford took a step back, but demanded that the Hwaseong plant Kia was building, (initially named the Asan Bay plant, but changed later to avoid confusion with Hyundai's Asan plant) be established as an independent entity and relinquish 50% ownership to Ford. Kim refused again. Later, Kia continued with the project on its own and produced its own model: the Sportage.

Despite being a milestone in the history of the global automobile industry, the first generation Sportage failed to achieve any significant success. The car was intended for city streets, but was built on a frame for cargo vehicles (passenger car monocoque frames used from second generation cars), rendering it relatively uncomfortable to drive. Above all, Kia set foot into the US market after Japanese companies.

The Sportage improved Kia's status, but it was also its downfall. Kia decided that it would no longer rely on overseas automakers and would continue to develop cars on its own. The decision was respectable, but the massive amounts of money spent strained the company financially.

Korea's oldest automobile manufacturer

Kia Motors was established in 1994 by Chairman Chul-ho Kim as a bicycle parts manufacturing factory named Kyungsung Precision Industry. At the age of 16, Kim traveled to Japan and learned to build bicycles. He went on to establish a factory famous for its technology in bicycle nuts and bolts. After saving up five million yen, Kim returned to Korea and started a company.

Being the oldest automobile manufacturer in Korea, a large number of Kia's products are "the first in Korea." In 1952, Kyungsung Precision Industry was renamed Kia Industries and produced Korea's first domestically produced bicycle, Samchully, in Busan. The company began manufacturing bicycles with motors in 1961. In 1962, it formed a technology alliance with Honda and released Korea's first motorcycle, the C100. Later that year, the company took its first step into the auto industry by forming another technology alliance with Toyo Kogyo (the predecessor of Mazda) to release the three-wheeled cargo vehicle, K-360 (356cc engine). Afterwards, the company released the T-1500 (1,484cc), a bigger version of the K-360 with a larger engine. The three-wheeled vehicles were essential for merchants.

Thanks to the brisk sales of the three-wheeled vehicles, Kia Industry went public in June 1973 and completed the construction of Korea's first integrated automobile factory, the Sohari plant (annual production capacity of 25 thousand units). Since Hyundai's first Ulsan plant was completed in 1975, Kia was two years ahead.

Failing to receive authorization to manufacture passenger cars, the Sohari plant spent its first year assembling trucks. The model being produced at the time was the small-sized truck, Brisa Pickup, which was virtually a passenger car. On April 5, 1974, President Jung-hee Park visited the factory without notice. The next day, Kia was cleared to begin manufacturing the family car variant of Brisa, which was based on the third-generation Mazda Famillia. Initially, 60% of Brisa parts were manufactured locally. The Famillia has an affinity to the Hyundai Pony as both were designed by Giorgetto Giugiaro. The name Brisa refers to the northeast trade wind blowing in the Caribbean. Anyhow, Kia differentiated the Brisa from the Famillia by applying front grills and tail lamps of its own design. In 1975, before the debut of the Pony, the Brisa accounted for 55% of the Korean passenger car market. Its low engine displacement reduced fuel consumption, making the Brisa a popular model for taxis. The Brisa was highly popular, selling 31,017 units by 1983. In September 1975, Kia exported ten Brisa Pickups to Qatar, which was Korea's first automobile export.

Acquisition of Asia Motors and separation of Samchuly Bicycle

After founder Chul-ho Kim passed away in 1973, his eldest son, Sang-moon Kim, became the Chairman and Kia Motors entered an era of change, undergoing a series of M&As, split/spin-offs and business establishment. First, in 1976, Kia Industries acquired Asia Motors, which currently serves as Kia's Gwangju plant. Asia Motors was founded in 1965 by entrepreneur, Moon-hwan Lee, who earned his fortune selling fertilizer in the Honam region of Korea. Lee established the company through a loan deal with Fiat, SIMCA (Fiat's French branch at the time; sold to PSA in 1979) and SIAVE. Asia Motors was picked up by Dongkuk Steel in 1969. In 1970, it partnered with Fiat and began manufacturing the Fiat 124. Though the car was popular among the middle and upper class population due to its unique angulated design, it was discontinued after three years because Fiat refused to extend the contract.

After getting picked up by Kia, Asia Motors was operated as a separate brand. Asia specialized in buses, trucks and other commercial vehicles and supplied vehicles to the military. Despite being a household name in the commercial vehicle market, its business was limited to Korea. In an attempt to reduce costs for producing a variety of models in small quantities, Asia Motors formed a technology partnership with Hino Truck in 1978.

After acquiring Asia Motors in 1976, Kia Industries established Kia Machine. Kia Machine started off in 1977 manufacturing machine tools. In 1979, it began producing car transmissions and supplied them to Kia Industries. Kia Machine remained a core parts supplier until it was acquired by Hyundai Motor. Kia Machine was renamed Kia Heavy Industries in 1996 and again to Hyundai Wia following its acquisition by Hyundai Motor.

The year Kia Machine was founded in 1976, Kia Industries spun off its motorcycle division and established Kia Industrial, which became Daelim Motor. Kia Industrial was picked up by Daelim Industrial in 1982 as its motorcycle unit and was renamed Daelim Motor. Kia's bicycle division was separated in March 1979 and became an independent entity named Samchuly Bicycle. Today, Samchuly Bicycle is Samchuly, whose majority shareholder is Seok-hwan Kim (27.1% stake owned), the grandson of Kia Motors founder Chul-ho Kim. Until Kia Motors was acquired by Hyundai Motor, Seok-hwan Kim worked as the executive leading the finance department and export division.

The Bongo Legend

Struggling from the fallout of the oil shock and the passenger car manufacturing restriction, Kia Industries recorded 50 billion won in losses between 1980 and 1981. It seemed Kia Industries was going under. Kia Industries was forced to downsize, selling off five of its 18 subsidiaries. In 1981, Chairman Sang-moon Kim took responsibility for the company's downfall and relinquished his 25% stake in the company to the employee shareholder union to be used to cover employee welfare. After 37 years as a family-owned business, Kia Industries was left in the hands of a professional businessman. The Chairman appointed Kia Machine President Sun-hong Kim, who was one of the first employees hired by Kia Industries, as his successor.

After years of efforts to improve the company's financial health, Kia Industries finally found a goose that laid golden eggs. This was the so-called Bongo Legend. In July 1980, Kia Industries took the first generation Mazda Bongo and released a one-ton truck. The following year, the truck was modified and released as the Bongo Coach. This vehicle was such a hit that its name, Bongo, became synonymous with van in Korea. The farm truck Ceres released in 1983 also sold well. Employees forfeited bonuses, while the company made efforts to save costs and improve productivity. By 1983, Kia Industries became one of the most profitable companies among Korea's top 50 corporations.

On the back of technology provided by Ford and Mazda, Kia Industries released the Pride and established a solid presence in the Korean family car market. In 1990, the company was renamed Kia Motors. Under the slogan "Technology Kia," Kia Motors spent massive amounts of money to release self-developed cars, such as the Sephia, Credos and Sportage. It also invested heavily to vertically integrate production processes, such as the acquisition of Kia Special Steel (currently, SeAH Besteel). However, excessive investments usually come back to stab companies in the back. Sun-hong Kim's grand dream ultimately turned out to be the very cause that endangered Kia Motors.

CHAPTER 17

Hyundai Takes Kia Under Its Wing

In order to overcome the financial struggles caused by snowballing losses, Sun-hong Kim decided to gamble. As a result, Kia released the mid-size sedan Credos as the follow-up to the Concord. The Credos was an ambitious endeavor on which Kia spent 510 billion won. Kim was confident that the Credos would be a success because he believed it to be superior in performance and design. However, the market response was lukewarm. Kia's marketing campaign for the Credos placed heavy emphasis on "exquisite handling." But, it was so far ahead of its time that it failed to appeal to consumers. Moreover, the Credos was more expensive. The 1.8-liter Credos was priced at 11.5 million won, while its competing models, the Daewoo New Prince and the Hyundai Sonata II, were each priced at 9,85 million and 9.5 million.

There is a saying, "If the product is good, people will buy even if it is expensive." This may seem true, but it usually applies to luxury brands. True, Kia had made great technological advances, but it was not a prestige brand. The failure of the car and the marketing strategy weighed down heavily on the enterprise. Decisions of CEOs tend to have a massive influence on the company. And Kim had pushed Kia to its doom

Financial struggles

From 1983 to 1985, Kia Industries increased its capital by 20-25 billion denomination each year because of difficulties in receiving loans. Hence, all capital expenditure had to be funded through capital increases. At the time, Kia was raising 60% of its funding through new share issuances. Another reason for its funding preference was because the separation between ownership and management eliminated the need for the majority shareholder to increase ownership to maintain control of the company. In 1983, Kia Industries issued 25 billion won in new shares, which were sold to Mazda (2 billion invested; 8% stake) and Itochu Corporation (0.5 billion invested; 2% stake). Mazda and Itochu owned common shares, but were unable to participate in management as their financial alliances with Kia stipulated that the shares be considered non-voting shares.

In 1986, Ford took part in the capital increase and acquired a 10% stake for 11 billion won. After the single segment production mandate was abolished in 1986, Kia was allowed to resume production of family cars in 1987. Along with the decision to produce the Pride and the Concord, Kia, Mazda and Ford formed an alliance, in which Kia managed production, Mazda, car development, and Ford, sales in the US. During this process, Kia had overseas companies own 20% of its stocks. Having secured funds via new share issuances, Kia proceeded with the construction of the Asan Bay plant (annual production capacity of 100,000 units) and acquired Daehan Heavy Machinery from Korea Development Bank in 1986 to reinforce its automotive parts division. The Asan Bay plant completed in 1989, is currently the Hwaseong plant.

Kia Industries was renamed Kia Motors in 1990, following the inauguration of Chairman Sun-hong Kim. Daehan Heavy Machinery was renamed Kia Special Steel. Kim set forth the motto "Technology Kia" and began to invest massive amounts of money. In 1992, Kia developed its own front-wheel drive platform, which was used to manufacture Sephia. In 1993, it developed a 4WD SUV platform, which was used in the Sportage. Kia spent 900 billion won in developing the Sephia and 440 billion in the

Sportage. Even by today's standards, this was a massive amount. Hyundai spent 500 billion won in R&D each for the Equus and Genesis, and 450 billion each for the YF Sonata and the LF Sonata. At the time, Daewoo Motor spent 45 billion won to come up with the Cielo, Sephia's competing model.

The problem was that despite spending all that money for R&D, the cars were not selling. Moreover, excessive capital expenditure had pushed Kia Special Steel into a heap of debt. For the first time in 13 years, Kia recorded a net loss of 69.6 billion won in 1994. Kia was in so much financial trouble that it was unable to pay its employees proper wages or bonuses.

M&A rumors emerge

The possibility of Kia Motors getting acquired by another company began to emerge in the mid-1990s. Rumors began to escalate from 1995. The daily trading volume for Kia Motors stocks hovered between 200 thousand and 300 thousand. Kia Motors had 745,000 shares issued. The reason for the M&A rumors was partially attributable to financial troubles stemming from poor unit sales, but the majority shareholder's small stake was also a cause. There was a strong chance that Mazda, which held a 7.5% stake in Kia Motors, would sell its Kia stocks because it was the most financially troubled company among Japanese automakers. Kia's advanced technology made it a compelling M&A target. Coincidently, Korea had eased legal restrictions on hostile takeovers before joining the OECD. The government abolished regulation that prevented anyone, except for the majority shareholder at the time of listing, to own over 10% of a company's stocks. Mergers through tender offers began to occur and institutional investors began exercising their voting rights to protect the interests of minor shareholders.

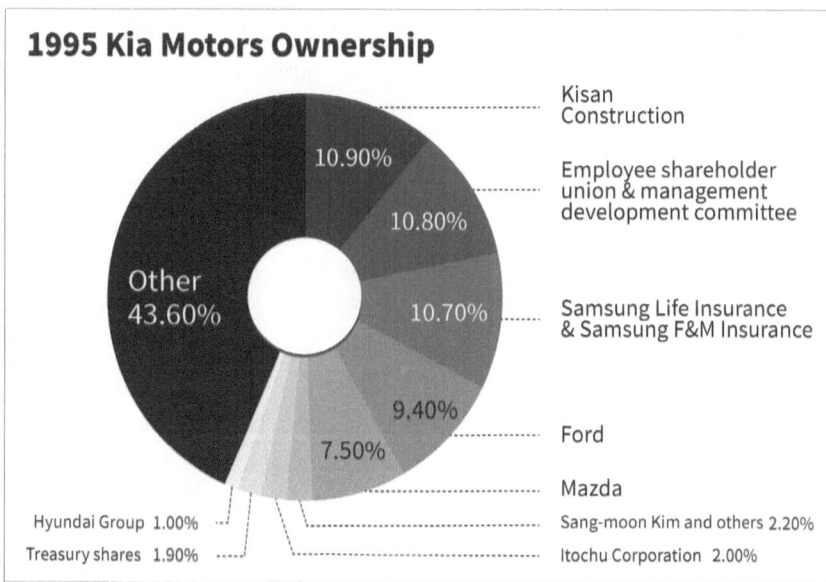

1995 Kia Motors Ownership

- Kisan Construction — 10.90%
- Employee shareholder union & management development committee — 10.80%
- Samsung Life Insurance & Samsung F&M Insurance — 10.70%
- Ford — 9.40%
- Mazda — 7.50%
- Sang-moon Kim and others — 2.20%
- Itochu Corporation — 2.00%
- Treasury shares — 1.90%
- Hyundai Group — 1.00%
- Other — 43.60%

The Samsung Group was a name that was always included in M&A rumors. The Wall Street Journal reported that the financially troubled Kia Motors was highly likely to be taken over by the Samsung Group. Samsung was considered the top candidate for acquiring Kia Motors, because Samsung Life Insurance had purchased a large number of Kia stocks in 1993. By the end of the third quarter of 1993, Samsung Life Insurance increased its stake in Kia Motors to 8%, claiming it was only an investment. Combined with Samsung Fire & Marine Insurance and other Samsung affiliates, the Samsung Group owned more than 10% of Kia Motors shares. The employee shareholder union, which was the largest shareholder of Kia Motors, owned only 7.73%. According to the securities trading act at the time, insurance companies and banks are allowed to own up to 10% and securities companies 5% of listed companies, but were unable to exercise voting rights during shareholder meetings. Strong protests from Kia Motors and pressure from the public forced Samsung Life Insurance to lower its stake to around 6-7% the following year.

In 1995, Samsung ventured into the auto industry by investing 5.6 billion dollars in the Sinho industrial complex in Busan. Being a late entrant, Samsung was constantly rumored to acquire Kia. The rumors proved to be true as Samsung participated in the bid for Kia Motors as soon as it was up for sale. In the end, Samsung was outbid by Hyundai Motor.

Hyundai Motor acquires Kia Motors

In October 1998, Kia Motors was placed under court receivership by the government and its creditors. At the same time, Sun-hong Kim stepped down from his position as CEO. This was the result of management troubles at Asia Motors, Kia Special Steel and Kisan Construction amid the sharp contraction of the Korean automobile market. Another cause was Kia Motors' excessive debts, which damaged its financial standing. At the end of 1996, Kia Motors' capital adequacy ratio stood at a mere 16%.

Asia Motors crumbled due to its unsuccessful investment in large-size and light commercial vehicles. Kia Special Steel was also struggling due to unfeasible investments. From 1992 to 1996, Kia Special Steel spent a trillion won to increase its production capacity four fold, but utilization rates remained below 50%. Kia Special Steel was suffering losses from 1993 until it was placed under court receivership. Kisan Construction, which managed construction duties for Kia Motors, including the Asan Bay plant, was deemed an affiliate of Kia Motors by the Fair Trade Commission in January 1997 because Kia employees owned 12.74% of its shares. Once incorporated into the Kia Group, Kia Motors was forced to provide surety for Kisan's debts, adding to Kia Motors' financial troubles. By the end of 1997, Kia Motors had 5.1 trillion won in debt, which is excessive considering the company turned in sales of 6.4 trillion won and an operating profit of 167 billion won in 1997.

Ju-yung Chung(middle) and MK Chung(middle right) during a visit to Kia Motors' Hwaseong plant in 1999. Nyeom Jin, who was the court-appointed supervisor for Kia Motors' workout, attempted to sell Kia Motors to Ford in a closed deal, but negotiations fell through as the two parties were unable to narrow their differences over debt reduction and other terms. In October 1998, Hyundai Motor prevailed over Samsung and gained ownership of Kia Motors and Asia Motors. The conditions of the deal were that Hyundai Motor raise 1.2 trillion won via capital reduction and a subsequent capital increase and inject the funds into Kia Motors, while the creditors invest 2.5 trillion won and provide a 7.1 trillion debt reduction.

Once the acquisition of Kia Motors was decided, MK Chung went to his father, Hyundai Group Honorary Chairman Ju-yung Chung, and expressed his desire to head Hyundai's automobile wing. MK was the chairman of the Hyundai Group, but had control over only Hyundai Precision & Industries and Hyundai Motor Service among Hyundai's automotive subsidiaries. Hyundai Motor was headed by Mong-gyu Chung, the son of Hyundai Motor Honorary Chairman Se-yung Chung. Ju-yung Chung had MK participate in the management of Hyundai Motor and in the normalization of Kia Motors' operations. In 1998, Hyundai Group announced that its subsidiaries would be divided into five subgroups – automobile, electronics, construction, heavy industries and chemicals, and financial services – and the automobile unit would be merged into a single entity. MK was promoted to Chairman of Hyundai Motor and Kia Motors, and his cousin, Mong-gyu, was demoted to Vice Chairman.

In March 1999, Ju-yung Chung called his brother, Se-yung Chung, and asked if it was wrong to give MK control over the Group's automobile unit when he was the eldest son. Ju-yung Chung was saying that he wanted MK to have full control of Hyundai's automobile business. His brother replied that there was nothing wrong. As a result, Se-yung Chung left the company he managed for 32 years. Se-yung Chung and his family exchanged their Hyundai Motor stocks for Hyundai Development stocks and separated Hyundai's construction units from the Hyundai Group.

CHAPTER 18

New Beginning: Launch of the Hyundai Motor Group

"The Hyundai Motor Group will separate from the Hyundai Group and walk its own path."

The HMC (Hyundai Motor Company) Group was launched on September 1st, 2000. Local media began spewing out articles of MK Chung heading an independent conglomerate dedicated to the automobile business. Ten Hyundai Group affiliates, including Hyundai Motor, Kia Motors, Hyundai Precision & Industries (currently, Hyundai Mobis), Hyundai Pipe (currently, Hyundai Hysco) and Hyundai Space & Aircraft, was separated from the Hyundai Group. The main cause of the separation occurred six months earlier, when MK Chung and his brother, Mong-hun Chung (Ju-yung Chung's fifth son), clashed to gain control of the Hyundai Group. MK and his brother were appointed co-chairmen of the Hyundai Group, but the younger brother was made sole chairman by the Hyundai CEO council on March 27th.

Another reason for MK's decision is likely to have been his confidence in heading an automobile company. The Galloper Legend and Kia Motors completing its workout in a record 22 months were all his accomplishments.

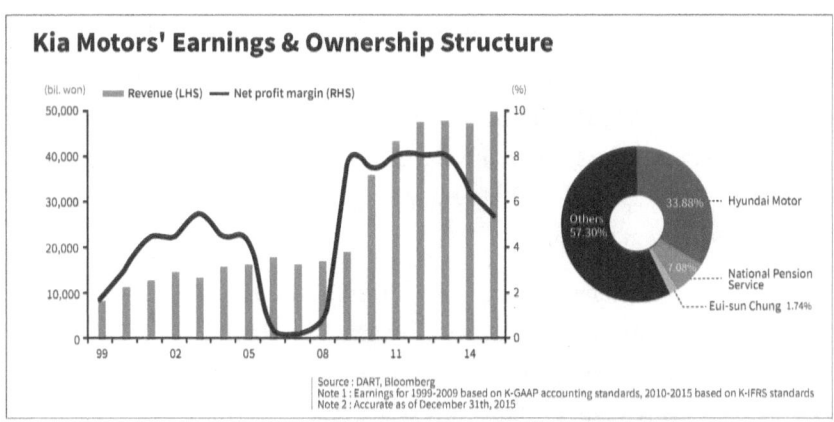

Kia Motors' Earnings & Ownership Structure

At the end of 2013, the Hyundai Motor Group owned 181 trillion won in assets, making it the second largest conglomerate (state-run corporations excluded) in Korea after the Samsung Group, which has 331 trillion won in assets. When it parted ways with the Hyundai Group, the Hyundai Motor Group was ranked fifth. As the Hyundai Motor Group became the largest automaker in Korea and fifth largest in the world, its subsidiaries achieved fast growth. The Group maximized efficiency by achieving vertical integration of production processes through Hyundai Wia, Hyundai Glovis, Hyundai Steel and various other subsidiaries. The number of its subsidiaries increased from ten at the time of its separation, to 212 as of 2012.

Kia Motors swings earnings to positive in 22 months

The year after it was picked up by Hyundai Motor in October 1998, Kia Motors recorded a net profit of 15.7 billion won, turning around from the 94.9 billion won loss in 1998. Kia Motors entered court receivership in a state of impaired capital (5.2 trillion won in net debt), but came out with 2.26 trillion won in net assets. Its debt ratio dropped from 810% to 172%, well below government guidelines. The feat was the result of the Hyundai Group placing the automobile wing under a single leader and an intensive restructuring process after taking over Kia Motors. The restructuring process covered platform standardization, parts sharing and reduction of product development periods.

141

Supervising the improvement of Kia's financial health, MK discontinued any model deemed unable to compete in the market, such as the Credos, the Avella, the Sephia and the Potentia. Only a handful of models survived – the Bongo, the Carnival, the Sportage and the Pride. By leaving models that sell and by equipping better engines and parts, Kia Motors sales began to climb.

The efforts produced instantaneous results and Kia Motors completed its workout 15 months after getting acquired by Hyundai and 22 months since entering court receivership. To this day, Kia Motors is one of the best examples of swift management normalization. Kia Motors completed its workout in the shortest period in history.

After Hyundai Motor acquired Kia Motors, Kia Motors was merged with Asia Motors, Kia Automobile Sales, Asia Automobile Sales and Taejeon Automobile Sales. The only remaining Asia Motors model is the full-size luxury bus, Granbird. Kia Special Steel was sold off to the SeAH Group and was renamed SeAH Besteel.

Fate of the Kia Motors founding family

Although Kia Motors found a new owner, the family of Kia Motors founder, Chul-ho Kim, remains engaged in the automobile business. A good example is the SECO Group, which owns companies like Seojin Automotive, Eco-Plastic and AIA. Kim's son-in-law, Chang-soo Bae, received an automotive parts company from Kim and established Seoul Steel, which was renamed Seojin Industrial after relocating to Gunpo in 1972.

Seojin Industrial earned most of its revenues from Kia Motors. After Kia's bankruptcy, Seojin Industrial sold 49% of its shares to Tower Automotive for 40 million dollars (56 billion won based on the won/dollar exchange rate at the time) in 1999 to form a joint venture. However, 33 billion won was used for capital increase resulting from share repurchases. Afterwards, it issued convertible bonds to Tower Automotive, which allowed the Tower Group to increase its stake in Seojin Industrial to 66%

two years later. In the end, Chang-soo Bae's son, Chairman Suk-doo Bae, sold the remaining shares to the Tower Group.

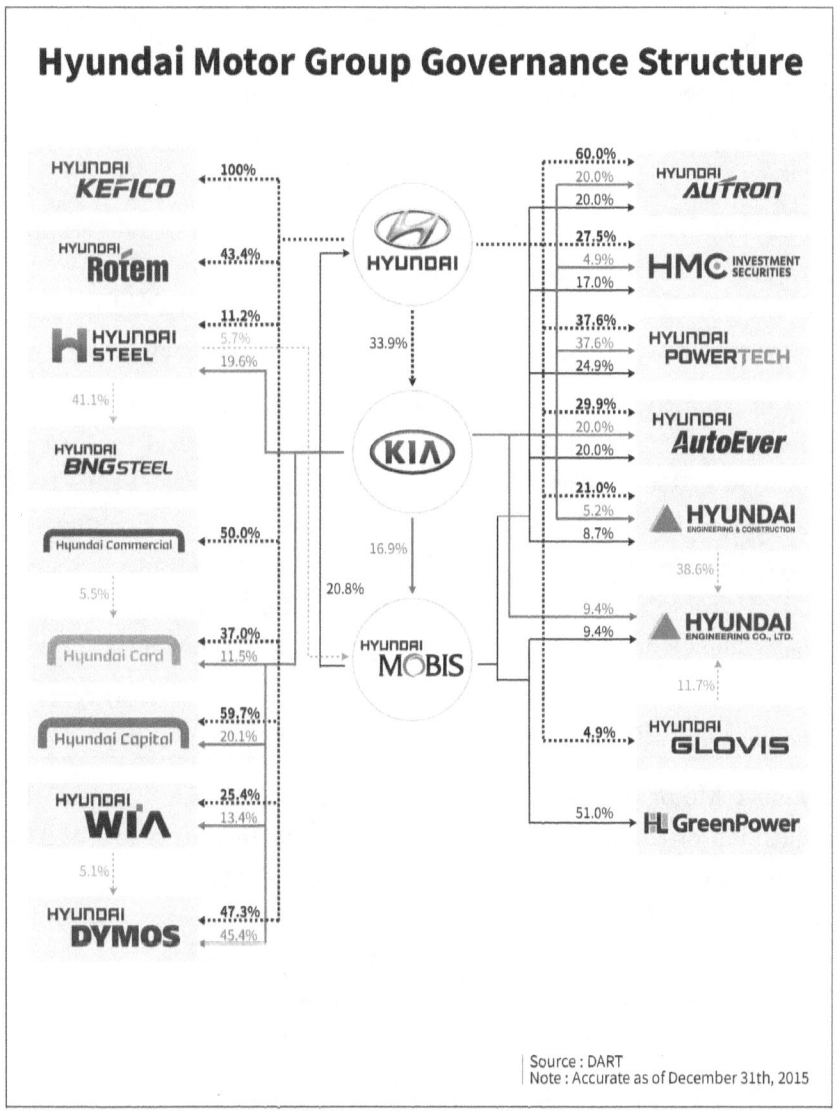

The Tower Group went bankrupt in 2006 as GM began struggling and Seojin Industrial was sold to the private equity fund, Cerberus Capital. When Seojing Industrial was put up for sale seven years later, Bae regained ownership of Seojin Industrial. During this time, Bae had been growing Seojin Automotive, which supplied clutches to Hyundai Motor and other automakers. Bae's son currently works as an interior designer at Mercedes-Benz.

LEEHAN, an automotive parts supplier founded by In-chul Park, the grandson-in-law of Chul-ho Kim and CEO of Seojin Industrial in 1979, is currently headed by Ji-hoon Park, the great grandson of Chul-ho Kim. Kim's grandson, Suk-hwan Kim, is currently the CEO of Samchuly.

Sun-hong Kim was sentenced to four years of prison for providing surety for insolvent subsidiaries and embezzlement, but was released on probation in 2000. He was pardoned in late December, 2002, by the Dae-jung Kim Administration. After Kia Motors' acquisition, an investigation by the Securities Supervisory Board revealed that over seven years since 1991, Kia Motors had engaged in window dressing and covered up a total of 4.5 trillion won by manipulating its electronic accounting books.

Hyundai Motor Group focuses on M&As

Hyundai Motor also underwent many internal changes. Prior to the acquisition of Kia Motors, the company suffered losses (net loss of 33.2 billion won; net loss margin of 0.4%) in the wake of Korea's financial crisis and cut its workforce by ten thousand via voluntary resignations. After obtaining Kia Motors, Hyundai Motor Service and Hyundai Precision & Industries were merged. Hyundai Motor Service's heavy machinery division was transferred to Hyundai Heavy Industries.

After the Hyundai Motor Group declared its independence, MK had the Group's headquarters relocate to Yangjae-dong, signaling the beginning of the Yangjae-dong era. In November 2000, Hyundai Mobis purchased the 2.7% Hyundai Motor stake held by Ju-yung Chung and became Hyundai

Motor's majority shareholder. The Group's cross-ownership structure was completed during this time.

Following its separation, the Hyundai Motor Group signed a joint venture deal with Daimler-Chrysler. The Group formed a partnership by selling a 10.5% stake in Hyundai Motor to Daimler-Chrysler for 484 million euros over two transactions: one in 2000 and the other in 2001. The Group was not selling its stocks. It converted Hyundai Motor's Jeonju plant into a joint venture, with each company owning half. In exchange, Hyundai Motor would receive truck technology from Daimler-Chrysler.

When Daewoo Motors was being sold, the two participated in the bid aiming for joint acquisition. However, the partnership came to a swift end when the establishment of the joint passenger car company (slated to be established in 2002) was postponed indefinitely and Daimler-Chrysler signed a joint passenger car production deal with Beijing Motor without consulting Hyundai Motor.

Some speculate that the two companies wanted different things from the partnership. Hyundai Motor wanted to discourage Hyundai Group Chairman Mong-hun Chung from exerting any influence over the company and operate safely under Daimler-Chrysler's protection. Meanwhile, Daimler-Chrysler wanted headway into the Asian market and, ultimately, takeover Hyundai Motor. So, the alliance was doomed from the start. In August 2004, Daimler-Chrysler sold its Hyundai Motor stocks for 740 million euros in a block deal through the stock exchange.

Driven by its automotive subsidiaries, the Hyundai Motor Group expanded its influence. It took over various companies and established companies when needed. Its first priority was reorganizing its automotive parts subsidiaries, the core of which was Hyundai Mobis.

In early 1990, Hyundai Precision & Industries CEO Jung-in Park walked into to the chairman's office looking stiff. His hands were holding a thick report that would determine the fate of Hyundai Precision & Industries. The essence of the report was that in order to enhance its competitive edge, Hyundai Precision & Industries needed to launch a module business, which fulfilled all of Hyundai Motor Group's needs. Having received MK's approval, Park was given control of Hyundai Motor and Kia Motors' entire production lines.

Hyundai Precision & Industries was renamed Hyundai Mobis after relinquishing its rolling stock division to the Korea Rolling Stock Technical Corporation in 1999 and acquiring the repair divisions of Hyundai Motor and Kia Motors in 2000. In June 2005, Hyundai Mobis gained ownership of Korea Automotive Systems (formerly, Kia Precision Work) from Korea Flange.

In July 2005, Hyundai Motor acquired Hyundai Autonet, an automotive electronics company specializing in AVN (audio, video, navigation) that spun off from Hyundai Electronics, from the Korea Deposit Insurance Corporation for 237.1 billion won. The Hyundai Motor Group acquired Kia Motors' AVN supplier Bontec in February 2006 and merged it with Hyundai Autonet. Hyundai Autonet was taken over by Hyundai Mobis in May 2009. Bontec-Hyundai Mobis merger was attempted in 2002, but was scrapped due to controversy over the 30% Bontec stake held by Hyundai Motor Group Vice Chairman, Eui-sun Chung. The merger happened after Siemens purchased Eui-sun Chung's stake. Kia Motors' key parts supplier, Kia Heavy Industries (currently, Hyundai Wia), was renamed Wia following its acquisition by Korea Flange in October 1999. Wia was sold to the Hyundai Motor Group in December 2001.

The aspect that differentiates the Hyundai Motor Group from other international automakers is the integration with a steel company. Since it is difficult to run an automobile company and a steel company at the same time, most automobile manufacturers seek to form partnerships with steel companies. For instance, Volkwagen AG partners with Arcelor Mittal, BMW with the ThyssenKrupp Group, Toyota with Nippon Steel and Honda with JTE Steel. Ju-yung Chung entered the steel business by establishing a steel pipe factory named Kyungil Industries (currently, Hyundai Hysco) in 1975 and the acquisition of Incheon Steel, an electric steel mill company that produced rebars, in 1978. The late Chairman competed against Pohang Iron & Steel (currently, POSCO) to secure the rights to the Gwangyang steel mill project, but was discouraged from doing so. Ju-yung Chung and MK Chung made repeated attempts to build a steel mill, but were derailed each time.

In 1997, MK received approval to build a steel mill in Hadong, South Gyeongsang Province, but the project was canceled in light of the financial crisis that hit Korea. In 2000, Incheon Steel merged with Kangwon Industries (currently, Hyundai Steel's Pohang mill) and acquired Sammi Specialty Steel (currently, BNG Steel), which had applied for court receivership. In June 2001, Incheon Steel was renamed INI Steel. During a worldwide bid for Hanbo Steel in October 2004, the INI Consortium outbid 15 companies from seven countries, including the US, the UK and Japan, and established the foundation to launch a blast furnace-based steel business. In 2006, INI Steel was renamed Hyundai Steel. As a result, Hyundai Motor and Kia Motors are able to purchase automotive steel plates at competitive prices. Hyundai Steel would go on to absorb Hyundai Steel would go on to absorb Hyundai Hysco's cold-rolled steel division in 2013 and Hyundai Hysco in July 2015.

The reform of the financial units must also be mentioned. During its early days, Hyundai Motor was almost liquidated by toxic debt. Hence, the company is well aware of the importance of finance and its connection with automobiles. After releasing the Cortina, Hyundai introduced installment plans for car purchases without adequately establishing an installment payment system. Soon, the amount of delinquent payments accumulated to over three times the amount of the company's 800 million-won capital.

In 1993, the Hyundai Group spun off its auto finance and home mortgage divisions to establish Hyundai Auto Finance. The company was renamed Hyundai Financial Services in 1995 and then, Hyundai Capital in 1999. The Hyundai Motor Group acquired Diners Card Korea in 2001 and changed in into Hyundai Card. Between 2004 and 2006, the Group sold a 43.3% stake in Hyundai Capital to GE Capital and a 43% stake in Hyundai Card GE Money to form a strategic alliance. The alliance with GE enabled Hyundai Card and Hyundai Capital to establish market presence as GE's credit standing made it easier for them to raise funds and they were able to learn GE's advanced marketing and financing techniques. In 2007, Hyundai Capital spun off its industrial financing unit (financing for commercial vehicles, construction machines and other industrial equipment), which became Hyundai Commercial. The Hyundai Motor Group acquired Shinheung Securities (currently, HMC Investment Securities) in 2008 and Green Cross Life Insurance (currently, Hyundai Life) in 2011.

When GE decided to sell off its non-essential financial assets in 2015, Hyundai and Kia each re-acquired 3.2% and 20.1% stakes in Hyundai Capital.

Equipped with an encompassing variety of subsidiaries, the Hyundai Motor Group automobile output began to skyrocket. MK's focus on quality and his son's focus on design enabled the Group to establish production bases around the world. The Hyundai Motor Group was a latecomer in the auto industry. Despite its handicap, the Group's automobile output tripled from 2.44 million units in 2000 to 8.02 million units in 2015, which was a feat never achieved in the automobile industry's 130-year history.

CHAPTER 19

MK's Gambit: Venturing into the World

On September 25th, 2000, Hyundai Motor Group employees were gathered at the new headquarters in Yangjae-dong, Seoul, to participate in the Group's launching ceremony. The Hyundai Motor Group had just declared its independence from the Hyundai Group. Everyone looked tense. The main doors opened and MK Chung walked in, accompanied by Hyundai Motor Group executives. NK walked up on stage. Once everyone settled down, MK stepped forward and said, "We need to have the fifth best quality in the world by 2005 and become the fifth largest automaker in the world by 2010. This is the Hyundai Motor Group's future." The plan presented would become known as the GT5 Vision. Everyone swallowed hard because the Hyundai-Kia Automotive Group (Hyundai Motor and Kia Motors) was producing 2.63 million units per year, which was around tenth in the world.

In July 2001, Hyundai Motor CEO Dong-jin Kim (currently, Vice Chairman) was called into MK's office. MK was absorbed in his thoughts and did not talk. Moments later, MK opened his mouth and said to Kim, "I think it is time. Make plans to build a plant in America." MK had been considering a foray into the US market since 1998. He had finally made up his mind and initiated a project that would become Hyundai's Alabama plant.

Four years later, the Alabama plant began manufacturing NF Sonatas, marking the genesis of USA-made Hyundai cars. That year, the Hyundai-

Kia Group sold 3.35 million cars and was ranked seventh in the world. Eventually, the Hyundai-Kia Group became the world's fifth largest automobile manufacturer and has been holding that position since. On April 25th, 2005, Time magazine published an issue with MK on the cover and a story about the Hyundai Motor Group's success. On January 18th, 2010, MK was on the cover of Fortune magazine.

Hyundai Motor had come a long way since it began manufacturing Ford Cortinas in 1967; it has over 70 models, which include Pony, Sonata, Grandeur, Santa Fe and Genesis. Hyundai's accomplishments were the result of aggressive efforts to release competitive cars, improve quality and build overseas production bases. The journey was not easy because bold entail risks. A great amount of effort is needed to ensure that endeavors are successful. The Hyundai-Kia Automotive Group was able to expand because it overcame the devastating failure of the Bromont plant in 1993 and pushed to build a new plant in the US. The Automotive Group currently has eight overseas production bases, which allowed its output to surpass the seven million mark in 2012 and the eight million mark in 2014.

A bold gamble: two hail Mary moves

After gaining control of Hyundai Motor, MK's first action was to achie economies of scale through the Hyundai-Kia merger. But this was not enough. In order to become the fifth largest company, the company needed to expand overseas. Hence, the company decided to venture into the US.

It was risky. If the US foray was not successful, Hyundai Motor would suffer massive losses and the losses could cause the entire Group to crumble. Hyundai Motor closed down the Bromont plant in 1993 for this very reason. The larger problem was consumers' negative opinion of Hyundai cars. Initially, the Excel caused major damage to the Hyundai brand. The Excel gained popularity thanks to its 4,999-dollar price tag, selling 260,000 units in the first year. But, frequent breakdowns caused consumer grievances to pile up and unit sales began to plunge from the third year. As a result, the company was forced to discontinue the Excel in the US. Getting stereotyped is extremely problematic. Reports of the Audi 5000's unintended acceleration in the US caused massive headaches for Audi and Audi has yet to recover from it. Hyundai Motor needed to gamble.

While proceeding with the US foray, MK called two meetings each day - the first was called upon arriving at the office and the second in the afternoon to draw conclusions.

Modularization was suggested as a strategy. The company would divide cars into a few large pieces, or modules, which would be sent to the US and assembled there. Hyundai modularized power packs, cockpits, doors and front bumpers. Modularization improved productivity as assembling a small number of modules was much easier than assembling 20 thousand parts at once. Defective parts could be located during the modularization phase, making it easier to replace and improving quality. In 2004, Hyundai Motor's first modularization facility was established at its Alabama plant. Later, the company introduced modularization processes to all of its plants.

The company also needed to change people's perception about the quality of Hyundai cars. In December 1998, prior to the construction of the Alabama plant, Hyundai decided to introduce a 10-year/100,000-mile guarantee. The finance department opposed vehemently because guarantees meant an increase of costs and would damage profitability. Hyundai's guarantees in the US are one of the reasons Korean consumers criticize Hyundai for "earning money in Korea and spending it in the US." Regardless, Hyundai knew it was not going to gain consumer confidence in the US without providing extraordinary measures. So, Hyundai proceeded with its plan. In 2000, it also established a quality control division within the Group to focus on improving product quality.

Hyundai was successful. JD Power's survey on the quality of Hyundai and Kia's cars shows that Hyundai ranked 34th out of 37 in 2000, but rose to seventh in 2004 and third in 2006. When excluding prestige marques, such as Mercedes-Benz, Lexus and Infiniti, Hyundai was ranked 16th out of 23 companies in 2002, but reached first by 2009.

Pursuit of markets

Using the Alabama plant, which began production in 2005, as an example, the Hyundai-Kia Automotive Group began building production bases around the world. The company built plants in: Nosovice, Czech Republic, in 2008; St. Petersburg, Russia, in 2011; Piracicaba, Brazil, in 2012; and Sichuan, China, in 2014. Hyundai Motor built production bases without stopping. The beginning of production at each plant was two to three years apart, indicating that construction of a new plant was underway by the time the last plant began operating. Before the Hyundai Motor Group took flight, Hyundai Motor was already operating the İzmit plant in Turkey (completed in 1997), the Chennai plant in India (completed in 1998) and the Beijing plant (completed in 2002). Hence, Hyundai had eight factories in seven countries. After production began at its first overseas plant in Yancheng, China, in 2002, Kia Motors proceeded to establish a production base in Žilina, Slovakia, in 2007 and in Georgia, USA, in 2009.

In the early and mid-2000s, the US was the main engine for the Hyundai-Kia Automotive Group's growth. Recently, China has become key to the Group's growth. With the completion of its third plant, Hyundai's Beijing production facility is capable of churning out one million cars per year Actual output topped the one million mark for the first time in 2013, with Hyundai Motors selling 1.03 million cars. In 2015, the company sold 1.06 million units. Hyundai's success in China is attributable to Yuedong and Langdong, the China-exclusive models based on the Avante. Hyundai solidified its presence with the release of the Elantra and the EF Sonata. Hyundai's fast production capacity increase in China led to the coining of the expression "Hyundai speed." Kia's Yancheng plant produced 620 thousand units in 2015, accounting for nearly half of the company's total overseas output of 1.33 million units.

By increasing overseas production capacity, the Hyundai-Kia Automotive Group was able to actively react to local demand and cut logistics costs. Profitability also benefited from low labor costs. Furthermore, overseas plants are showing better productivity than Korean plants. Based on 2013 statistics, Hyundai's HPV (hours per vehicle) stands at 28.4 hours at its Korean plants, 17.8 hours at its Chinese plants and 14.4 hours at its US plant. Overseas plants also boast better line balancing efficiency than the Korean plants. Naturally, overseas plants look more appealing to management executives. In 2012, the Hyundai-Kia Group's overseas output exceeded Korean output. For the first ten months of 2014, overseas plants were responsible for 56% of the Group's total output. In 2015, overseas plants were responsible for 55% of the Group's total output.

10 million-unit era

Design innovation was also a contributor to the Group's success. The most prominent change was initiated by Vice President Eui-sun Chung (then-President of Kia Motors). Eui-sun Chung announced Kia's focus on design during the Paris Motor Show in June 2006 and recruited Peter Schreyer as a key part of his vision.

Along with Volkswagen's design chief Walter de Silva and Jaguar's design chief Ian Callum, Hyundai-Kia Automotive Group's design chief Peter Schreyer is currently one of the three best car designers in the world. Schreyer was chief of design at Audi and the Volkswagen. Eui-sun Chung, who was the President of Kia Motors at the time, repeatedly tried to recruit Schreyer. In August 2006, Schreyer gave in and became the CDO at Kia Motors. Based on his design philosophy of simplifying lines, Schreyer designed the mid-size sedan K5, the SUV Sportage R, the Soul and other models, establishing the identity of Kia cars. Schreyer designed Kia's family look, the so-called "Schreyer grille," which has become a symbol of Kia's K Series.

Kia's design created a sensation in the global market. In 2009, the Kia Soul received Red Dot Design Award for product design. Kia's Europe-exclusive Venga received the iF Design Award in the transportation category. Watching Kia flourish from Schreyer's contributions, Ferdinand Piëch is said to have regretted letting Schreyer go.

In January 2013, Schreyer assumed designing duties for Hyundai Motors as well. Hyundai had introduced "fluidic sculpture" as its design philosophy in 2009, but experts pointed out that it did not establish a brand identity. So, Schreyer was given the new task of giving life to the design of Hyundai cars. After the uplift from Schreyer, the Group recruited a large number of foreign talent in 2015. The Group recruited Albert Biermann, the chief of development at BMW's M division, and appointed him the head of Hyundai's high-performance model division, N. Hyundai aspires to imbue N with technology acquired through its participation in the World Rally Championship since 2014. The N nameplate represents Hyundai's Namyang R&D Center. The Group also recruited two people from Volkswagen into its senior ranks: Bentley's design chief Luc Donkerwolke became the head of Hyundai's design center and former head of the Lamborghini brand, Manfred Fitzgerald, was placed in charge as Genesis marque's strategy chief. Donkerwolke and Fitzgerald have been given important roles in the mission to merge Hyundai's luxury model, Equus, into the Genesis brand and launch Genesis as an independent, prestige marque.

The Hyundai-Kia Automotive Group's growth spurt was triggered by active ventures into overseas markets, establishment of overseas production bases and innovative design. The global financial crisis triggered by the subprime meltdown of 2008 provided an opportunity for the Group to expand its presence in the global market. The financial crisis entailing the Korean won depreciation has also helped the Group's venture into the global market.

However, the situation has changed. The won has begun to gain strength, while automakers have recovered from the fallout of the financial crisis and have gone on the offensive. Toyota's annual output is on the brink of hitting the 10 million-mark. Meanwhile, GM and the Renault-Nissan Alliance are pursuing M&A opportunities and partnerships to reach the 10 million-mark as soon as possible.

The Hyundai-Kia Group is not watching idly. Hyundai is moving to build a new plant in Chongqing, China, and Kia in Mexico. Hyundai is also expanding its plants in Russia and China. And now, the competition has boiled down to technology. Standards for exhaust emission, crash performance and fuel efficiency have become strong, while consumers have become harder to satisfy. As a result, automakers are forced to compete harder.

Along with increasing R&D spending, companies are seeking technological partnerships and M&As to eliminate any weaknesses. On the other hand, the Hyundai-Kia Automotive Group has been relatively cliquey. The Group's attempt to tackle problems by itself has been criticized for causing isolation in the industry. Others argue that the Group is actively seeking technological partnerships beneath the surface. One has to wonder if the Hyundai-Kia Automotive Group is truly isolated. Nonetheless, the technology race has begun.

CHAPTER 20

Hyundai Motor Group:
Lone Wolf or Busy Under the Surface

"The more friends you have, the better."

These were the words Carlos Ghosn, Chairman of the Renault-Nissan Alliance, spoken to reporters on April 7th, 2010, in Brussel, Belgium. Sitting across the table was Dieter Zetsche, Chairman of the Daimler Group. That day, Ghosn and Zetsche had gathered to officially announce a capital tie-up between the two groups. According to their agreement, Daimler would obtain a 3.1% stake in Renault, while Renault and Nissan gained similar stakes in Daimler. Daimler gave 32.9 million Daimler shares to the Alliance in exchange for 89 million Renault-Nissan shares. Although the stake exchanged was small, it was a union between two companies, with a full range of prestige brands (Mercedes-Benz and Infiniti) and mass-production brands (Renault, Nissan, Smart). The two parties agreed to joint-develop engines and subcompact cars, purchase parts together to reduce costs and share production plants. They would also develop electric vehicles together. The most significant result came out in 2013, when Nissan released the Infiniti Q50, which was equipped with Benz's 2.2 liter diesel engine. The Q50 is selling well around the world and is pulling Infiniti out of the abyss.

Toyota has partnered with BMW. The two agreed to joint-research clean diesel engine technology in November 2011 and fuel cell technology in June 2012. They are also working together to research reinforced plastic for reducing car weight and next-generation car batteries. The essence of the alliance is to create synergy between Toyota's hybrid car and fuel cell technologies and BMW's advanced diesel engine technology. The industry is waiting for the results of the Silk Road 2 project, which is due in 2018. The project is likely to result in a high-performance, mid-ship sports car – like the Porsche 911 – that is equipped with a plug-in hybrid engine.

The partnerships do not end here. In January 2014, the Fiat Group gained full ownership of Chrysler and has renamed itself FCA (Fiat Chrysler Automobiles).

True to the saying, "No one stays an enemy or friend forever," relationships within the automobile industry are constantly in flux. On the other hand, the Hyundai-Kia Motor Group has been silent. The Group has not announced any mergers, financial alliances or technology partnerships. Anytime a company is put up for sale, the Group is always mentioned as a strong candidate to acquire it. Yet, the Group denies all rumors and states that it will focus on only automobiles. The Hyundai-Kia Group has maintained a do-it-yourself approach to any technology. So, one has to wonder whether the Hyundai-Kia Automotive Group is a lone wolf or just moving diligently below the surface.

Ford and Pony: Partnership at the start

Hyundai Motor kicked off with a partnership. Its first partner was Ford. Ju-yung Chung chose Ford because it showed no interest in obtaining stakes or participating in management.

Hyundai's first joint venture with Ford was the Cortina. Hyundai imported CKD parts for the Cortina from Ford of Britain and assembled them. The partnership remained intact until Hyundai proposed a joint venture, to which Ford demanded ownership of at least 50% and full management control. After a year of negotiating, the two agreed to a joint-establishment of an engine company. However, talks ruptured during working-level negotiations. In January 1973, the Korean government retracted its approval of Hyundai's joint venture with Ford.

This was the first time Hyundai felt the need to stand alone. The failed joint project with Ford turned out to be a blessing in disguise. Hyundai decided to develop its own model, which resulted in the Pony. Deep down, the Pony was the fruit of collaboration with numerous automakers and automotive parts companies. Lacking the capability to build its own car, Hyundai sought technological assistance from companies in Japan, UK, US and Italy and used it as the foundation of its growth.

Hyundai developed its first engine in 1991. After seven years of research, the Manbokri research center developed the 1.5 liter Alpha engine, which was equipped on the Hyundai Scoupe. The first mid-size engine used was the 2.5 liter Delta engine, which was equipped on the EF Sonata in 2001. The EF Sonata also came with the 1.8 liter and 2.0 liter Sirius engines. By the time the NF Sonata was released in 2004, all engines were replaced with Hyundai's self-developed engines – the 2.0 liter Seta engine and the 2.4 liter and 3.3 liter Lambda engines. The development of diesel engines began in 1997. Hence, Hyundai's diesel engines have yet to rise to the level of German or French diesel engines.

Uneasy relationship with Daimler

On November 21st, 2013, the domestic auto industry was shaken by the news that the Daimler Group had purchased a 12% stake in BAIC (Beijing Automotive Industry Holding Company) for 625 million euros. Moreover, Daimler had secured two seats in the BAIC's board of directors, giving it authority to participate in decision-making processes. It was the first time a foreign company purchased stakes in a Chinese state-run automobile manufacturer. The problem was that Hyundai's joint venture partner in China was BAIC. Hyundai was reminded of its liquidated joint venture with Daimler a decade earlier, although Hyundai and Daimler claimed that the stake holding change would not affect each other.

In September 2000, Hyundai gave Daimler a 10% stake and had one representative from Daimler join its board. This was similar to the Daimler-BAIC partnership. At the time, Hyundai's Jeonju plant was changed into a joint venture with Hyundai and Daimler owning equal shares. They also agreed to a technology exchange. But, the partnership dissolved without producing any results.

The two companies had agreed to establish a joint venture in 2002, but it was postponed indefinitely. Then, Daimler signed a joint passenger car production deal with Beijing Motor, causing its partnership with Hyundai to rupture. In May 2004, the partnership ended with Daimler selling its Hyundai Motor stake. Hyundai's ties with Ford, Mitsubishi and Daimler only strengthened its resolve for technological independence. Hyundai has not pursued technology and financial alliances or M&As with any automaker since.

Parts suppliers over automakers

Hyundai Motor turned its attention to parts suppliers. While remaining reluctant to form alliances or engage in joint ventures with automakers, Hyundai is actively seeking collaborations with parts suppliers. This is the reason people believe Hyundai is moving diligently beneath the surface.

Hyundai focused on improving automotive electronics. To this end, it acquired Hyundai Autonet in 2005 and Bontec in 2006, seeking independence in automotive electronics. On August 1st, 2012, Hyundai broke its ties with Bosch after purchasing its stake in Kefico. Kefico was an automotive electronics manufacturer established in 1987 via a collaboration between Hyundai Motor (50% stake), Bosch (25%) and Mitsubishi Electric's subsidiary Melco (25%). Later, Bosch bought Melco's stake. After Hyundai gained full ownership, Kefico became Hyundai Kefico. At the same time, the Hyundai Motor Group renamed its software platform company, Hyundai Carnes, to Hyundai Motor Electronics and then to Hyundai Autron. Through Hyundai Autron, the Group began developing automotive semiconductors. Hyundai Autron has yet to produce significant results. The plan for technology independence in automotive electronics had hit a dead end.

In a joint effort with Delphi, Hyundai Motor is currently developing a GDCI (gasoline direct-injection compression ignition) engine, which would improve fuel efficiency by 25%. This indicates that Hyundai is accumulating knowhow through collaboration with parts companies, not automobile companies. The Hyundai Motor Group's parts companies are also actively engaging in joint ventures and technology partnerships. On August 8th, 2013, Hyundai Wia and the Japanese turbo charger company IHI established a joint venture named HWIT (Hyundai Wia IHI Turbo). The two companies built a factory in Seosan, South Chungcheong Province, Korea, and will begin mass production of turbo chargers in 2015. Hyundai Wia owns 51% of HWIT and IHI 49%. The contract will remain valid for ten years after production begins (2015-2024). Initially, IHI demanded 50% ownership of HWIT as it had never launched a joint venture with a stake below 50%. But, Hyundai refused and IHI had no choice but to agree to a 49% ownership. After operating various joint ventures, the Hyundai Motor Group had learned the importance of having management control.

Before HWIT, Hyundai Wia worked with Magna to establish Wia-Magna Powertrain. On May 24th, 2010, Wia-Magna Powertrain completed a factory in Asan, South Chungcheong Province, and began production. Magna International's subsidiary, Magna Powertrain, supplies 4WD systems to automakers, such as Benz. The Asan plant manufactures electronic coupling, which is a core component in 4WD systems. The HTRAC (4WD system) applied to Hyundai's new Genesis was developed through a technology alliance with Magna. The new Genesis is the first Hyundai vehicle equipped with the ASB (active seat belt) system. The ASB system tightens the seat belt of passengers when it anticipates a collision or the vehicle strays from its lane. The development of the ASB system began on November 24th, 2011, through a partnership between Hyundai Mobis and Takada. Hyundai Mobis handled the designing and production of the ECU, while Takada managed the motor and gears. Commercial production of the ASB system was announced on December 12th, 2013.

Partnerships were also formed for transmission. For many years, Hyundai Powertech imported transmissions from ZF Friedrichshafen AG and acquired related technology. Hyundai Powertech developed a rear-wheel drive, 8-speed automatic transmission, which was used in the Genesis. Hyundai Powertrain no longer purchases passenger car transmissions from the ZF Group, but continues to receive transmissions for commercial vehicles. Hyundai Dymos, which supplies commercial vehicle transmissions to Hyundai Motor, has yet to develop an automated manual transmission, which ZF Friedrichshafen is currently supplying. Collaborations with parts companies remains in progress.

Attention shifting to Aston Martin

Any financial alliances or M&As between automakers always present risks. One instance is Porsche, which attempted to takeover Volkswagen, but ended up getting taken over. Even if the M&A is successful, the financial drain may cause the company to struggle. No one can deny that the best option is to work hard to earn profits, use the profits to develop technology, use the technology to advance manufacturing techniques, build more expensive cars and repeat the process. Toyota is the embodiment of this approach. In running the company, Hyundai Motor's management is maintaining a conservative stance, which resembles that of Toyota.

Some suggest that Hyundai Motor could enhance its brand recognition in the global market by acquiring a luxury brand. A potential target is Aston Martin.

Aston Martin was established in 1913 by the British businessman, Lionel Martin. Aston Martin has been associated with James Bond as it has appeared in several 007 movies. The 2012 movie, Skyfall features a 1964 DB5. There are only four 1964 Aston Martin DB5s remaining in the world and each are worth nearly 11 million US dollars.

Kuwait investment management firm, Investment Dar, acquired Aston Martin from Ford in 2007. Investment Dar purchased a 64% stake for 766 million dollars. With Aston Martin struggling from poor sales, Investment

Dar decided to sell the company. Aston Martin produced 4,200 cars in 2011, down 40% from the 7,200 in 2007. The price for acquiring Aston Martin is known to be around 800 million dollars. The Indian automaker, Mahindra & Mahindra, attempted to acquire Aston Martin in 2012. However, Aston Martin was sold to the Italian private equity fund, Investment Industrial. Among the major automobile marques, Aston Martin is the only one owned by a private equity fund. In 2014, Daimler acquired a 5% stake in the British sports car maker, but its role seems to be limited to cooperative efforts. Therefore, Aston Martin may still be taken over by global automakers, such as Hyundai Motor.

Aston Martin would be a nice match for Hyundai Motor. The designs of Aston Martin cars have a strong resemblance to Hyundai's hexagonal grill and fluidic sculpture design. The emblem of Hyundai Genesis sports wings is like the Aston Martin emblem. Since Aston Martin is the pinnacle of the "modern freedom" Hyundai is pursuing, the acquisition of Aston Martin would provide an opportunity for Hyundai to learn advanced automotive technology and designing techniques. The halo effect from Aston Martin would be able to sway consumers considering the purchase of a Hyundai - the Genesis in particular. In the long run, Aston Martin may generate synergy with the Genesis brand. In September 2014, the Hyundai Motor Group purchased the KEPCO headquarters site in Samsung-dong for 10 billion dollars. The Group plans to build a 105-story office building on the plot. If Aston Martin is sold at around one billion dollars, the acquisition would be worth considering given that it would provide a larger boost in enterprise value and long-term growth momentum than the purchase of the KEPCO headquarters site.

Industry-Altering Event #3

Oil Shocks

The 1970s were a nightmare for automobile companies due to the oil shocks of 1973 and 1978. The oil shock was triggered by the wars that broke out in the Middle East. During the first oil shock, the price of Middle Eastern oil increased fivefold from 2.59 dollars per barrel in early 1973 to 11.65 dollars in just a year. The impact of the first oil shock seemed to be dispersing by 1978. But, political turmoil in Iran and the Islamic Revolution in early 1979 triggered a second shock. Iran, which was responsible for 15% of the world's oil production, banned all oil exports. To make matters worse, oil companies cornered the market and manipulated the market, causing chaos in the international oil market. Oil prices rose above 30 dollars per barrel by August 1980 and reached 34 dollars by October 1981. Former Volkswagen President Danial Goeudevert described the aftermath of the oil shock, saying "The two oil shocks left highways empty and streets filled with bicycles during weekends. Not even Porsche could avoid the impact of the slumping automobile market."

The oil shock provided an opportunity for Japanese companies to overthrow US automakers, which were the industry leaders at the time. As oil prices surged, the US federal government raised CAFE (corporate average fuel economy) standards, creating problems for the automobile industry. CAFE was raised to 7.7km/L for cars manufactured in 1978 and after and to 11.7km/L in 1985.

The new CAFE standard hit US automakers hard. Japanese cars already met the fuel economy requirements because smaller cars were the main focus of

Japanese companies. German companies had competitive models line-up in the smaller segments. The problem was US companies. GM was forced to spend billions to meet the new CAFE requirements. Rear-wheel drive systems were changed to front-wheel drive, 8-cylinder engines were replaced with smaller and more efficient 4-cylinder and 6-cylinder engines. Chrysler and Ford were forced to do the same.

GM released subcompact cars, but many were defective because they were rushed. The fact that GM fired its skilled automatic transmission engineers during the first oil shock only added to GM's problems. The company was also forced to sacrifice design for fuel economy. Bob Rutz states that the Cadillac de Ville and Fleetwood were shortened by 10cm to meet the fuel economy requirement. In the end, the reputation of American cars hit rock bottom in the US market. Consumers began to believe that the technology of Japanese companies was more advanced. The negative opinion of consumers about American cars was a problem, but the US government's near-sighted CAFE standard adjustments only made matters worse.

A similar development was witnessed in Korea. Following the collapse of the Yushin Dictatorship in 1978, the Legislative Council for National Security rose to power. The Council initiated an automobile industry reform based on the theory of comparative advantage. With car sales dropping amid rising oil prices, the Council had automobile companies specialize in one type of car to make them more competitive. Hyundai Motor was ordered to make only passenger cars and Kia Motors only trucks and buses. With its production restricted, Kia Motors turned in 50 billion won in losses between 1980 and 1981. As a result, owner Sang-moon Kim was forced to sell his stake in the company. It would not be wrong to say that Kia Motors began losing its competitive edge during this period.

Fiat Chrysler Automobiles

CHAPTER 21

Italy's Automobile Empire: From Fiat to Ferrari

"Unit sales will be increased by 2.5 million by 2018."

These words were spoken by Sergio Marchionne, CEO of Fiat Chrysler Automobiles (FCA), on May 6, 2014, during the Investor Day event held at the Chrysler headquarters in Auburn Hills, Michigan. Unlike his usual emotionless demeanor, Marchionne beamed as he spoke. He promised that FCA would increase annual unit sales from 4.35 million in 2013 to 6.8 million in 2018 and that the newly launched joint ventures in India and China would sell a combined 0.7 million units. This seemed to imply the company was shifting its focus from Europe and America to Asia. The CEO also said that while unit sales climbed, the company would be reducing its debt, promising to reduce the net debt of 10 billion euros by 90%. In short, Marchionne was saying that FCA would attempt to overcome its past strains and achieve solid growth. He smiled and went on to say that his "D-Day" was the day FCA achieved its 6 million unit sales target.

Fiat is the most popular marque in Italy, while Chrysler is one the top three automobile names in North America.

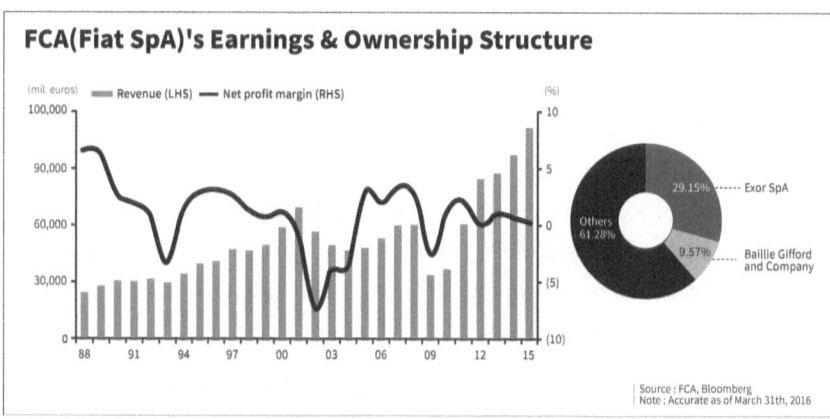

FCA(Fiat SpA)'s Earnings & Ownership Structure

Source : FCA, Bloomberg
Note : Accurate as of March 31th, 2016

Fiat and Chrysler joined as the FCA in January 2014 when Fiat acquired the remaining 41.5% of Chrysler shares from the UAW Retiree Medical Benefits Trust, which is a voluntary employees' beneficiary association (VEBA). Fiat paid 4.35 billion dollars for the shares, which includes 700 million dollars in four annual installments paid to the VEBA. Fiat previously owned a 58.5% stake in Chrysler. The merger made FCA the seventh largest automaker in the world.

Fiat is a 115-year-old Italian automobile manufacturer that battled Volkswagen for hegemony in the European market. After a series of M&As, Fiat developed into a massive enterprise that owns many highly desirable marques, like Ferrari, Maserati and Alfa Romeo. It was also a colorful history, plagued with incompetent management and economic recessions; at one point it almost went bankrupt. Having achieved economies of scale and gained a distribution network in the US through the acquisition of Chrysler, the FCA is now eyeing China, India and other emerging markets.

FCA has a brand portfolio that includes the SUV manufacturer Jeep and the supercar company Ferrari, making it an increasing threat to the world's top five automobile companies.

Most popular brand in Italy

Fiat is a company based in Turin, a city in northern Italy, 200km west of Milano. Fiat is an acronym for *Fabbrica Italiana Automobili Torino* (Italian

Automobile Factory of Turin). In a number of aspects, the structure of the Fiat Group resembles the HMC Group.

In addition to passenger cars and commercial cars, the Fiat Group has businesses operating in agricultural and construction machinery, metallurgy, production systems, aviation, parts, publication and communication, and insurance. Like the HMC Group, the Fiat Group has a massive influence on the Italian economy. Fiat was founded in 1899 and became a publicly traded company in 1906.

In 1969, Fiat Automobiles took over Lancia, the third largest company in Italy, while acquiring stakes in Ferrari. In 1975, following the first oil shock, Fiat established the industrial vehicle company, Iveco, in the Netherlands. Fiat acquired Alfa Romeo in 1986 and Maserati in 1993, becoming a dominant player in the Italian passenger car market.

Imbuing sports car DNA in Fiat

Ferrari was founded in 1929 by Enzo Ferrari as Scuderia Ferrari. Ferrari has a long history with Alfa Romeo as the company was established while Enzo Ferrari was a driver on Alfa Romeo's racing team. In 1939, Enzo Ferrari left Alfa Romeo after discovering that Alfa Romeo was planning to absorb his racing team and kick him out. This was when Enzo Ferrari began developing cars. His first car was the Tipo 815, unveiled in 1940. Enzo Ferrari began manufacturing this vehicle in 1947 under the Ferrari marque. Most of the profits from selling cars were invested in the Scuderia Ferrari F1 racing team. Enzo Ferrari's business philosophy was "selling cars to run a motor racing team." It was an idealistic vision fitting for his background as a race car driver, but it was also the downfall of his company.

The Ferrari brand was picked up by the Fiat Group in 1969. The Group acquired a 50% stake that year, before increasing its ownership to 85% by 1985 and placing Ferrari under its control. In 1987, Fiat beat GM to gain ownership of the state-run Alfa Romeo Group. The one thing Ferrari, Maserati and Alfa Romeo have in common is the racing DNA. Maserati was established in 1914 and was taken over by the Orsi family in 1937.

Ownership was relinquished to Citroen and then to Fiat in 1993. Maserati celebrated its 100th anniversary in 2014.

The "one-trick pony"

A one-trick pony refers to a simpleminded person with one talent. The expression is also sarcastically used in reference to the Fiat Group's management strategy that almost led to its demise. Due to the poor performance of Fiat cars and snowballing loses, the Fiat Group had accumulated 6.6 billion dollars in debt by early 2003. The Group's management strategy brought on the crisis.

During the 1970s and 1980s, Fiat was flourishing. It had become a massive empire, large enough to overthrow Volkswagen and become the leading automobile manufacturer in Europe. However, the management's poor judgment slowly eroded the company's competitive edge. Traditionally, Fiat placed more focus on domestic sales than overseas sales and on smaller cars that medium and large-sized cars. Fiat was complacent with the Uno in the 1980s and the Punto in the 1990s. It failed to react to diversification in market demand and began losing ground in the European market. Up until 1990, Fiat boasted a 13.8% share in Europe and was ranked second after Volkswagen, but its market share plunged to 8% in 2002 and 5% by November 2004.

Management could no longer watch sales slide. So, it decided to play its trump card: internationalization. Fiat engaged in a "world car project"– an ambitious plan to develop a new model, the Fiat 178, with aspiration to manufacture and sell one million units in non-European markets. The company injected a staggering 1.5 billion dollars into the project, only to end in failure. Because of the financial crisis that hit Latin America in the 1990s and poor sales in Poland, Turkey and other countries, the company managed to sell 400 thousand 178s, less than half of the initial target. Another factor behind the failure was the Fiat Group's efforts to expand its operations to insurance, energy and heavy machinery. The costs of pursuing new business opportunities limited funding for R&D (research and development), weakening the company's competitive edge. By 2002, Fiat was facing the worst crisis in its history.

On the edge

Facing imminent doom, the Fiat Group decided to initiate a complete restructuring of Fiat Automobiles with hopes of the company recovering its competitive edge. Management concluded that it needed to lay off 12,000 employees and close factories. The labor union was outraged and offered to cut working hours and wages to ensure everyone kept their jobs, while demanding that Fiat Automobiles be nationalized in exchange for funding from the government.

The Fiat Group considered nationalizing its automobile wing, but GM, which was one of Fiat Automobiles' creditors and a partner, argued against it. The government was also in a difficult position as nationalization of Fiat Automobiles would violate EU market competition guidelines. Hence, the nationalization plan was scrapped. In hindsight, GM had an ulterior motive for opposing the nationalization: it wanted to take over Fiat. In fact, in May 2002, some media outlets were suggesting Fiat Automobiles should be sold to GM, which owned 20% of its stakes.

GM gives up Fiat Automobiles

After Giovanni "Gianni" Agnelli, honorary chairman of Fiat, passed away in January 2003, investors wanted Fiat to exercise its put options against GM, believing GM's acquisition of Fiat was the only solution. In 2000, Fiat exchanged 20% of its stocks for 5.1% of GM stocks, while signing a put option contract that would allow it to sell the remainder of its shares to GM after 2004. Later that year, in March, Umberto Agnelli, the newly appointed chairman and younger brother of Giovanni Agnelli, made a surprise announcement: the Fiat Group had no intention of selling Fiat Automobiles to GM and promised that the Agnelli family would revive the company.

GM was also reluctant to buy Fiat Automobiles because its earnings had deteriorated even further. Fiat Automobiles had suffered a 0.1 billion-euro loss in 2001, a 3.9 billion loss in the following year and a 1.9 billion loss in the year after that. Over the course of four years (2001-2004), the company had accrued over 7.9 billion euros in losses. The total value of the company's asset was estimated at 2-2.5 billion euros, while it had nearly 4 billion euros in outstanding debt. GM concluded that normalizing the operation of GM Europe, which had recorded 2.6 billion dollars in accumulated losses since 2000, would be a better than taking over the crumbling Fiat Automobiles. The Italian government was also skeptical of the acquisition, because the ensuing massive restructuring process would cause unemployment numbers to rise and increase the government's burden.

On May 13, GM and Fiat agreed to void the put option contract for 2 billion dollars in compensations paid to Fiat. Fiat Automobiles recruited Sergio Marchionne, the then vice president of finance at the Fiat Group, as its new CEO. Being a financial expert, Marchionne sold Fiat's insurance subsidiary for 2.5 billion dollars and the aviation subsidiary for 1.7 billion dollars in just 50 days after his arrival. He put his foot down and announced that the business diversification would end and the company would commit fully to cars. Marchionne came up with numerous plans to normalize operations, like increasing R&D expense to 1.2 billion dollars, cutting costs by 1.1 billion dollars, limiting output in Europe to 1.6 million units per year and releasing new models to boost sales in Europe.

The closer

The Italian Canadian Marchionne is notorious for being a workaholic. He works more hours than any other automobile company CEO. He works seven days a week, adding diligence to his exceptional financial management skills, developed during his career as an accountant, and his straightforward personality. His attributes allowed him to gain leverage in the company. He solidified his position within the Fiat Group by successfully merging Fiat with a North American company.

Upon arriving at the company in late 2004, Marchionne immediately initiated a structural reform. He rearranged the company's organization horizontally and had the 80 divisions report directly to him. Marchionne carries five smart phones. On US holidays, he travels to Italy to work and during Italian holidays, he is in the US. In 2009, Business week named him the hardest-working CEO in the world. At times, Marchionne finds himself in situations where he is forced to be a workaholic. When Marchionne arrived at Fiat Automobiles, there was a report on his desk saying the company had accumulated a total loss of 12.0 billion dollars. For the former Vice President of Finance, it was the most urgent issue on his agenda.

Marchionne immediately began restructuring and developing new cars. In 2005, he fired 2,000 management-level employees and replaced them with young and skilled mid-level managers. The restructuring process strengthened the company's financial health. In just two years, Fiat Automobiles turned around to a 400 million-dollar profit. The company also began spending relentlessly to develop new cars.

The updated Fiat 500, released in 2007, allowed Fiat's European sales to recover. In 2009, Marchionne had Fiat acquire Chrysler, which was struggling in the aftermath of the subprime meltdown. Marchionne made the right decision. Chrysler became the buoy that sustained Fiat during Italy's financial crisis. Chrysler's line-up of SUVs and medium-to-large-size sedans supplemented Fiat's line-up perfectly. Marchionne now had more cards in his hands.

CHAPTER 22

Chrysler Begins to Wobble

On November 2, 1978, the front page of the Detroit Free Press had two articles. One was titled "Chrysler Losses Worst Ever" and the other, "Lee Iacocca Joins Chrysler." The latter was a report that Lee Iacocca, the mastermind behind the Ford Mustang, was hired as the CEO of Chrysler. At the time, Chrysler was a sinking ship that had turned in a 160 million-dollar loss for the third quarter of 1978. With his hands on the steering wheel, Iacocca spearheaded the development of the Caravan, the world's first minivan, expanding Chrysler's market and veering it back on the road to success.

Chrysler was founded in the early 20th century, during the dawn of the automobile industry. It was the first to conduct wind tunnel tests on cars and the first to release cars with streamlined design. Chrysler was also the first to commercialize power steering systems and power windows. Chrysler grew on the back of its advanced technology and designs. With the acquisition of Dodge and AMC, it emerged as one of the "Big 3" US automobile manufacturers, along with Ford and GM. However, Chrysler's journey was not all roses and rainbows – its existence was threatened by the oil shock, advances of Japanese cars and poor management strategy. It had many different owners throughout its history: Daimler-Benz, private equity funds and the Fiat Group. Among the Big 3, Chrysler has the most colorful past.

Emerging as one of the big 3 after M&As

Officially, Chrysler was established in 1925, but its history can be traced back as far as 1909. The origin of Chrysler is the United States Motor Company founded by Jonathan Maxwell and Benjamin Briscoe. Maxwell left United States Motors Company and started Maxwell Company in 1913. In 1920, Maxwell recruited Walter P. Chrysler, who would become the first executive vice president at GM. At Maxwell Company, Chrysler led the acquisition of Chalmers Motor Car in 1992. In 1924, he rolled out the Chrysler 70, which was named after him. Chrysler became the president of Maxwell Company in 1925, and the company's name was changed to Chrysler.

Chrysler's growth spurt began at this point. In 1928, the company acquired the Dodge Brothers Company and became the third largest automobile company in the US after GM and Ford. After taking over numerous car companies of varying sizes in the 1950s, Chrysler placed its sights on Europe in the 1960s. Chrysler bought the French automaker, Simca, in 1963 and renamed it Chrysler France. In 1967, the company acquired the British automobile company Rootes Motors and the Spanish company Barreiros Diesel, whose names were changed to Chrysler United Kingdom and Chrysler España, respectively.

In 1971, Chrysler purchased a 15% stake in Mitsubishi and launched joint businesses. Mitsubishi cars were sold through Chrysler's sales network. Chrysler had built a global manufacturing and sales network that encompassed Europe and Japan.

The Airflow legend

Chrysler unveiled a car in 1934 that surprised the automobile industry: the Airflow, which was influenced by the streamlining design movement. When designing the Airflow, Chrysler conducted extensive wind tunnel tests, a test to study air flow on objects in a tubular passage with air blown through it at high velocities. The purpose of the test was to develop a design that minimized wind resistance. At the time, cars had a box design. Once

Airflow gained attention, other companies began adopting streamlined designs. Chrysler changed the course of automobile designs.

The C-300 born in 1955 is a classic that lives on as the 300c. The 300hp power V8 Hemi engine used in the C300 is considered one of most well-made engines in history. The 300 in C-300 refers to the engine's 300hp output. The massive output and strong design earned the C-300 a place among the most prominent American muscle cars.

Even while leading the US automobile industry with innovative technology and design, Chrysler was unable to avoid trouble. The foundation of the company was shaken by the oil shock that swept the world. The European wing, which was established via local M&As, was struggling. Chrysler sold all three of its European subsidiaries to Peugeot, but it was not enough to quell the crisis. Must as Maxwell Company did in 1920, Chrysler sought help outside the company and recruited Lee Iacocca, the "Father of the Mustang."

Lee Iacocca puts the reform hammer down

"I believe it is time for you to leave."

It was 3pm on July 13, 1978, at Ford headquarters in Dearborn, near Detroit. In his office, Ford Chairman Henry Ford II told Lee Iacocca that he had to leave, and it was the best for the company.

Iacocca played a crucial role in Ford's rise to prominence. Iacocca had led the development of one of Ford's most popular nameplates, the Mustang, which earned him the nickname, "the Father of the Mustang." However, Ford II was afraid of Iacocca replacing him as the head of Ford and fired him.

Ironically, what Henry Ford II believed was "best for Ford," turned out to be the best for Chrysler. In November 1978, four months after leaving Ford, Iacocca joined Chrysler and was given full control. Iacocca used his power to initiate a complete overhaul of the company. At the time, Chrysler had 35 vice presidents. This was a problem, because the vice presidents were unable to cooperate properly with each other. The company's funds were depleting due to poor sales, rising inventories from excessive production and pointless use of funds. In 1978, GM led the US market selling 5.4 million cars, followed by Ford, which sold 2.6 million. Chrysler managed to sell only 1.2 million cars. To make matters worse, two thirds of the customers that bought Chrysler cars were dissatisfied. Chrysler would fade into history if the situation continued.

Over the course of three years, Iacocca fired 33 out of the 35 vice presidents. He had removed the tumor weighing the company down. With one vice president packing and leaving each month, people began to get nervous. Along with streamlining the workforce, Iacocca also began reforming the company's product line-up. One of the more famous results of the line-up reform is the Voyager, the 7-passenger minivan released in 1984. The Voyager combined the strengths of wagons and vans: it was larger than wagons, but smaller and more practical than vans. The Voyager created a new segment and immediately established a solid presence in the blue ocean market. Chrysler's subsidiary Dodge released its own minivan, the Caravan. The Voyager was subsequently benchmarked by various companies: the Toyota Sienna, the Honda Odyssey and the Kia Carnival. With Iacocca's innovative products, Chrysler regained its former glory in the 1980s – the company's US output bottomed out at 758 thousand in 1980 and doubled to 1.72 million units by 1988.

Chrysler obtains Jeep

The 1980s was a good decade for Chrysler. Many great things were happening with Lee Iacocca at the helm. Then, in 1987, the company obtained a cash cow: AMC, the fourth largest car company in the US.

Established in 1954, AMC was the owner of the Jeep brand. The Jeep was developed for the military during WWII. At the time, the Pentagon wanted a vehicle that had a top speed of 80km/h, weighed less than 590kg, had a load capacity of 0.25tons and could carry three passengers. The request was fulfilled by Willys-Overland's Willys MB. After the war, the

Willys MB gained popularity among civilians for its unique angular design and off road performance. As the original SUV, Jeeps remain a steady seller to this day.

In addition to M&As, Chrysler sought to expand its markets through partnerships. The 20-year relationship with Mitsubishi is one such effort. In 1971, Chrysler established a cooperative relationship with Mitsubishi by purchasing a 15% stake in the company. Chrysler had Mitsubishi utilize Chrysler's US dealership network to sell its cars. Chrysler continued sharing its sales network until Mitsubishi established its own network in 1981. The partnership also had a technological aspect: Mitsubishi supplied 4-cylinder engines to Chrysler. Currently, Hyundai Motor is supplying engine blocks to Chrysler and Mitsubishi because Hyundai gained its engine manufacturing technology from Mitsubishi. When Mitsubishi went public in 1988, Chrysler increased its stake to 20%. The partnership continued for over 20 years, until Chrysler sold its Mitsubishi shares in 1993.

After severing its ties with Mitsubishi, Chrysler began searching for a new partner. In the 1990s, global automakers were frequently engaging in M&As to increase their size. It was a time when Daimler-Benz Chairman Jürgen Schrempp's prediction that six companies would survive was the widely-accepted opinion. The prediction was upsetting for Chrysler, which was the smallest among the American Big 3. In 1998, three years after Schrempp became chairman, Daimler-Benz and Chrysler merged. Daimler-Chrysler immediate emerged as a force to be reckoned with. However, Schrempp's prediction turned out to be wrong, and Daimler-Chrysler began to struggle. Once again, Chrysler was left vulnerable.

CHAPTER 23

Porsche Pursues Volkswagen

The third largest car manufacturer in the world is born.

In May 1998, something happened that shocked everyone in the auto industry. Daimler AG announced its acquisition of Chrysler for 39.5 billion dollars. The official title of Jürgen Schrempp, who spearheaded the deal, changed from Daimler AG Chairman to Daimler-Chrysler Group Chairman. Daimler-Chrysler was the perfect automobile empire with a brand portfolio that had no holes. Daimler-Chrysler owned Dodge, Jeep, Mercedes-Benz and Chrysler, meaning it had a car in every segment. The industry praised the merger, calling it the "merger of equals" and a " marriage made in heaven."

However, happiness does not last forever. In less than a decade since announcing the merger, the "marriage made in heaven" became the "worst decision ever." Daimler and Chrysler failed to mix and the lack of chemistry caused Daimler and Chrysler to erode each others' capital. Chrysler divorced Daimler and united with Fiat. Thanks to the field leadership of Sergio Marchionne, Chrysler's operations normalized and a new family was born: Fiat Chrysler Automobiles (FCA).

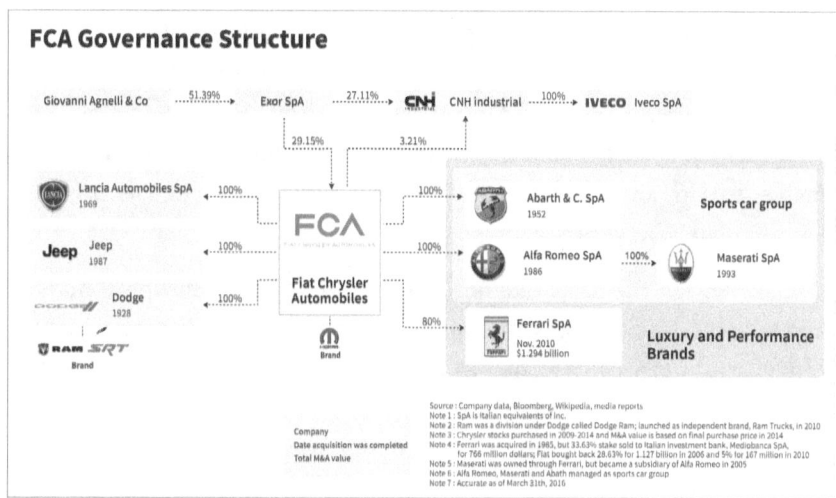

FCA Governance Structure

Every hunter's prey

After relocating to Chrysler, Lee Iacocca was a breath of fresh air. However, there are limits to improving the financial health of a company. So, Chrysler stumbled into another crisis.

There were a few reasons for Chrysler falling back into trouble. In the 1990s, the production capacity of US automakers was higher than local demand. To make matters worse, Japanese companies were increasing their market presence. With Honda and Toyota manufacturing quality cars at affordable prices from their US plants, US companies were losing on their home turf without putting up a proper fight. The situation was particularly brutal for Chrysler, which had lost its position as the third largest automobile company in the US to Toyota and had Honda on its tail.

Its long partnership with Mitsubishi began to creak. Chrysler and Mitsubishi had equally contributed in building a production plant in the US, DSM (Diamond Star Motors). At DSM, Chrysler was able obtain the technology for developing and manufacturing small-sized cars. In light of its financial strain, Chrysler relinquished its stake in DSM to Mitsubishi between 1989 and 1991. Mitsubishi renamed the plant (Mitsubishi Motor Manufacturing of America).

Chrysler was at a disadvantage against GM and Ford. While GM and Ford had presences around the world, Chrysler relied on the US market for 95% of its sales. The AMC Group acquired from Renault in the 1980s worsened Chrysler's financial struggles. AMC owned Jeep, but Jeep was unable to do anything under Chrysler, which was unable to fund development of new cars.

Chrysler felt the desperate need to venture into the European market. At one point, Chrysler was attempting to sign a joint production deal with Renault, but eventually turned to Fiat. Fiat needed a presence in the US, and Chrysler a presence in the European and Fiat's subcompact car technology. The relationship between the two companies had already begun in 1990.

After Iacocca left, Chrysler became the target of the "enterprise hunter," Kirk Kerkorian. Kerkorian's investment firm, Tracinda, held a 10% stake (36 million shares) in Chrysler. On April 12, 1995, Tracinda announced that it would purchase Chrysler. Kerkorian said it would buy the remaining 90% stake at 55 dollars per share, 40% higher than its closing price the previous day. At that price, the deal would be worth 22.8 billion dollars, making it the largest takeover in history up to that point. Interestingly, Iacocca, who owned 5 million dollars worth of Chrysler stocks, sided with Kerkorian.

Robert Eaton, the then-Chairman of Chrysler, officially announced he was against the deal. The Chrysler labor union also expressed their dissent. The union criticized Kerkorian for being a mere profiteer. The dispute between Kerkorian and Chrysler ended with Kerkorian becoming a board member. However, Chrysler's management was unable to run the company arguing with the new board member.

Grand wedding and discord

Amid the turmoil, the Schrempp-led Daimler AG seemed like a savior when it reached out. Daimler wanted a mass brand and footing in the world's largest automobile market, the US. Chrysler wanted advanced technology, funding and access to the European market. Hence, it was widely considered as a match made in heaven. However, things went very differently. Even though it accepted Chrysler into its family, Daimler AG refused to let Chrysler into its home turf. This was disappointing for Chrysler, because it was expecting collaboration. Concerned Chrysler would damage its prestige, Benz refused to interact with Chrysler. So, even after the merger, Chrysler continued to suffer losses as escalating competition in the US market continued to damage sales.

It was in 2003, five years after the merger, when the first car derived from the parts shared between Benz and Chrysler was released. In November 2000, a Benz executive was named the new CEO of Chrysler. That man was Dieter Zetsche, the current Chairman of the Board at Daimler. Once a person from Benz began leading the company, Benz and Chrysler began interacting. Their first joint effort resulted in the sports car, the Chrysler Crossfire. Zetsche was satisfied with the design and decided to begin mass production, but funding was the problem. The solution came when a Benz executive saw the Crossfire at the 2001 North American International Auto Show and said that if the car was a little shorter, it would be able to share platforms with the Benz SLK. Schrempp launched an EAC (Executive Automotive Committee) to supervise parts sharing and collaborations between Mercedes-Benz and Chrysler. The EAC dispatched Benz engineers to Detroit and redesign the Crossfire to share 39% of its parts – including engine and transmission - with the Benz SLK. The development period was shortened by over 50% to less than 24 months. Subsequent collaboration led to a wagon, the Chrysler Pacifica, which used parts from Benz's E-Class vehicles.

Parts sharing and platform unification are essential to improve competitiveness and cut the costs of newly developed models. The executives of Daimler AG were aware of the perks. However, they were worried about damaging the value of the Benz marque. The belated collaborations between the two were not enough to revive Chrysler.

Ultimately, Chrysler was unable to benefit from Benz. After its stint with Chrysler, Daimler AG attempted to take over Mitsubishi Motors and form an alliance with Hyundai Motor, both of which ended in failure. Schrempp's aggressive attempt to increase size turned out to be a double-edged sword. Taking responsibility for poor earnings, Schrempp resigned with two years remaining in his term. Schrempp's successor was Zetsche, who severed ties with Chrysler.

In May 2007, Daimler AG sold 80.1% of Chrysler stocks to the private equity firm, Cerberus Capital Management. It was nine years after the Daimler-Chrysler merger in 1998. The stake was sold for 7.45 billion dollars, which was around a fifth of the 36 billion Daimler AG spent to acquire Chrysler. Daimler sold the remaining 19.9% stake to Cerberus in 2009.

A new home

Left alone, Chrysler's era seemed to be coming to an end. Some speculated that Chrysler would close. The situation was so dire, Cerberus Capital Management offered to sell Chrysler for a dollar to the US government. On April 30, 2009, Chrysler filed for Chapter 11 bankruptcy protection. The Obama Administration came up with a solution for Chrysler: a merger with the Fiat Group. This was the moment Fiat and Chrysler's 47 thousand employees boarded the same ship. The merger was spearheaded by Fiat Group Chairman Sergio Marchionne.

During his visit to Chrysler headquarters in June 2009, Marchionne promised Chrysler employees that he would revive the company. Not many employees seemed ready to place faith in the chain-smoking man wearing a sweater and jeans. Two years later, everyone would become believers when Chrysler, under Marchionne's leadership, repaid 7.6 billion dollars in loans from the American and Canadian governments ahead of schedule.

While the Daimler-Chrysler union was a merger in name only, Fiat made efforts to make the merger a true union. Six months after gaining control of Chrysler, Marchionne announced a five-year plan: Italy's brand of design and craftsmanship would be imbued into Chrysler to improve its competitiveness and profit margins, before forming a unified group as soon as possible.

Marchionne reduced the number of executives and tore down the large, luxurious offices used by his predecessors. He established his office on the fourth floor of the Technology Center and made it no different from the offices of the chiefs of engineering, design and production. Being the workaholic that he was, he restructured the organization horizontally and demanded the 25 executives report directly to him. Under Marchionne's leadership, Chrysler's unit sales, which plunged to 1.32 million in 2009, skyrocketed to 1.52 million in 2010, 1.86 million in 2011, 2.19 million in 2012 and 2.4 million in 2013. Chrysler had begun to recover after its merger with Fiat.

Pushing ahead under a new name

In September 2011, Marchionne became the Chairman of FCA. Two years and four months later, on January 1, 2014, Fiat acquired the remaining 41.5% of Chrysler shares from the UAW Retiree Medical Benefits Trust for 4.35 billion dollars, which includes 700 million dollars in four annual installments paid to the VEBA.

Upon gaining full ownership of Chrysler, Fiat became a massive automobile manufacturer with 197 thousand employees worldwide, including the 80,000 in Italy. FCA emerged as the seventh largest car manufacturer, selling over 4.3 million units per year. FCA owns Fiat, Alfa Romeo, Lancia, Abarth, Fiat Truck, Maserati and Ferrari through Fiat Automobiles and Chrysler, Jeep, Dodge, Ram, Mopar and SRT through Chrysler. The strategy to combine the two companies' strengths produced quick results. The Chrysler 300C and the Jeep Grand Cherokee were redesigned with a sophisticated Italian touch and carefully finished, allowing them to discard the typical raw look of American cars. The market responded with a jump in sales. Chrysler's fast growth during the recovery of the US market provided a buffer when Fiat's sales plunged during Italy's economic slump.

Once the merger processes were completed, the group's name was changed to FCA. Fiat uprooted from Turin, which was its home for 115 years, and relocated to the Netherlands, where the FCA was registered. The company's stocks were transferred from the Milano Stock Exchange to the New York Stock Exchange in October 2014, after which the company announced its plans to focus on expanding its presence in the US.

Marchionne announced a five-year plan, beginning in 2014, in which the company would focus on developing new models and investing a total of 48 billion euros to increase unit sales by 60% to 7 million units and boost sales 52% to 132.0 billion euros. The net profit target was set at 4.7-5.5 billion euros, which is more than twice the 1.95 billion recorded in 2013. Some observed that the target was overly aggressive, but Marchionne was confident.

Resignation of Mr. Ferrari: Dawn of a new age

An emergency press conference was held on September 10, 2014, at the Ferrari headquarters in Mirabella. Ferrari Chairman, Luca di Montezemolo, had announced that he was resigning after leading the sports car company for 23 years. Montezemolo said he would leave Ferrari on October 15 and Marchionne would be appointed as his successor.

Montezemolo was born in 1947 to an aristocratic family in Bologna, Italy. His family was close to Giovanni Agnelli, founder of Fiat. Montezemolo's father was friends with Giovanni Agnelli's grandson, Gianni Agnelli. After Gianni Agnelli became the chairman in 1966, Fiat took over Ferrari, meaning that Montezemolo's connection with Ferrari was not a coincidence. Montezemolo graduated from the University of Rome with a degree in law and from Columbia University with a degree in international business. Upon returning to Italy in 1973, Montezemolo became the manager of Ferrari's F1 racing team and assisted Enzo Ferrari. When Enzo Ferrari died in 1988, Gianni Agnelli appointed Montezemolo as the Chairman of Ferrari.

Montezemolo immediately began restructuring. In 1993, he recruited Jean Todt to lead Scuderia Ferrari. Todt is currently the Chairman of Fédération Internationale de l'Automobile (FIA), which supervised various international motor racing events. In 1996, the legendary Michael Schumacher was recruited into Scuderia Ferrari. The Ferrari team won F1 championships in 1997 and 1998. Between 2000 and 2004, the Ferrari team dominated the F1 – Schumacher won the title five straight years with the team winning 57 out 85 races over the five year span.

Montezemolo changed people's perceptions about the Ferrari. He limited output to around 7,000units, increasing the value of the brand. As a result, Ferraris became cars "money could not buy," As a result, Ferrari's unit sales increased from 2,289 units in 1993 to 7,664 in 2015. It was a significant improvement but failed to exceed its initial target. Meanwhile, Ferrari's net profit jumped from 2 million euros in 1995 to 290 million euros in 2015.

On the surface, Montezemolo was pressured to resign because of Scuderia Ferrari's poor performance, but people within the industry speculate that it was the friction between Montezemolo and Marchionne.

Marchionne wanted to list Fiat on the New York Stock Exchange and use Ferrari as the catalyst to boost sales. He believed Fiat would become a more compelling investment for shareholders if Ferrari's output was increased from 7,000 to 10,000 units. People in the auto industry believe this is where the two men collided, resulting in Montezemolo's resignation. For Marchionne, who wanted to strengthen his grip on FCA, the heavyweight Montezemolo was a thorn in his side.

During his resignation speech, Montezemolo said that an era was closing and Ferrari would begin a new chapter. Ferrari was listed on New York Stock Exchange in October 2015, a year since FCA had transferred to New York. Before going public, 10% of Ferrari shares were owned by Piero Lardi Ferrari, the son of Ferrari founder, Enzo Ferrari, who had been the vice chairman of the company since 1988. The remaining 90% was owned by FCA. FCA listed a 10% stake and distributed the stocks to its shareholders. In the long-term, FCA plans to allocate the remaining Ferrari shares to its shareholders and completely separate the company. Marchionne attempted to merge with GM, Ford or other companies to solve FCA's massive debts, but was rejected each time. Hence, he decided to generate some growth momentum by listing Ferrari and selling FCA's stake. Ferrari and FCA are both entering a new era. As FCA prepares to set foot into the new age, the industry has its attention on FCA's next course of action.

Groundbreaking Classics #3

Mini and Eldorado – Defining the Era on Opposite Sides of the World

The British Motor Company (BMC) Mini and the Cadillac Eldorado have different backgrounds, sizes and clientele, but they both are cars that reflect the situations that define the era.

The Mini is a British economy car, while the Eldorado is an American luxury car. A comparison of their lengths show how different their sizes were. The Mini was 3 meters long, where the Eldorado was 5 meters. Their engines differed in both displacement and output. The Mini had an 850cc 4-cylinder engine producing 34.5hp, but the Eldorado had a 5,400cc 8-cylinder engine producing 211hp.

In one word, the Mini could be described as practical and the Eldorado abundant. At the time, gas prices were skyrocketing in the UK due to the Suez War (the second Arab-Israeli conflict, 1956-1957) that broke out because of Egypt's decision to nationalize the Suez Canal. With the country still recovering from WWII, the British economy was in a state in which it was extremely difficult for cars to sell. As a result, the British sought small and practical cars. Thus, the Mini was born. On the other hand, the Eldorado reflects the economic boom Americans enjoyed in the 1950s, after the US accumulated a massive amount of wealth during the war. The name is also a giveaway. Eldorado comes from El Dorado, the legendary city of gold. Meanwhile, the name Mini comes from the word miniature.

The Mini targeted ordinary citizens, while the Eldorado was marketed to the rich. Upon its release, the Mini was well-received by the British and became one of the most popular cars in the UK. On the other hand, people driving Eldorados were movie stars, politicians and businessmen. US President Dwight Eisenhower was an Eldorado enthusiast, so much so that he rode in an Eldorado – not the presidential state car – on the day he was sworn into office. Elvis Presley also bought his mother an Eldorado as a gift. Despite such glaring differences, both cars were successes in their respective markets.

There is one thing they have in common: the secret of their success. While one was small and practical and the other large and luxurious, they were both made with state-of-the-art technology. In order to use space efficiently, the Mini had a transverse engine, meaning the engine was installed vertically instead of horizontally. The Mini was also the first car to come with an independent suspension system, in which each wheel is supported independently. Independent suspensions may not have been common today, if it were not commercialized by the Mini. The Eldorado also employed cutting-edge technology, like power steering systems, automatic transmission and power windows.

Both cars are similar in the fact that they both trigger nostalgia and are often seen in movies. The Mini has appeared in the BBC comedy Mr. Bean, and the movies Italian Job (1969) and Bourne Identity (2002). The Eldorado appeared in the 1989 movie Pink Cadillac, earning it the nickname Pink Caddy. The car was also featured in True Romance (1993), Gone in 60 Seconds (2000) and other films.

EMPIRE VII

Ford

CHAPTER 24

One Car Every 16 Seconds: The Popularization of Cars

"Cars are no longer the toys of aristocrats."

When speaking about the leading automobile manufacturers in America, Ford is always mentioned. Better yet, it is impossible not to mention Ford when talking about the history of the global automobile industry. Ford's founder, Henry Ford, is the man that drove the advancement of the automobile industry – not just in 20th century America. He was instrumental in popularizing cars through mass production. His business philosophy was making cars cheap and affordable for anyone. All of Ford's most prominent models - from the Model T to the Mustang – are results of this philosophy.

The auto industry made great advances when Ford and GM competed for hegemony of the US market. Henry Ford's bullheadedness got his company to the top, but was also the cause of its downfall.

In the early years, Ford expanded by acquiring Lincoln and Mercury. Later, it increased its size by absorbing brands, such as Aston Martin, Jaguar, Land Rover and Mazda. Ford was on the verge of completing an empire that spanned across the US, Europe and Japan. However, the poor earnings of its subsidiaries transformed the company into a house of cards. Then, Alan Mulally was recruited from Boeing. Upon taking the reins, he trimmed down the company to two brands – Ford and Lincoln. Mulally's decision was timely and Ford become sturdier. When the collapse of Lehman Brothers in 2008 triggered the subprime meltdown that ravaged the US, GM and Chrysler both filed for Chapter 11 bankruptcy protection and sought government aid. Ford was the only company among the American Big 3 that did not need a bailout.

Car for the masses

Henry Ford was born in 1863 in a farm in Greenfield, Michigan, as the son of Irish immigrants. When he turned 16 in 1879, he became an apprentice machinist at Michigan Car Company, where he learned about internal combustion engines. He also had a stint with Thomas Edison when he joined Edison Illuminating Company in 1891. Recognized for his talent, he was promoted to Chief Engineer, after which he began developing a car in his workshop behind his house. In 1985, Ford produced the Quadri cycle, a four-wheeled vehicle with tires. Eight years later, he would completely devote himself to manufacturing automobiles.

In 1903, at the age of 40, Ford founded the Ford Motor Company with his business partner with 100 thousand dollars in capital. He used a new method to start the company, in which a certain stake in the company was distributed to investors. By 1908, Ford Motor produced Model A, B and K, but they were too expensive for ordinary citizens to buy. Moreover, the company had difficulty selling its cars due to escalating competition from existing companies.

Following the failure of the luxury sedan Model K, which was sold at 2,500 dollars, Henry Ford had an epiphany to make cars that the general public could afford. He concluded in order to achieve any level of success was to make motorized vehicles essential for ordinary people, not just an expensive toy for the wealthy. Thus, the Model T was born. The Model T was priced at 825 dollars, which was less than half the price of contemporary cars, which were sold at an average price of 2,000 dollars. Later, the price of the Model T dropped below 300 dollars. Around this time, Ford introduced the eponymous Ford production system, revolutionizing modern production processes and rewriting industrial history. Ford was thinking of ways to reduce production costs through mass production, when he invented the world's first conveyor belt-based assembly system in 1913. This triggered the change from a cottage industry to a mass-production regime.

The Model T was literally a sensation. Ford sold 2.01 million units in 1923 alone, producing a car every 16 seconds. Until the nameplate was discontinued in 1927, Ford had manufactured 15 million units. So, Henry Ford had achieved his dream of popularizing motorized vehicles by giving birth to an affordable car for all.

Curse of the Model T

Ford successfully lowered the price of cars, but wages moved in the opposite direction. Since 1914, the minimum wage of a factory worker working eight hours a day was set at 5 dollars. Because people were lined up at Ford's front door with dreams of becoming a Ford employee, the company had no problem building a competent workforce. At the time in the US, a laborer working nine-hour shifts earned 2.38 dollars a day. Hence, Ford is credited for expanding the middle class.

Being satisfied with the Model T, Henry Ford insisted on carrying only one model. So, the Model T's design remained almost unchanged since it was first released in 1908. Over time, the car became outdated. Once sales began slipping, Ford dealers demanded that Ford come up with a new model.

However, Henry Ford believed the Model T's popularity would last. He was so confident, the company did not spend a single penny in advertisements from 1917 to 1923. While the Model T continued to flourish during the 1910s and 1920s, Henry Ford made the grave mistake of ignoring market changes. After remaining the leading automobile manufacturer for the better half of the 1920s, Ford was pulled down from its pedestal and GM emerged as the largest automobile company in the late

1920s. To this day, Ford has failed to reclaim its throne even once. On May 31, 1927, Ford ceased production of the Model T, stopping at 15,007,033 units.

Afterwards, Ford rolled out the Model A, but sales did not meet expectations. Henry Ford's self-righteous management method had allowed his company to control half of the US car market until 1924. However, his arrogance was also the company's downfall. In 1937, Chrysler became the second largest car company and Ford was pulled down to third.

Unable to trust his own son, Edsel, Henry Ford continued to head the company until 1945, when he turned 82 years old. He relinquished management rights to his grandson Henry Ford II and resigned. The industrialist returned to Greenfield with his wife and spent the last two years of his life there. On the day of his funeral, Ford's assembly lines were all stopped for a minute as the seven million workers honored Henry Ford. While his body was being buried, all drivers in Detroit stopped their cars. American economist John K. Galbraith said that Henry Ford was stubborn and that stubbornness was initially a great advantage in running his business, but was equally destructive later on. Galbraith goes on to say that success prevented Ford from seeking advice and counsel as he believed deep down his foolishness was genius.

Mustang and Iacocca

Succeeding his grandfather as the CEO, Henry Ford II led Ford from 1945 to 1979. During this time, he reinvigorated the company. Ford II was president of Ford, before becoming chairman in 1960. During his reign, Ford became a publically traded company in 1956. Yet, the Ford family was still the owner of Ford Motor Company as they owned 40% of the company's stocks. When talking about the more prominent figure within the Ford Motor Company during this era, not many people point to a member of the Ford clan. The favored choice is not even Ford's first CEO, Robert McNamara. The name that will most likely pop up is Lee Iacocca - because he spearheaded the development of the sports car, the Mustang.

The Mustang was true to Henry Ford's philosophy of making affordable cars – it was a sports car for the general population. Upon its release in 1964, 400 thousand Mustangs were sold. By 2013, a total of 10 million units were sold under the nameplate. The car was so popular, people claimed that "one out of two sports cars sold in the US is a Mustang." The Mustang was a reincarnation of the Model T and it allowed Ford to stage a major comeback.

Lee Iacocca joined Ford in 1945 as a salesman. Acknowledged for his accomplishments, he was promoted to president in 1970. However, his relationship with Ford II began to fall apart due to a rivalry that developed between the two. The Chairman of Ford was feeling threatened by the up-and-coming president of Ford. As a result, Ford II fired Iacocca in 1978. Iacocca was shocked because he thought he would end his career at Ford, but was forced to leave. Iacocca would go on to find a new home at Chrysler, where he achieved another success by developing the Voyager. Iacocca had his revenge, which upset Ford II.

The empire's shaky growth

Through production process and product innovation, Henry Ford laid the groundwork for the industry and consumption culture of the 20th century: mass production and mass consumption. While being excellent in building cars, his ability to manage a brand was his shortcoming. In 1922, Ford purchased the Lincoln Motor Company for 8 million dollars. Lincoln is the first brand Ford acquired and continues to exist to this day. Using the cash earned from the success of the Mustang, Ford went on to acquire and establish numerous new brands.

Mercury was launched in 1939 as a brand filling the gap between Lincoln and Ford. In 1958, Ford launched Edsel, which was named after Henry Ford's son. However, Edsel was dismantled in just 27 months. The Merkur, launched in 1985, also disappeared after four years.

Ford was also active in M&As and partnerships. Its first partnership was formed with Mazda in 1971. The partnership developed into a capital tie-up in 1979 when Ford exchanged its property in Hiroshima for a 25% stake in Mazda. Ford gained control of Mazda in 1996 after Mazda began to struggle. Ford acquired Jaguar (UK) in 1989, Aston Martin (UK) in 1994, Volvo (Sweden) in 1999 and Land Rover (UK) in 2000. As a result, Ford became a massive entity with presences in Britain, Sweden and Japan.

After Lee Iacocca, a number of professional CEOs headed Ford – Harold Poling served as chairman from 1990 to 1993, Alexander Trotman from 1993 to 1998 and Jacques Nasser from 1998 to 2001. When it was acquiring the British luxury brands, Ford was stable. It compiled 56 billion dollars in net profit from 1993 to 2000, of which 60% (33 billion) was earned from 1998 to 2000. However, some luxury brands failed to generate any profit and became a liability. While all of this was happening, Jacque Nasser made strenuous efforts to expand the aftermarket business. As a result, the company began to suffer losses. Ford posted subpar earnings for four quarters straight, from the second quarter of 2011 to the first quarter of the following year. After peaking at 37 dollars in 1999, Ford shares plunged to 8 dollars in 2002. Ford II's son, Bill Ford, stepped up and began to clean the mess, but troubles only increased. To tide over this difficult situation, Bill Ford recruited Alan Mulally, who disassembled and reassembled the company with keen insight.

CHAPTER 25

Mulally's Insight Saves Ford

In 2005, the aircraft industry rustled with excitement. Boeing, which always was the runner up, had outperformed the undisputed industry leader, Airbus, in terms of received orders. The catalyst of the overturn was the Boeing 787 Dreamliner. The Dreamliner's fuselage and wings were made of carbon fiber-based materials – instead of the conventional aluminum – making it lighter and more fuel-efficient.

Five years later, in March 2011, the US automobile industry experienced a similar surprise. Ford sold 212,777 cars that month, outperforming GM's 206,621 units sold. Ford had reclaimed the throne for the first time since 1998. One man was at the center of both events: Alan Mulally. Mulally worked at Boeing for 37 years, where he proved his prowess in business management. Mulally was handed the keys to Ford, which was crumbling from poor sales and financial strains of arduous M&As. After a thorough restructuring and improvement of product quality, Mulally ordered company engineers to improve the competitiveness of Ford's power train and design to re-establish Ford as an automobile powerhouse in the US.

As the head of Ford, Bill Ford attempted to rescue the sinking company by hiring Mulally as the CEO. Among the big three automobile majors, Ford was the only company still headed by a member of the founder family and the only company that did not ask for a life line during the 2008 financial crisis that swept the nation.

The self-damaging "full-service" strategy

In 1999, two people were running the company. The Ford Automotive Operations head, Jacques Nasser, was promoted to president and CEO of Ford. Later in March, the company recruited Wolfgang Reitzle out of BMW and appointed him head of PAG (Premier Automotive Group), the organization that managed all of Ford's premium brands.

Nasser was born in 1947 in Lebanon. He joined Ford as a financial analyst for Ford's Australian unit in 1968. He was promoted to head of Ford's Australian operations, then to Chairman of Ford Europe, Vice President of Ford Motor Company and Vice President of product development. Having built his career outside the US, Nasser hoped to conduct a reform to eradicate the bureaucracy prevalent at the company's headquarters. Along with Nasser, Reitzle was recruited and given the reins to PAG. There was no doubt that Reitzle – given his history at BMW – was the perfect man for the job. Ford acquired Jaguar in 1989, Aston Martin in 1994, Volvo in 1999 and Land Rover in 2000. Retizle was given the mission of increasing PAG's overall unit sales from 650 thousand in 1998 to 1 million by 2004.

Nasser had a vision of taking Ford beyond the boundaries of an automobile manufacturer and transforming it into a full motor vehicle servicing company. His "transformation & growth" strategy focused on expanding the aftermarket and premium vehicle businesses. Nasser aimed to increase aftermarket sales from 300 million dollars in 1997 to 1 billion in 2002. He noticed that a 20,000-dollar car required 68,000-dollars in maintenance, gas and insurance coverage throughout its life span and he wanted Ford to tap into that market. In April 1994, to move his plans forward, Nasser had Ford use 1.6 billion dollars to acquire the Scottish automobile maintenance chain, Kwik-Fit, which operated 2,000 service centers in Britain. Ford also acquired the remaining 18% stake in the car rental company, Hertz.

However, Nasser's plan did not work. Ford's aspirations were foiled by the economic slump that hit Europe and the US in 2001 and intensifying competition within the American market. Strenuous investments added to the poor business environment and pulled the company's earnings down. Ford's operating income fell from a 7.2 billion-dollar profit in 1999 to a 3.5 billion loss in 2000 and a 5.5 billion loss in 2001. Nasser was forced to relinquish command in October 2001, two years and nine months after he was promoted to the position. Henry Ford's great grandson, William Clay "Bill" Ford Jr., was named his successor.

Bill Ford steps up

Ford was struggling in 2001, but it was not in a critical financial crisis. Although active M&As and new business ventures had resulted in losses and accumulating debt, Ford still had a large amount of cash piled in its safe. As of the end of 2001, Ford Motor Company still possessed 17.7 billion dollars in cash. Yet Nasser was pressured to resign because, above all, he had neglected Ford Motor Company, the heart of Ford. Under Nasser's command, Ford was unable to release any successful cars, aside from the Escape. To make matters worse, Ford dealers demanded Nasser to be fired because constant recalls had caused consumers to doubt the quality of Ford vehicles, causing sales to stumble.

Bill Ford immediately began to tighten screws within the organization. Ford Europe was already undergoing restructuring. The Dagenham plant in the northeastern area of London, UK, was closed in May 2000, cutting the workforce by 1,900. In June of the same year, the automotive electronics supplier, Visteon, was spun off. In August 2001, Bill Ford announced plans to lay off five thousand administrative employees. The layoffs were completed by June 2002. In January 2001, Ford decided to shut down an engine factory and three truck plants. He also announced a long-term restructuring mandate, which included the firing of 19 thousand part-time workers. Kwik-Fit was sold off in August 2002. Even with such efforts, Ford could not get back on track. Being unable to improve its financial health, Ford's stock price fell from a 1999-peak of 37 dollars to 8 dollars in 2002.

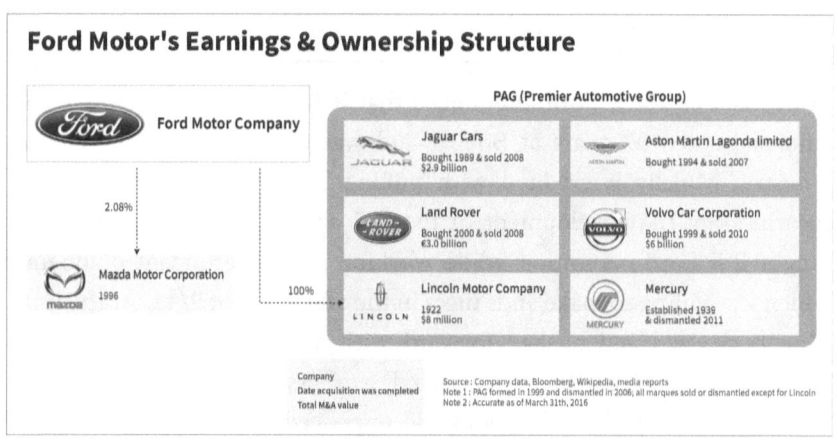

Toyota, Honda, Nissan and other Japanese automakers penetrated further into the American market, adding to the competition presented by Ford's traditional nemesis, GM and Chrysler. Hyundai Motor also invaded American shores and expanded its presence. For these companies, the fat and vulnerable Ford was a sitting duck.

Ford's sales fell 3.8% year-on-year to 178.1 billion dollars in 2005. In the first half of 2006, sales came in at 83.02 billion, down 7.4% from the same period of the previous year. Net profit plunged 44.0% year-on-year to 1.96 billion in 2005 and swung negative to a 1.31 billion loss in the first half of 2006. Ford needed a change. So, Bill Ford announced the Way Forward restructuring plan in January 2005 and the New Way Forward plan in September 2006. The defining difference between the two was the target year for swinging earnings positive: the former was aiming for 2008 and the latter for 2009.

Ford was particularly wary about the contracting pickup truck market. The pickup market had decreased to 2.3 million units in 2006, down from 2.5 million units. It was natural for Ford to feel threatened because it was leading the pickup truck market with its F series. Bill Ford needed reinforcement.

Alan Mulally's restructuring

In September 2006, Ford announced that it had recruited Alan Mulally, who had spent 37 years at Boeing and was a star CEO in the aircraft industry. Mulally is credited with pulling Boeing out of the abyss by spearheading the development of the 777 and 787 Dreamliner. Mulally caught Bill Ford's attention while working as vice president of Boeing, which was failing to make ends meet in the aftermath of 9/11. At the time, Mulally devised and pushed forward with a restructuring plan, which would cause 30% of the 94 thousand workers at Boeing's commercial aircraft division to lose their jobs. He improved the competitive edge of Boeing, which was also playing second fiddle to Airbus, while resolving labor disputes with finesse. It was no mystery why Bill Ford took an interest in Mulally. However, some were skeptical about recruiting Mulally, who had spent his entire career nowhere near the automobile industry.

Regardless, Alan Mulally relocated to Ford and pushed forward with the New Way Forward plan. By the end of the first quarter of 2007, Mulally had laid off 14 thousand workers, which represented a third of Ford's fixed-term contract workforce. He also decided to close 16 plants by the end of 2008, two more than the initially planned fourteen. The plant shutdowns would reduce Ford's North American production capacity to 3.6 million units, which was 26% lower than 2005 levels.

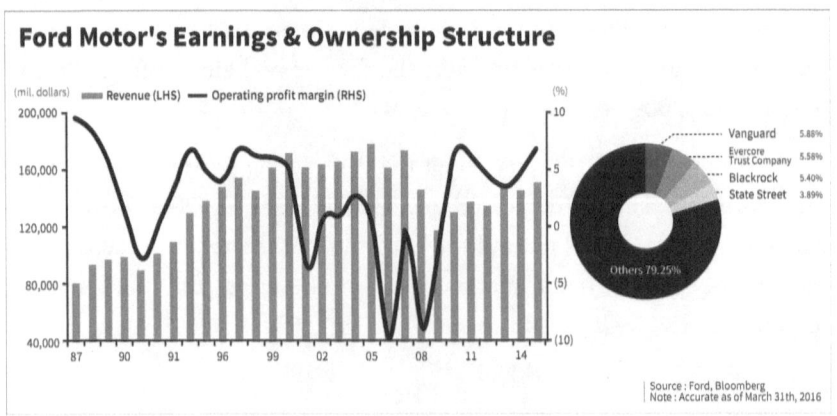

Ford Motor's Earnings & Ownership Structure

(mil. dollars) ▬▬ Revenue (LHS) ▬▬ Operating profit margin (RHS)

Vanguard 5.88%
Evercore Trust Company 5.58%
Blackrock 5.40%
State Street 3.89%
Others 79.25%

Source : Ford, Bloomberg
Note : Accurate as of March 31th, 2016

With the exception of Ford and Lincoln, Mulally boldly dismantled and sold off brands. Aston Martin was sold to Prod rive in 2007 and Land Rover and Jaguar to the Indian conglomerate, the Tata Group. The final brand, Volvo, was sold to the Chinese automaker, Geely. To increase Ford's cash holdings, most of the Mazda stocks were discarded. Ford had purchased 33.4% of the financially struggling Mazda's stocks in 1996 and had been in control of the company since. Ford sold a 20% stake in 2008 and another 8% in 2010. Currently, Ford owns only 2.08% of Mazda shares.

Despite obtaining funds by selling off brands, Ford needed more cash to get back on track. So, Ford offered its logo and all of its US assets as collateral for a 23.6 billion-dollar loan. Ford invested the borrowed money in its core business segments, which established the foundation that allowed it to withstand the subprime meltdown without a bailout. While GM and Chrysler were begging for a government life line, Ford was recording 83 million dollars in losses per day and its share price nosedived to 1.01 dollars. The company's credit rating was downgraded to Ba1, which was junk-bond status. However, Mulally seemed to have predicted the crisis. The restructuring had boosted Ford's financial health, giving the company enough strength to survive without any assistance.

Getting back up

During the North American International Auto Show (NAIAS) in January 2014, Bill Ford and Alan Mulally stepped on stage looking confident. Traditionally, Ford was the first to hold a big exhibition at the NAIAS. That day, the two men introduced the world to the all-new F-150 pickup. The truck was made of aluminum alloy, trimming its weight down by 317kg. It came with a downsized 2.7-liter EcoBoost engine that lowered engine displacement, but increased output. Automobile industry people at the exhibition were astonished but Bill Ford had another surprise for everyone as he announced that Ford would be releasing 23 new models in 2014, twice the number in the previous year, and build two new plants in China to increase production.

Ford's unit sales fell from 6.555 million in 2007 to 5.532 million in 2008 and 4.817 million in 2009, but took an upturn to 5.524 million in 2010 and 5.654 million in 2011. In 2013, unit sales reached 6.33 million, recovering to pre-financial meltdown levels. Unit sales came in at 6.635 million in 2015. Share price recovered to 12 dollars for the first time since 2008 and closed at 17.36 dollars on August 1, 2014.

The One Ford plan implemented in the aftermath of the subprime crisis provided a footing for Ford's recovery. In the past, vehicle development and production was inefficient due to the fact that Ford's overseas subsidiary and R&D division all operated separately. The focus of the One Ford plan was to form an organic connection between all of the company's business units to streamline the massive variety of models and platforms. The plan resulted in cost reduction and quality improvement. Ford expanded the use of EcoBoost engines in other models, while increasing hybrids and electric vehicles to prepare for the upcoming era of eco-friendly cars.

On July 1 of the same year, Mulally stepped down from his position as CEO. He was praised for achieving success during his eight years manning the helm at Ford. Eight days after leaving Ford, on July 9, Mulally became a member of the board of directors at Google, which is currently developing the Self-Driving Car. The automobile industry believes Mulally will play a crucial role in expanding Google's vehicle unit. Everyone will be watching as Mulally takes on his third challenge.

Bill Ford appointed Mark Fields as the new CEO. Fields has built a 25-year career at Ford and was the COO heading the North American operations prior to the promotion. Fields is credited with turning the North American unit around from its subpar earnings. Ford remains the second largest automobile company in America after GM, but has been pushed out of the top five in the global market. Ford plans to bulk up by increasing global sales, particularly in China. So, it should be interesting to watch how the next phase of Ford's adventure plays out.

EMPIRE VIII

Honda

CHAPTER 26

Stubborn Craftsman Reaches the Pinnacle of Technology

One December day in 1956, two middle-aged Japanese men were wandering the streets of Hamburg, Germany. The two men looked closely at the scooters and motorcycles passing by and took notes. The two had been traveling around Europe for two months looking at motor bikes and taking notes. The first man said, "The chassis must be small and light. In order to be competitive, it must be practical and capable of serving a variety of purposes, while requiring a small amount of cost to operate. It must be easy for even novices to ride comfortably. Then it will sell."

The other nodded and replied, "Let's make a motorcycle that a noodle restaurant delivery boy can control easily with one hand, while holding a delivery case in the other."

By August 1958, the Japanese motorcycle manufacturer, Honda, released a new model called the Super Cub C100. The two men traveling Europe for market research were Honda founder, Soichiro Honda, and chief of sales, Takeo Fujisawa. The Super Cub C100 they created still considered one of the most practical motorcycles in the world. The Super Cub C100 was nicknamed "the companion of ordinary people." Having successfully ventured into the motorcycle market with the Super Cub, Honda gained worldwide fame by entering motorcycle races and winning multiple titles. Later, Honda found its way into the automobile industry and developed into Japan's second largest automobile company after Toyota. Honda went on to win F1 championships. No one hesitates to say that Honda is the epitome of technology. Even as the company expanded its business to robots and aircrafts, technology has always been at the heart of Honda. Soichiro Honda, who was the founder and the key engineer at the company, established Honda as the unmatched leader in technology by steering away from M&As and concentrating on development. He also drew a clear line between ownership and management and lived by his creed that "shareholders are the owner of the company."

Model T bedazzles Honda

Soichiro Honda was born in 1906 in the village of Hamamatsu, near Shizuoka Perfecture, as the eldest son of nine siblings. At the age of six, Honda witnessed a Model T drive through the village and immediately fell in love with cars. Years later, he worked at his father's blacksmith shop, while repairing automobiles on the side. One day, he came across a job ad for of position at garage. Without hesitation, Honda went to Tokyo and became an apprentice at Art Shokai. After years of doing menial tasks and learning about automobile repair, Honda became a full-time mechanic. Six years later, in 1928, Honda returned home at the age of 22 and opened the Hamamatsu branch of Art Shokai. In just three years after opening, the garage had 50 employees and became the largest repair shop in Hamamatsu. After WWII, Honda sold the garage and started Honda Technical Research Institute in October 1946. The institute became Honda. While Toyota became renowned for its quality and production system, Honda became famous for its technological prowess.

The Super Cub C100 combined the advantages of easy-to-operate scooters and manual transmission motorcycles. The engine was placed in the lowest area of the chassis to lower the center of gravity. The frame was also lowered. As a result, the Super Cub C100 ensured riding stability, even for novices. This structure is called the "under bone" structure. Operation was simplified by developing a clutch that shifted gears without the use of hands. Just as Soichiro Honda desired, delivery boys could operate the motorcycle with one hand, while holding delivery cases in the other. The Super Cub C100 became an immediate success. Honda sold 90 thousand units in the first year and 160 thousand in the next. It was a steady seller than sold over 76 million units at the end of 2013.

Honda's interest was not limited to commercial motorcycles. He developed racing motorcycles that gave BMW Motorrad, Ducati, MV Agusta and other European motorcycle companies a run for their money. The best example of the outstanding performance of Honda motorcycles is the 1961 International Isle of Man TT (Tourist Trophy) Race, during which Honda won the 125cc, 250cc and 350cc segments. Even Ferdinand Piëch of Volkswagen admitted in his autobiography that he envied Honda's motorcycle and engine technology. Honda sold 10.34 million motorcycles in 2013. In terms of unit sales, Honda leads the motorcycle market. Honda's motorcycle sales came in at 1.6 trillion yen in 2013, accounting for 14% of its total sales.

Expansion to four-wheeled vehicles: F1 conquered

With the success in two-wheeled vehicles, Honda made the natural expansion to four-wheeled vehicles. With the Japanese government moving to regulate new automobile companies, Honda quickly launched its automobile business in 1962. The automobile division announced its arrival in a somewhat abrupt manner. In 1963, Honda released its first sports car, S600, and the light truck, T360. Without warning, Honda participated in the F1 in 1964. It was a reckless endeavor. It entered the German Grand Prix with the RA271, but suffered a devastating defeat. Honda entered three races and ended up retiring each time. In 1965, the situation was different. Honda entered eight races and won the last race in Mexico, proving its technological prowess. It was the first time in F1 history an Asian automaker won. Honda disappeared from F1 racing after its driver, Jo Schlesser, died during the 1968 French Grand Prix. It was 15 years before Honda returned to the F1 arena.

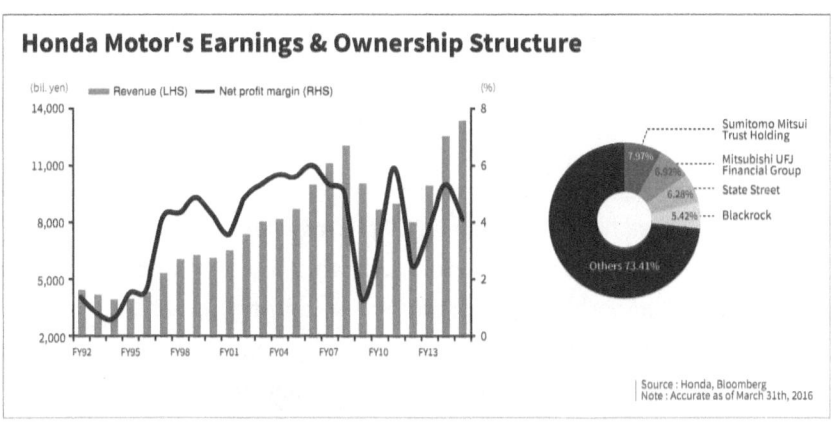

Honda Motor's Earnings & Ownership Structure

(bil. yen) ▪ Revenue (LHS) — Net profit margin (RHS)   (%)

Sumitomo Mitsui Trust Holding
7.97%
Mitsubishi UFJ Financial Group 6.92%
State Street 6.28%
Blackrock 5.42%
Others 73.41%

Source : Honda, Bloomberg
Note : Accurate as of March 31th, 2016

Upon returning to F1 racing in 1983, Honda caused a sensation by using cutting-edge wireless communication and computers to monitor the condition of its cars. This system has become a staple for F1 racing teams. During this period, Honda created a dynasty in the F1 arena. Over the next decade, it won multiple championships. The most notable achievement was in 1988, when the McLaren F1 team dominated the year with Honda engines, winning 15 out of 16 races. The rivalry between the McLaren teammates Aryton Senna and Alain Prost contributed greatly to the popularity of F1 racing.

In 1993, Honda withdrew from F1 to test itself in the Indy Racing League, but Honda did not stay away from F1 racing for long. Honda resumed supplying engines to F1 teams in 2000. It continued to supply engines to F1 teams for another eight years, until in 2008, when Honda withdrew to cut costs after it began to struggle in the wake of the global financial meltdown. Honda became a household name in the F1 world, winning 69 out of 151 Grand Prix events. Using its established technological prowess, Honda released the sports car NSX in 1990. The NSX gained massive support from motor enthusiasts around the world. Built to beat Ferrari, the NSX is still regarded as one of the best cars in history. After recovering from the damage of the financial crisis, Honda announced that it would return to F1 racing in 2015, supplying engines to the McLaren team. Since Soichiro Honda first made the rash decision to have Honda test its technology in 1964, Honda has participated in F1 racing unless it had a particular reason not to.

One and only capital tie-up

Late entrants need help from leaders. Obtaining technology and knowhow from leaders reduces trial and error, allowing late entrants to run the business more smoothly. In the automobile industry, most late entrants manufacture cars through joint ventures and technology alliances with other companies, but Honda was an exception. Soichiro Honda desired his own unique technology. Being an engineer himself, Soichiro headed the R&D department and concentrated on developing his own technology. Through such efforts, he achieved innovation that surprised the industry.

Yet Honda had one joint venture: in 1979, it partnered with the Austin Rover of the British Leyland Group (renamed Rover Group in 1986). During the first phase, Austin Rover manufactured Honda's Civic hatchbacks and Ballade (sedan variant of the Civic) in the UK. In 1983, the two companies signed an agreement that launched the XX Project (ended in 1988), which was a joint effort to develop a luxury sedan. In 1986, the two signed the YY Project contract to develop a subcompact car. The Rover Group produced all Honda cars sold in Europe, while Honda invested 5 billion yen to produce the YY engine locally. The two companies got closer overtime. In 1989, the Rover Group and Honda of the UK Manufacturing (HUM) exchanged 20% stakes. Due to poor earnings, the Rover Group Rover needed the support of Honda's quality and technology. On the other hand, the Rover Group was an effective production base for Honda, which was seeking to expand in Europe. Exporters predicted that the Rover Group would be taken over by Honda until BMW acquired it.

On January 31, 1994, the BMW Group announced that it would acquire the Rover Group. Despite having a 15-year relationship and a 20% stake, Honda was unaware of BMW's intention until it was announced. Burdened by piling losses, British Aerospace, which owned the Rover Group, had decided to sell.

BMW wanted the Rover-Honda partnership to last. Because the two shared a deep relationship and Honda was gaining a significant amount of profit supplying parts, BMW was confident Honda would not sever its ties with the Rover Group, but BMW was wrong. On February 21, 1994, Honda President Nobuhiko Kawamoto met with BMW President Bernd Pischetsrieder and said that due to the change in the Rover Group's ownership structure, Honda wanted to end its capital tie-up with Rover.

Honda was upset that despite owning 20% of the Rover Group's stocks, the Rover Group did not consult it before the acquisition. Moreover, Honda had no desire to form a relationship with BMW, which was its competitor in the motorcycle market. After the meeting, Honda sold its Rover Group shares.

Refusing to play second fiddle to Toyota

Toyota is Honda's biggest rival. Although the two companies were significantly different in size, they were competing against each other in markets around the world. The rivalry is traced back to the 1970s. Starting with subcompact cars in the 1970s, Honda and Toyota countered each other, expanding their model line-ups to mid-size sedans, luxury sedans, minivans and SUVs. During the 1970s, the Civic was competing against the Corolla for hegemony in the subcompact segment. During the 1980s, the Camry and the Accord competed to lead the mid-size sedan market.

The rivalry brought on the global Japanese car boom from the 1990s until the mid-200s. In 1991, Toyota released the Estima and took its first step into the minivan market. Three years later, Honda followed with the release of the Odyssey in 1994. The next year, the Odyssey outsold the Estima. In 1994, Toyota ventured into the CUV market with the release of the RAV4. Honda followed with the CR-V a year later. The rivalry stopped with the release of hybrid cars in the early 2000s as the Prius was a major success, while the Honda Insight failed to gain traction.

The two companies also showed differences in their premium brand strategy. In 1986, Honda announced its premium brand, Acura, in the US.

It was three years before Toyota launched Lexus. Acura was not received well, whereas Lexus became the top-selling luxury brand in North America as marketing and product clicked into place. In 2013, Lexus sold 34,757 cars in the US, while Acura sold only 15,751 units.

No one can deny that Honda and Toyota made great advances while competing against each other as they expanded in the global market. During the past several years, Honda recovered from its slump and returned to F1 racing, re-establishing itself as Toyota's largest threat. The development of the rivalry should be observed closely by all companies.

Unlike Toyota, which has kept the company in the family, Honda set aside any blood or personal relationships. Soichiro refused to pass the company on members of his family. The only stake the Honda clan has in the company is the 1% stake Soichiro Honda left to his wife. Soichiro Honda resigned from the company in 1973 and died from liver cancer in 1991. It has been 20 years since Soichiro Honda died, but his resignation speech is still quoted by many people.

"I spend 99% of the time given to me pursuing failure."

Industry-Altering Event #4

The Plaza Accord

During the 1980s, the trade war between the US and Japan began to escalate. Competition between the two countries was especially high in the automobile industry because exports of Japanese companies skyrocketed as US consumers began to show preference for smaller cars in the aftermath of the oil shocks. As their cars began selling well in the US, Japanese automakers began building plants in the US. Among the three Japanese automobile majors, Nissan was the first to build a US plant. Nissan built the NMMC assembly plant in 1980. Honda followed suit in 1982. In 1984, Toyota founded the NUMMI (New United Motor Manufacturing Inc) plant with GM. Toyota's first independent plant was built in May 1988 in George Town, Kentucky.

Having a massive political influence, the US automobile industry managed to get an import quota implemented in 1981. Under the quota, car imports would be restricted for three years and only 1.68 million would be imported in the first year of the quota. In short, the automobile industry wanted to minimize car imports until they could meet the raised fuel economy requirements. The quota became the trigger that caused Japanese automakers to launch luxury brands. Until then, the US high-end automobile market was divided among American and German marques. After Acura was launched in 1986 and Lexus and Infiniti in 1989, the US luxury car market began leaning toward Japanese brands.

The trade war spread to foreign exchange rates. In September 1985, the financial ministers of the G5 nations (US, France, Germany, Japan and UK) gathered at the Plaza Hotel in New York and resolved to correct the dollar appreciation caused by interfering with the foreign currency market. This was the Plaza Accord. Over the next two years, the value of the yen and the mark each increased 65.7% and 57% against the dollar. During this period, the value of the dollar plunged 30%. The resulting price competitiveness of US products allowed the US manufacturing industry to flourish overseas. On the other hand, the yen appreciation hit the Japanese economy hard.

Although the Japanese companies had failed after launching prestige brands and spent massive amounts of money in marketing to safe-land their premium marques in the US market, Japanese companies were not the only ones that suffered from the Plaza Accord. The mark appreciation created trouble for German companies. The plunge in exchange rate cut Porsche's sales and profit in half. BMW, which had been enjoying brisk sales in the US, saw its earnings take a nosedive. Foreign exchange rates were not the only cause of Porsche and BMW's struggles: after Black Monday, the US luxury car market began to show a preference for practical cars

Peugeot-Citroën (PSA)

CHAPTER 27

Pride of France Swallows its Pride to Survive

"France's pride, Peugeot, asks China for help"

On February 18, 2014, the supervisory board of the French automobile company, Peugeot-Citroën Automobile (PSA) approved the sales of 14% stakes to Dongfeng Motor and the French government. The *Wall Street Journal* reported the news to the world. The article referred to Peugeot as the pride of France, writing, "In World War II, the company's main factory was captured by Nazi German forces. But the family approved workers sabotaging German output, and Peugeot was allowed to remain independent after the conflict, while competitor Renault, accused of collaboration, was nationalized." The article reported that people were worried that the 200-year-old Peugeot may fall into the hands of the young truck manufacturer, Dongfeng Motor.

PSA went through its share of internal conflict. In 2013, PSA's unit sales in Europe fell 8.4% year-on-year to 1.31 million units. It was devastating for PSA, because it relied on the European market for 60% of its sales. Unless it gained capital from Dongfeng, large-scale restructuring and financial struggles were inevitable.

The French did not receive the news of PSA's partnership with Dongfeng well. To prevent PSA from falling into the hands of Chinese, the French government stepped forward and offered to participate in the capital injection, splitting the stake equally with Dongfeng to prevent PSA from falling into the hands of the Chinese. Dongfeng currently owns 14% of PSA and has two people on PSA's board of directors. The board replaced Thierry Peugeot with Carlos Tavares of Renault as the new Chairman of PSA.

Peugeot is only one of France's most prominent companies, having a century in the automobile manufacturer and another century as a steel company before that. Peugeot was the vanguard of the European auto industry since the beginning. Peugeot merged with the marketing genius Citroën in 1975 and has continued to operate to this day. Having a long history, Peugeot has seen its share of danger. Risk continues to find Peugeot, demanding new changes.

Oldest history after Benz

Peugeot's history is traced back as far as the 18th century. Its foundation was the steel mill established by Jean-Pierre Peugeot in Belfort in 1810. Jean-Pierre Peugeot manufactured saws, coffee grinders and sewing machines. His grandson, Armand Peugeot, began a bicycle manufacturing business in 1871, after observing bicycles while studying in Britain. By 1882, Armand Peugeot produced the highly successful bicycle, Grand Bi, which had front wheels larger than the rear wheels.

After the bicycle business grew, Peugeot turned to automobiles. He received help from the steam engine developer, Léon Serpollet, and produced his first car in 1889, the Serpollet Peugeot. The three-wheeled vehicle was entered in the Exposition Universelle. However, the Serpollet Peugeot did not sell well. Peugeot used the gasoline engine developed by Gottlieb Daimler to produce a four-wheeled gasoline engine vehicle, the Type 3, in 1891. The Type 3 was well received by the market. Sales increased from 19 units in 1892 to 40 units in 1894. In order to prove the durability of his products, Peugeot participated in the Paris-Brest-Paris race as a coach. The Type 3 proved itself by completing the 2,000km course in 139 hours. In 1894, Peugeot entered the world's first motor racing event, the Paris-Rouen Trial, with the Type 7. The Type 7 prevailed over 102 participants, driving 127km.

In 1896, Armand Peugeot founded Peugeot Automobiles, becoming the second automobile company established in Europe after Benz in 1886. Peugeot began to develop his own engine. The Type 15 released in 1899 sold 300 units, which represented 25% of France's total automobile sales.

In 1912, Peugeot released the small car, Bébé, which was equipped with an 855cc 4-cylinder engine developed by Ettore Bugatti. Bugattie's engine was the world's first DOHC engine, which had four valves and camshafts per cylinder. The reliability of Bébé was proven with its entery in the European Rally and Grand Prix and the American Indianapolis 500. Ettore Bugatti is the founder of the French super car brand Bugatti.

In 1931, Peugeot released the 201, which was equipped with a German suspension system. The 201 was the first car to bear Peugeot's name format, in which the middle digits are 0. In 1934, the company released the world's first hardtop convertible, 401 Eclipse. The 204, which is the fourth model of the 201 series, was the best-selling car in France from 1969 to 1971. By 1970, Peugeot was churning out 500 thousand cars each year, placing it second in France after Renault.

The marketing genius

Founded in 1919, Citroën is an auto company named after its founder, Andre Citroën. Andre Citroën advertised his company in a unique way: creating an event that was beyond anyone's imagination. Between 1925 and 1934, Citroën used 250 thousand light bulbs to display the letters "CITROËN" on the Eiffel Tower. This was recorded as the world's first outdoor advertisement. In 1921, Citroën attempted to drive across the Sahara to prove the durability of the newly released B2. In 1925, he demonstrated the safety of the B12 by driving around Paris with an elephant on it. Thanks to Andre Citroën's astonishing marketing campaigns, everyone in France had heard of Citroën. At the time, the

French joked that the first words babies learn were "mother", "father" and "Citroën."

Citroën also attempted to expand the boundaries of technology. One of Citroën's most famous technologies is the self-centering steering wheel: the Type A, Europe's first mass-produced car, popularized motor vehicles. In 1934, Citroën released Traction Avant, the world's first front-wheel drive vehicle. In the 1950s, Citroën began developing the DS, the follow-up to the Traction Avant. The DS was unveiled during the 1955 Paris Motor Show. Citroën received 734 orders for the DS19 in just five minutes and 12,000 during the first day. The DS is Citroën's premium nameplate. The name is derived from "deesse," which is French for "goddess."

Between 1955 and 1975, Citroën sold 1.45 million DS19s. The DS19 was one of the most popular cars in French history. In 1968, Citroën acquired Maserati and set foot into the luxury sports car market. In 1975, Citroën released its first diesel engine car, the CX. The CX was designated at the official state car for the President of France.

However, Citroën began to struggle in the midst of the 1974 oil shock and went bankrupt. The DS was not enough to sustain the company. In the end, Citroën gave in, and the French government handed the company to Peugeot. In short, Peugeot had taken over Citroën. Maserati was sold to the Argentinean race car driver, De Tomaso. It was later picked up by the Fiat Group.

Eventful years

After acquiring Citroën, Peugeot was renamed Peugeot-Citroën Automobile (PSA). In 1978, PSA purchased Chrysler's factories in France, Britain and Spain. PSA was able to strike a deal as Chrysler was struggling and needed to slim down its business, whereas PSA needed to expand its market. PSA united the factories under the name Talbot. That same year, PSA acquired Simca, a French automobile company established in 1935. As a result of such M&As, PSA's automobile output reached 2 million units in

France and 2.5 million units, when the Spanish and British plants were included.

Using its increased size, PSA actively began venturing overseas. It provided support to its American sales subsidiary established in 1958. In 1984, it ventured into the Chinese market with the establishment of Dongfeng Peugeot-Citroën, a joint venture with Dongfeng Motor. PSA actively formed technological alliances; for instance, it established a joint venture with Renault in the 1960s to develop engines and transmissions. In the 1970s, Peugeot shared designing and production technologies for vans with Fiat.

Despite the numerous M&As and technological partnerships, PSA went through its fair share of ups and downs. PSA kept its market share in France above 33% since 1983, but by 1993, its market share fell to 29.7% as the market integration resulting from the launch of the EU caused other automakers to establish presences in France. The strong run by Renault contributed to the disappointing figures, but Peugeot was also becoming outdated. It released only four new models between 1990 and 1993. The company was selling its mainstay 205 without any full changes since the model's release in 1983. The Citroen AX also remained unchanged since 1986.

With its domestic market share dropping and exports falling amid the Western European economic slump, PSA decided to discontinue its overseas operations to focus on strengthening its foundation. In 1991, PSA withdrew from its losing battle against Japanese automakers in the US. In 1997, it retreated from China and India.

Reoccurring crises and China

Glory was waiting at the end of the crisis. By 1999, PSA was the second largest automobile manufacturer in Europe after Volkswagen. Its unit sales in Western Europe surged from 2.15 million units in 1999 to 2.54 million in 2001. The market share gap between the two narrowed down from 6.6 percentage points to 4.4 percentage points. During the same period, PSA's global unit sales jumped from 2.52 million to 3.13 million, breaking the 3 million-mark for the first time.

PSA's unit sales increased because advances in its PSA's diesel engine technology coincided with increase in diesel engine car demand. In 2001, 36% of cars in Western Europe were diesel. Diesel engine cars were particularly popular in France, accounting for 56% of cars in the country. The increasing preference for diesel vehicles was favorable for PSA, which had the common rail diesel engines that produced were less noisy, and in addition had higher output and fuel efficiency. Having an edge in gasoline engines, Renault yielded its throne to PSA.

Reorganization also generated synergy. PSA had been operating Peugeot and Citroën separately. It was inefficient. PSA launched PSA S.A. as an entity unifying and managing product development, procurement and production of the two brands. Peugeot and Citroën handled only the sales and repair duties for the cars. Once overlapping businesses were unified and the R&D, product development, parts purchases and other processes were conducted together, PSA was able to save costs and reduce product development periods.

However, the good times did not last. PSA's operating profit peaked at 2.6 billion euros in 2002 and then began to slide. By 2009, PSA had turned in a 690 million-euro loss. PSA began to stumble, because it was unable to keep up with the increasing demand for better interior design and more luxurious materials as it struggled to withstand the onslaught of the economic crisis that engulfed Europe.

PSA could no longer hold its own and sought help outside. In February 2014, PSA decided to receive capital injections from Dongfeng Motor and the French government. The Peugeot family owned 25% of the company and had 38% of voting rights. Dongfeng Motor and the French government each provided 800 million euros in exchange for 14% stakes. As a result, the number of Peugeot family members on the PSA board of directors was reduced from four to two. Dongfeng Motor and the French government each got two people on the board.

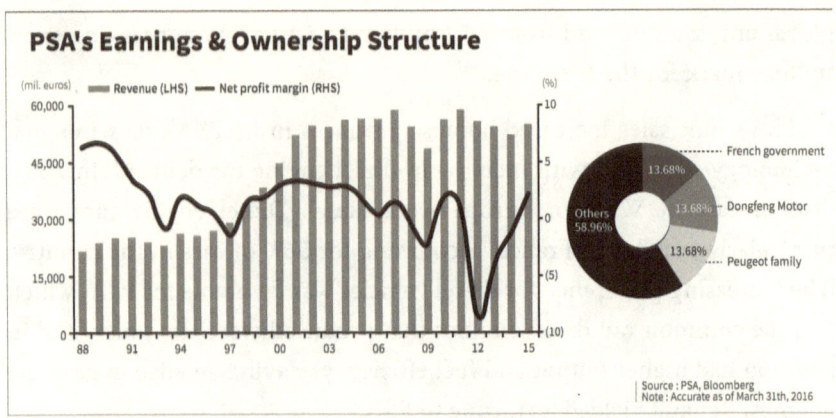

PSA's Earnings & Ownership Structure

Source : PSA, Bloomberg
Note : Accurate as of March 31th, 2016

According to the contract, Peugeot, Dongfeng and the French government cannot increase their stake in PSA for the next 10 years to ensure that resources are used to save PSA, not fight for more control. Each party has its own agenda. The Peugeot family probably wants to regain absolute influence in PSA. Dongfeng is likely to attempt to acquire PSA in order to obtain a major base for its expansion in Europe. The French government will want to retain its stake to preserve the jobs sustained by PSA in France - 90 thousand jobs at PSA and 200 thousand in related industries. The liquidity injection produced immediate results. PSA recorded a 2015 net profit of 1.2 billion euros (2.2% margin), generating profit for the first time in four years. The positive turnaround seems attributable to the joint R&D construction with Dongfeng and production cost cuts. With the governance structure reorganized, one has to wonder what PSA would look like in 2024. PSA already has gone through a lot during its long history, but it is at the beginning of a decade that is likely to be just as eventful as its past.

EMPIRE X

Daimler AG

CHAPTER 28

Daimler Empire: From Mini Cars to Trucks

Mercedes Benz held its IAA (Frankfurt Motor Show) eve event on September 9, 2013, at Messe in Frankfurt, Germany. During the event, Daimler Group Chairman Dieter Zetsche appeared on stage on the back seat of a new Benz S-Class with music playing in the background. Everyone in the audience cheered because no one was in the driver's seat. It was an autonomous vehicle.

Zetsche got out of the car and surprised the audience again, saying that the S500 Intelligence Drive successfully drove across a 103km-interval from Mannheim to Pforzheim and that Benz would develop a mass-production autonomous vehicle by 2020. Benz was the first company to develop an autonomous car that drove over 100km on open roads, not highways and test tracks.

The 103km course is called the Memorial Route and is the same one Karl and Bertha Benz test drove the Patent-Motorwagen 125 years ago. The route consists of winding country roads, expressway and busy downtown traffic. Zetsche went on to say, "Benz's ultimate goal is to realize automobiles that do not get into accidents and do not produce exhaust gas. Just as Gottlieb Daimler and Karl Benz invented a carriage free of horses, we will invent a car free of accidents and pollution."

From the Patent-Motorwagen to the autonomous car, Benz has advanced through technology. Benz has solidified itself as the Daimler

Group's prestige brand, and has expanded its business to all car segments, including mini cars, sports cars and commercial vehicles. There is practically no car Daimler cannot manufacture. Daimler is the embodiment of the history of the automobile industry and car manufacturing technology.

Karl Benz and Gottlieb Daimler

In 1883, Karl Benz started the world's first automobile factory, Benz & Cie, in Mannheim, Germany. Two and a half years later, Benz produced the world's first motor vehicle, the Patent-Motorwagen. In 1893, Benz developed and sold Victoria, which had front wheels capable of turning in various angles. Until 1900, Benz sold around 600 Victorias each year.

At the time, Benz's rival was Gottlieb Daimler. In 1886, Daimler developed a frame for installing a motor, which was named "horseless carriage." In 1890, Daimler founded DMG(Daimler–Motoren–Gesellschaft). That year DMG produced and sold 96 cars. DMG began using the Mercedes marque at this point. Mercedes was the name of Austrian businessman Emil Jellinek's daughter. Jellinek purchased 36 cars and made a few proposals to Daimler. He also requested exclusive sales rights to some regions of Europe and in the US and that the cars be named after his daughter. Daimler accepted and when the name received a positive market response, he began to name all his cars Mercedes.

Mercedes Benz and the world's firsts

During WWI, Benz & Cie and DMG both manufactured vehicles for the German army. When the German economy entered a severe slump in the 1920s, the two companies merged as the Daimler-Benz AG. All cars manufactured by Daimler-Benz were named Mercedes-Benz.

Just as it was from its establishments, Mercedes-Benz was technologically more advanced than other companies. The high-performance Mercedes SSK released in 1928 drove 20,000km non-stop in

13 days without breaking down once. This durability is commendable, even by today's standards. In 1935, the company released the 260D, the world's first diesel engine passenger car. The company produced two thousand 260Ds until 1940. In 1951, the company introduced the concept of the "crumple zone," which absorbs shock to prevent passengers being injured. Mercedes-Benz was the first to apply seat belts and ABS brakes in mass-produced cars. In 1959, the company conducted the world's first crash test.

In 1954, Mercedes-Benz released the masterpiece, 300SL. The 300SL was built as a racing car and was the first car to feature gull-wing doors. The concept of gull-wing doors had been around for some time, but was not applied for safety reasons. Mercedes-Benz tackled the safety issues and was able to apply the aesthetically pleasing gull-wing doors. The 300SL came with a 3.0 liter 6-cylinder engine, producing up to 215 horse powers and a maximum speed of 250km/h. Until 1963, Mercedes-Benz manufactured 3,258 units.

Chrysler sold off – Dream of building an empire crumbles

Through Mercedes-Benz, Daimler-Benz AG collaborated with many companies in many ways, including through M&As, equity investment and technology alliances. Being a prestige marque that sold a small number of cars, collaborations were necessary for the company to achieve economies of scale. Ultimately, most of Daimler-Benz AG's collaborations ended in failure. The high chance of collaborations ending in failure may be the reason Toyota, Honda, Hyundai and other companies prefer to stand alone, rather than joining hands with others.

The largest M&A in Daimler-Benz's history was the acquisition of Chrysler in 1998. Headed by then-Chairman of Daimler-Benz AG, Jürgen Schrempp, the deal was worth 36 billion dollars. With the acquisition of Chrysler, Daimler-Benz obtained Dodge and Jeep. So, it had completed an empire that covered every car segment. Daimler-Chrysler was the third largest automobile manufacturer at the time. However, the marriage lasted only a decade, and the two companies went their separate ways. Having existed as separate entities in a single body, the organization was inefficient and Daimler's insularity impeded Chrysler's technological advancement. Assuming responsibility for the unsuccessful M&A, Schrempp resigned and was succeeded by Dieter Zetsche.

Daimler-Chrysler's efforts to expand its business did not stop. On March 27, 2000, Daimler-Chrysler announced a capital tie-up with Mitsubishi, in which Daimler would purchase a 35% stake in Mitsubishi for 2 billion euros. Through the partnership, Daimler-Chrysler hoped to improve its competitiveness in the European subcompact segment market and expand to the Asian market. The company even had a long-term target of earning 25% of its sales from the growing Asian market. Daimler went on to increase its ownership to 37.3%. It was natural for Daimler-Chrysler to begin thinking about a takeover.

In April 2004, Daimler announced a capital increase of 750 billion yen for the struggling Mitsubishi, with Daimler providing 450 billion, the Mitsubishi Group 100 billion and numerous institutional investors 200 billion by 2007. Daimler's ulterior motive was to assist the struggling Mitsubishi to increase its control. The problem was, Chrysler was also under financial distress. Due to opposition from shareholders and executives, Schrempp retracted the support to Mitsubishi. Daimler began selling its Mitsubishi stocks in November 2005. In 2007, it sold Chrysler and changed renamed itself Daimler AG.

As a part of its investments in eco-friendly cars, Daimler bought shares in Tesla. The company hoped to use its stake to secure batteries, powertrains, and other parts for use in the full electric-powered versions of the Benz A and B Classes and the SMART For two. In May 2009, Daimler secured a 9% stake in Tesla for 50 million dollars, before the company went public. Daimler's stake decreased to 4% after Tesla's IPO in May 2010 but enjoyed a 1,560% return as it sold the shares for 780 million dollars in October 2014. Even after Daimler sold its shares, Tesla and Daimler remain partners in electric vehicle production.

Daimler's most prominent collaboration with a hyper car brand was with McLaren. McLaren was a motor racing team and sports car manufacturer that had a long-standing rivalry with Ferrari in the F1 world. McLaren was founded in 1963, when the New Zealander Bruce McLaren, a driver and engineer from the Cooper Team, started the Bruce McLaren Racing Team. The McLaren team first entered F1 in 1966 and won the Belgium Grand Prix two years later. Bruce McLaren died in 1970 while test driving a car at the Goodwood Motor Circuit in Britain. However, the McLaren Team continued to write history. Emerson Fittipaldi, Niki Lauda, Alain Prost, Ayrton Senna and other famous F1 drivers all won titles with the McLaren Team. After Honda withdrew from F1, the McLaren team was seeking a new engine supplier and partnered with Mercedes-Benz. The collaboration expanded to non-race cars, resulting in the SLR McLaren in 2003. McLaren assumed chassis design and production. The car was equipped with Benz's supercharged 5.4 liter 8-cylinder engine and was modified to produce 626 horse powers. The Benz-McLaren partnership ended in 2014, and today the McLaren Racing Team purchases its engines from Honda.

The hectic birth of the Smart

For a long time, Benz had built a reputation as a premium automobile manufacturer. As a result, consumers automatically connected Benz with its S-Class cars. It was the fruit of the strong presence and competitiveness of the S-Class. The S-Class line began with the release of the Mercedes Simplex 60hp in 1903. The 60-horse power Simplex surprised the world by reaching a top speed of 109km/h. In 1928, Benz released the W08 and presented one as a gift to the Pope, earning the nickname "Pope Mobile" The history of the Pope Mobile continues to this day. The name "S-Class" was first used in 1972.

Due to its history, only a small number of people know that Benz manufactures city cars. People are aware of the Smart marque, but not many know that the brand is owned by Mercedes-Benz. To put it simply, Benz is selling city cars indirectly. The Smart brand began with the watch manufacturing company, Swatch, which is owned by SMH (Swiss Corporation for Microelectronics and Watch making Industries). SMH Chairman Nicholas Hayek decided to build a two-seat city car with high fuel economy, but was unable to do it by himself. He began searching for a partner and found one in Volkswagen in July 1991. When Ferdinand Piëch became Chairman of Volkswagen in 1993, he ended the partnership, saying that Volkswagen would develop a city car alone, so SMH partnered with Benz in 1994. The two companies established a joint venture called Micro Compact Car (MCC), with SMH owning 49% and Daimler AG 51%. The MCC brand became Smart, which is the combination of "S" for Swatch, "M" for Mercedes and art. The first fruit of the partnership was the Smart City, unveiled in July 1998. Once the car was developed, SMH withdrew from the venture, as Hayek had become aggravated by constant clashes with Benz. For instance, Hayek wanted a hybrid vehicle, but Benz insisted on a gasoline engine. Benz acquired the remaining stake for MCC and has been running the company since.

In 1982, after years of focusing on S-Class and E-Class vehicles, Benz released the compact sedan, 190E, which developed into Benz's C-Class. In the early 2000s, Benz released the front-wheel drive subcompact line of A-Classes and B-Classes. As a result, Benz had a complete model line-up that spanned from city cars to large-size vehicles.

Benz also actively nurtured its commercial vehicle division; Daimler AG first began producing commercial cars for the military. After the war ended, it fully engaged in truck and bus manufacturing. Benz owns a number of commercial vehicle brands, including FUSO (joint venture between Benz Truck and Mitsubishi), Freightliner and Western Star. However, the Daimler Group needed a plan to gain hegemony in the saturating premium sedan market. Change seemed necessary.

CHAPTER 29

Tri-Star Becomes Younger

"I plan to leave the company by the end of the year."

On June 28, 2005, Daimler-Chrysler Chairman Jürgen Schrempp expressed his desire to resign from his post. The announcement came as a surprise, because Schrempp had two years left in his term. The press immediately heralded the news that the man who led the world's third largest automobile manufacturer for a decade, was stepping down. Ironically, Daimler-Chrysler's share price jumped 9% that day, indicating investors welcomed Schrempp's decision. Coming out from a blunder-stricken reign, which included the merger with Chrysler and capital tie-up with Mitsubishi, Schrempp's last decision was exquisite. After Schrempp's resignation, Dieter Zetsche, who was leading Chrysler, was appointed as the new Chairman. Zetsche was sharp and fearless in restructuring the struggling empire. After divorcing Chrysler, Zetsche's Benz discontinued Maybach production and discarded any business segment that failed to function adequately. Zetsche's extreme measures produced results. The Daimler AG regained its health and Mercedes-Benz was stronger than ever. The emperor had returned.

"Schrempp discount"

Schrempp began his career at Daimler-Benz as an apprentice mechanic in 1961. He was 16 years old. In 1995, 34 years later, Schrempp was appointed chairman. He began at the very bottom and worked his way to the top.

In 1998, Schrempp lead Daimler's acquisition of Chrysler, one of the three largest automakers in the US. The problem with the acquisition was the price: Daimler paid a whopping 39.5 billion dollars to acquire the financially troubled Chrysler. After the merger, Daimler's share prices began to fall. Daimler-Chrysler's market capitalization, which had once peaked at 115.3 billion dollars, nosedived to 44.9 billion dollars. Investors joked about Daimler's share price, saying it included a "Schrempp discount."

Schrempp attempted to turn the tables in his favor by investing a massive amount of money in Mitsubishi, which ultimately ended in failure. He also made an unsuccessful attempt to collaborate with Hyundai Motor in the commercial vehicle segment. Schrempp had nowhere to run. To make matters worse, Deutsche Bank, Daimler-Chrysler's majority shareholder and Schrempp's guardian angel, announced that it would divest and lower its Daimler-Chrysler share from 10.4% to 6.9%. Deutsche Bank was moving to end its 80-year relationship with Daimler. Quoting a Daimler executive, *Financial Times* reported that Schrempp realized that he would be unable to complete his vision within his term and believed it was the opportune moment to resign.

The violin-playing, beer-serving star CEO

On the outside, Dieter Zetsche had the features that made him look like the stereotypical "kind, old German gentlemen" - tall, with a white mustache and a warm smile. While working as the CEO of Chrysler in 2001, Zetsche actually performed a sketch wearing overalls in a marketing stunt to advertise a product. While introducing the new S-Class at the 2005 Tokyo Motor Show, he played the violin with an orchestra. During an event unveiling the A-Class in 2012, Zetsche personally served beer. Zetsche had a reputation for freely mingling with people at various events.

Underneath his pleasant exterior, Zetsche was a decisive CEO who pulled the Daimler Group out of its lump. After becoming the Chairman, he fired 26 thousand workers to make up for Chrysler's one billion-dollar loss in 2005. In 2007, Daimler sold Chrysler for 7.45 billion dollars and renamed itself Daimler AG. The capital tie-up with Mitsubishi was also liquidated.

Born the son of an engineer in Istanbul, Zetsche studied electrical engineering in college. In 1976, he joined Daimler-Benz AG and worked at the R&D center. After earning a PhD in engineering in 1982, he became specialist in developing electronics and products. When deployed overseas, he even had a stint in sales and marketing. Thanks to his time overseas, Zetsche is fluent in six languages, including German, English and French.

After restoring Daimler AG's financial health, Zetsche's next agenda was improving Benz's competitiveness. In 2011, Benz was behind BMW and Audi in terms of operating profit margin, which indicated Benz was less profitable than its competitors. In 2013, Benz came in third in terms of worldwide unit sales after BMW and Audi. Zetsche decided on two decisive measures: the dismantling of the "old" Maybach brand and placing the future of Benz in the hands of young designers.

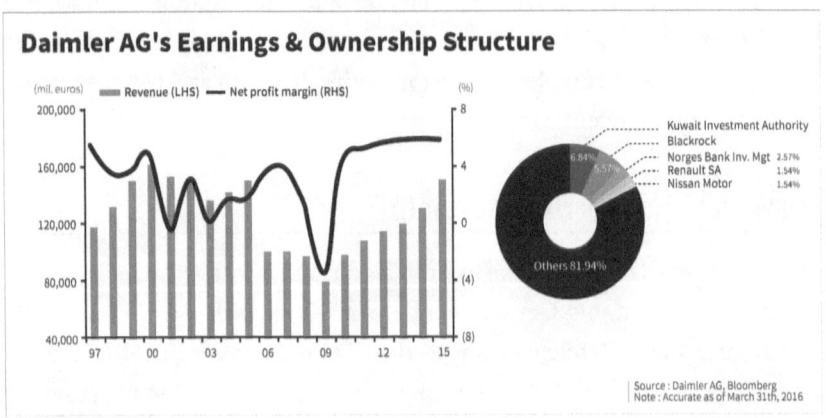

Daimler AG's Earnings & Ownership Structure

Source : Daimler AG, Bloomberg
Note : Accurate as of March 31th, 2016

Discontinuation of Maybach

In an interview with Frankfurter Allgemeine Zeitung on November 27, 2011, Zetsche said he concluded that investing in the S-Class – not Maybach – would be more reasonable. He went on to say Daimler would stop Maybach production in 2013. Wilhelm Maybach is one of the key contributors that established Benz's reputation as a premium automobile manufacturer. Wilhelm Maybach worked with Gottlieb Daimler. Without Maybach, Daimler might have become a footnote in automobile history.

The Maybach DS8 Zepplin, which would develop into the Maybach cars, was developed by Wilhelm Maybach and his son, Karl. After his father passed away, Karl Maybach completed the Zepplin. The Zepplin was 5.5 meters in length and deserved to be called the most luxurious vehicle in Germany. Having been crafted by the man that polished Mercedes-Benz, the Zepplin allowed Maybach to join the ranks of the top luxury brands.

Hoping Maybach would regain the praise it enjoyed in the 1930s, Daimler AG invested over a billion dollars in Maybach to establish a massive plant and bespoke production system. However, the market was far from impressed. Daimler aimed to have Maybach sell 1,000-1,500 vehicles per year, but the brand averaged only 200. In 2011, Daimler attempted to join hands with Aston Martin to develop Maybach as a last resort. However, the partnership was voided and Daimler decided to discontinue the Maybach nameplate.

Instead, Daimler AG decided to concentrate its resources on the Benz S-Class. It had an ambitious strategy of improving the S-Class to make it capable of competing against BMW and Rolls-Royce. The Maybach brand lives on as a single high-end model within the Benz S-Class – the Maybach S-Class. Zetsche entrusted the task to the young designer, Gordon Wagener.

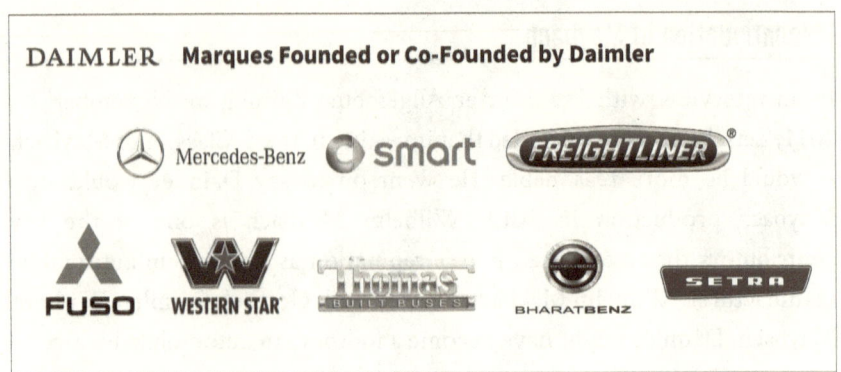

Tri-Star Becomes Younger

Gordon Wagener was born in 1968, in Essen, Germany. He graduated from the University of Duisburg-Essen with a degree in industrial design. He went on to study transportation design at the British Royal College of Art. He joined Benz in 1997 and became the Head of Design in 2008. Wagener was 39 years old at the time.

It was a drastic promotion by Zetsche, which proved to be the right decision. Benz's main customer base had moved to the next generation, so cars needed to appeal to people 20 years younger, which was why Wagener was entrusted with the mission to make Benz cars younger. For five years after becoming the head of design, Wagener redesigned all of Benz's models – from the A-Class (hatchbacks) to the S-Class (luxury sedans). Consumers welcomed the new look. Benz saw unit sales increase, even for its high-performance brand, AMG. Daimler AG's unit sales increased from 2.35 million units in 2013 to 2.54 million in 2014 and another 12% year-on-year to 2.85 million in 2015. Based on sales figures for sedans, Mercedes Benz sold two million units in 2015, regaining its position as the leading luxury car seller in 11 years since losing to BMW in 2004. It was five years earlier than the 2020 target stated in Zetsche's interview with the Financial Times.

AMG and F1

When talking about Benz cars, it is difficult not to mention their explosive performance. The performance of Benz cars is exemplified by AMG and F1. AMG is a 47-year old automobile tuning company. The company was founded in 1967, when Daimler-Benz engineer Hans Werner Aufrecht and his partner Eberhard Melcher started their own business in Großaspach to develop high-performance engines. AMG represents the first letters of the co-founders' names and the company's location.

In 1971, AMG announced the 300 SEL 6.8 AMG. In 1987, it released the Benz 300E 5.6 AMG. In 1993, Daimler bought over half of AMG and began jointly developing high-performance cars. The first result of their collaboration was the C63 AMG. That year, AMG became a registered trademark. AMG became a member of the Daimler AG after Aufrecht sold his stake to Daimler in 2005.

To maintain quality, AMG has a "one engine per person" rule, in which one person builds an engine from start to finish. The name and signature of that person is engraved into the engine. AMG has a growth strategy entitled "Performance 50." The strategy includes plans for expanding the AMG Performance Center, designing strategies to reduce weight, the goal being to release a new car in time for its 50th anniversary. The strategy is expected to lead to demand boosts in China, Korea, Russia, Brazil and other countries. AMG has established AMG Performance Centers in 24 countries since 2008 and aims to have around 350 performance centers by 2017.

Benz also returned to F1 racing. It took 40 years for Benz to forget the disaster of June 11, 1955. That day, during the 23rd hour of the 24 Hours of Le Mans, Benz's 300SLR exploded in the stands, causing the deaths of nearly 80 people, including the driver. Benz took full responsibility for the disaster and removed itself from motor racing. In 1993, Benz reappeared in the motor sports world as an engine supplier. In late 2009, Benz acquired the championship team, Brawn GP, and launched the works team, Mercedes GP. After accumulating a few years of experience, the Mercedes GP has been performing at a high level since 2014. During the early days of motor sports, the Benz's silver, streamlined racing machine was referred to as the "Silver Arrow." For Benz, the "Silver Arrow" symbolizes its days of glory. Quoting Gordon Wagener, the "20-year younger Silver Arrow" has begun to race again.

Groundbreaking Classics #4

The Sports Car "Porsche 911" and the Muscle Car "Mustang"

Dream cars. Anyone with affection for cars is likely to have at least one car they dream of owning. The Porsche 911 and the Mustang are likely to be among the most popular choices of dream car.

The Porsche is the most prominent sports car in Europe, and the Mustang in North America. While the Porsche 911 is a high-end vehicle available to a small number people, the Mustang is the sports car of everyday people.

Released in 1963, the Porsche 911 was the first to see daylight. The Mustang was rolled out in 1996. The 911 was developed by Porsche founder, Ferdinand Porsche. Along with his eldest son, Ferry, Ferdinand Porsche began to develop a sports car; the result was the Porsche 356 in 1948. The 356 was Porsche's first sports car and the predecessor of the 911. The 356 had a mid-engine design, making it easier to find the center of gravity. However, this design came with a lot of noise and vibration evident to the driver and passenger. So, Ferdinand Porsche pushed the engine back, to a RR (rear-engine, rear-drive) layout. The RR layout has been used continuously and has become one of the main features of the 911. However, because the heavy engine is located at the back, the RR layout has been criticized for lacking stability when driving at high speeds. Porsche overcame this setback with technology and proved its performance on the circuit. Porsche cars, including the 911, have won over 23 thousand titles in motor sports events over a 50-year period.

The Mustang was developed by Lee Iacocca, a legend in the US automobile industry. The strategy behind the Mustang was to manufacture an inexpensive sports car that would appeal to college freshmen and other younger people.

Iacocca wanted the car to be less than 4,572mm long and cost less than 2,500 dollars. Iacocca cut production costs by using chassis, suspension and other parts from existing models. This is how the Mustang was able to be a cheap, well-made sports car with outstanding performance.

The mustang is a breed of wild horses. The Mustang became known as a muscle car, because its overbearing design resembled a muscular body. The running horse emblem of the Mustang became an icon that defined the culture of American youths. In 1965, Ford collaborated with a race car driver, Carroll Shelby, and produced the high-performance Mustang Shelby GT350. The GT350 was equipped with an 8-cylinder engine, producing over 300 horsepowers. As of 2014, Ford has sold over 10 million cars under the Mustang nameplate, which is celebrating its 50th birthday.

EMPIRE XI

BMW Group

CHAPTER 30

Quandt Family's Decision Saves BMW

"We must protect BMW from Daimler-Benz. We cannot give the company up."

It was on December 9, 1959, during a shareholder's meeting at BMW headquarters in Munich that a BMW employee stood and said his piece. His words were met with applause from labor union members and shareholders. That day, the main agenda of the meeting was to decide whether BMW should be sold to Daimler-Chrysler AG. The board of directors had proposed the idea as a way to save the financially troubled company. Union members and minority shareholders opposed vehemently and demanded that BMW attempt to survive on its own. One middle-aged man sat silently watching, while absorbed deep in his thoughts. The man was Herbert Quandt, one of the majority shareholders of BMW. Quandt stood up and spoke.

"I was initially going to side with the board and agree to sell the company to Daimler-Benz, but I am deeply moved by the love for BMW that the employees and shareholders have displayed. So, I've changed my mind. I will do everything I can to prevent BMW from falling into the hands of another company." Cheers exploded in the auditorium.

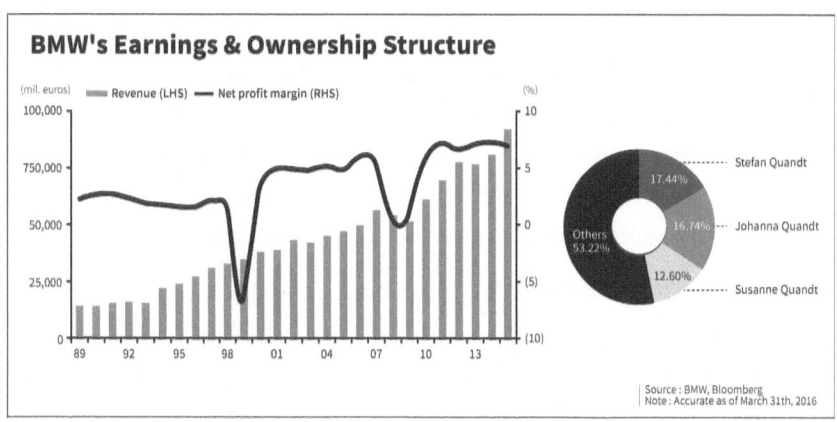

Having decided against selling BMW, Herbert Quandt and his younger brother, Harald, emptied their personal wealth and increased their ownership of BMW from 30% to 50%. The labor union responded with better productivity and quality. Consumers began to buy BMW cars which became more entertaining to drive over time. As a result, BMW's unit sales began to skyrocket.

In 2006, 47 years after Herbert Quandt made his decision, BMW prevailed over Mercedes-Benz and Audi and became the leading marque among Germany's three premium automobile brands. BMW had avenged itself on Benz. BMW started as an aircraft engine manufacturer, but transformed itself into a motorcycle company, before expanding to the automobile business. Now, BMW has become a conglomerate, owning multiple brands, including Rolls-Royce and Mini.

Fall from grace

In 1913, the German engineer Karl Rapp established an aircraft engine manufacturing company Rapp Motorenwerke in Munich and began supplying aircraft engines to the German military. A few years earlier, in 1910, Gustav Otto - also an engineer - began manufacturing aircraft engines. In 1916, Karl Rapp took over and absorbed Otto's company, which was going through financial difficulties. The resulting company was later renamed Bayerische Motoren Werke, or BMW, because Franz Josef Popp, an Austrian engineer working for Rapp, became the new owner. Once Popp took control of the company and renamed it, Rapp left the company. Although the founder was gone, the company flourished thanks to the competitive aircraft engine developed by Marx Fritz, who was a skilled engineer. Later, Fritz went on to use his engineering skills for BMW's motorcycle business, which became the foundation for BMW's growth.

The background of the BMW emblem was blue and white. Blue represented the state of Bavaria and white the Alps. The circle was divided into quarters with each color arranged diagonally to symbolize a spinning propeller. The emblem seemed to reflect BMW's history, as it transited from aerial vehicles to land vehicles, from two-wheeled vehicles to four-wheeled vehicles.

During WWI, BMW earned its fortune supplying 12cylinder fighter plane engines. After Germany lost the war, the company began to collapse at an alarming rate, because under the Versailles Treaty, Germany was prohibited from manufacturing all weapons, including aircraft engines, for three years.

Hence, BMW turned its eyes to the ground. Desperate to survive, BMW entered the motorcycle industry in 1923 and the automobile industry in 1928. BMW's first motorcycle, the R32, was developed by Fritz. The R32 was unveiled during the Paris Motor Show and the Berlin Motor Show in 1923. Having experienced manufacturing aircraft engines, BMW began to stand out in the motorcycle industry. The most cutting-edge engine at the time was the two-cylinder flat engine, or boxer engine, in which the cylinders were positioned horizontally facing each other, with the pistons moving in between. By 1925, BMW had won nearly 100 titles in various motorcycle racing events. This translated into sales; BMW's sales continued to grow. By 1938, BMW had produced a total of 100 thousand motorcycles.

BMW entered the automobile business in 1928, when it bought the automobile company Dixi for 10 million marks. Dixi was founded in 1896 in the town of Eisenach. Founder Heinrich Ehrhardt relinquished control of the company to engineer Willi Seck in 1903, and the company was reorganized as Dixi in 1904. Dixi released the R8, which had a 4-cylinder enginegenerating14 horsepower, in 1909 and manufactured 650 units. Dixi was taken over by the rolling stock company Goathaer Waggonfabrik in 1921. In 1927, Dixi signed a license deal with the British motor company, Austin Motor, and produced the two-seat Austin Seven. The following year, Dixi found a new owner in BMW and remained the core of BMW's car manufacturing operations until production was stopped by Hitler in 1939. Among the number of cars produced by Dixi, the two-seat racing car BMW 328 released in 1936 was considered as one of the best vehicles of its time. The BMW 328 was equipped with a steel frame, rear axle and independent suspension on its front wheel, all of which was the amalgamation of BMW's technology. Between 1936 and 1940, the 328 entered 172 races and won 141. The car accomplished one of its most significant feats during the 1938 Mille Miglia, a 1,000-mile race. That year, the 328 won the race averaging 166km/h, establishing its superior durability and performance. With this achievement, BMW established its reputation as a prominent automaker.

Quandt family

Once again, BMW manufactured airplanes and airplane engines during WWII. With Germany having lost the war, darkness loomed over BMW. In 1948, BMW was on the verge of entering court receivership when banker Hans-Karl von Mangoldt acquired the company. The motorcycle and aircraft engine manufacturer resumed its automobile business in 1951, but was not as successful as in the past. By 1959, BMW was struggling financially. Management began warming up to the board of directors' suggestion of selling the company to Daimler-Benz. If the Quandt brothers had not intervened, BMW may have become an automobile production base for Daimler.

The Quandt clan still stands at the top of BMW's governance structure. The history of the Quandt family is traced back to Herbert and Harald Quandt's father, Günther Quandt. Günther Quandt began his career as a business man taking charge of his father's rope business and his maternal family's textile company. The two World Wars presented major opportunities for Günther Quandt. He accumulated his wealth supplying munitions and used the money to takeover other companies. In 2011, the Quandt family admitted to collaborating with the Nazis and allowed a 1,200-page report on its past to be published. By the time Günther Quandt died in 1954, the Quandt family owned approximately 200 companies, including the battery manufacturer AFA. Günther Quandt and BMW both have ties with Hitler. Günther Quandt's second wife, Magda, divorced Günther and married Joseph Goebbels, who was a close associates of Hitler and his followers.

Herbert Quandt was born of Günther Quandt's first wife. He was responsible for making the twin kidney grille the symbol of BMW. At the age of 9, Herbert Quandt was afflicted with a retinal disease and became nearly blind. Fortunately, his other senses were perfect. The twin kidney grille was first used in the 303 series released in 1933. When the grille was removed from the 1955 Isetta and the 1959 BMW 700, Herbert Quandt ordered it to be used, saving the kidney grill from fading into history.

When Herbert Quandt died in 1982, the reins of BMW were passed on to his third wife, Johanna, and her two children. Before marrying Herbert Quandt in 1960, Johanna Quandt had been working as her future husband's secretary since 1950. Being nearly blind, Johanna was an essential person for Herbert. Johanna Quandt gained knowledge of business management by reading books on the subject to her husband. From 1982 to 1997, Johanna Quandt served as a member of the supervisory board at BMW. Her daughter, Susanne, was given stakes in BMW and the chemical company Altana. She is currently the richest woman in Germany. In 1990, she married Jan Klatten, who she met during an internship at BMW. Herbert Quandt's son, Stefan, married software engineer, Katharina, in 2005.

In August 2015, Johanna passed away at the age of 89. Between 2003 and 2008, her stake was given to her son Stephan (49) and daughter Susanne, both of whom were members of the BMW board. Meanwhile,

Johanna retained the attached voting rights. Even after Johanna's death, the Quandt family continued to hold a 47% interest.

Hahnermann's Law fuels BMW's resurrection

While BMW was picking itself up off the ground in 1961, Herbert Quandt recruited a man from Auto Union (currently, Audi). The man was the marketing genius, Paul Hahnemann. Hahnemann was appointed the executive for overseeing sales. He placed emphasis on a niche strategy for marketing and product development. According to his strategy, if a model is stretched into a series, cars could maintain a fresh image. This garnered the attention of consumers and translated into sales. An instance of Hahnemann's strategy was to release a new four-door model one year, a convertible variant in the next year and a high-performance version in the year after that. In other words, through constant performance enhancements and model variations for seven years, the company could maintain the attention of the media and that of consumers. This is the so-called "Hahnemann's Law."

BMW could remain on an upward trajectory using this strategy, which is widely used today. In 1963, BMW paid dividends to its shareholders for the first time in 20 years. Hahnemann also received the spotlight for making provocative comments directed toward Benz, earning him the nickname, "Mr. BMW." The image Hahnemann built for BMW was "A successful businessman who wants to brag about his success to his neighbors will drive a Mercedes-Benz, while a man that accomplished greatness, but does not feel the need to gloat, will buy a BMW."

CHAPTER 31

Design Innovation:
Recovery from Failed Rover Acquisition

"The Rover acquisition has caused the company a massive amount of losses."

On February 5, 1999, an emergency board meeting was called. Members of the supervisory board gathered at the BMW headquarters in Munich. A deafening silence hung in the air. Board members were handed a report that said the Rover Group, acquired in 1994, suffered a massive amount of losses and accumulated at 7 billion-dollar deficit during the past five years. BMW's majority shareholder Stefan Quandt, who had called the meeting, looked grim. BMW's management was divided into two groups - the management board and the supervisory board. The meeting had been called so that the supervisory board could question the management board. At the same time, members discussed restructuring plans for Rover.

The doors to the conference room reopened seven hours later. Chairman Bernd Pischetsrieder walked out. Half an hour later, the CEO Wolfgang Reitzle appeared at the door. Both announced their resignations. On the surface, Pischetsrieder and Reitzle were voluntarily leaving the company, but the two men had virtually been fired. The board appointed manufacturing chief, Joachim Milberg, as the new CEO.

Pischetsrieder and Reitzle resigned, taking the blame for the worst M&A in the company's history. However, their resignation did not make up for the losses the company incurred. BMW was still burdened by the 7 billion-dollar deficit and the Rover Group. Susanne and Stefan Quandt made another decision: selling the Rover Group at a cheap price. In 2000, the Rover Group was sold to the Phoenix Consortium for a mere 10 pounds. BMW had purchased the company for 135 million dollars in 1994. The decision to sell the Rover Group dirt cheap could only be made by members of the Quandt family, the company's "monarchs" who ruled the company from behind the scenes. After discarding the deficit-stricken headache, BMW did not incur any further losses. The company swiftly got back on track thanks to its engine manufacturing expertise and the dynamic performance of its cars. The company's prominence was further solidified when the designing efforts of Chris Bangle created a sensation in the automobile industry. Despite failing to create any chemistry with the Rover Group, BMW was able to obtain the Mini and Rolls-Royce marques. With support from BMW's technology and marketing, Mini and Rolls-Royce have become lucrative brands for the BMW Group. As a result, BMW had regained its former glory.

Rover Group: A deal gone sour

The Rover Group's supervisory board decided to sell the company in 1999. Until the deal was completed in 2000, the Rover Group caused an additional billion dollars in losses to BMW. That one poor decision caused BMW to watch8 billion dollars disappear into thin air over a six-year period.

The Rover Group owned three marques: the mass production brand Rover, the "Rolls-Royce of the desert "Land Rover and British city car brand Mini. Rover produced front-wheel drive vehicles that did not fit with BMW's mainstay models. Despite receiving a large amount of fund injections, Land Rover was unable to perform at a satisfying level. For BMW, the Rover Group acquisition turned out to be an expensive course in SUV technology. Land Rover's 4WD technology was instrumental for the release of the BMW's mid-size SUV, X5, in the late 1990s. The addition of SUVs provided a giant boost to BMW's unit sales as SUVs sold extremely well in the US. Thanks to robust SUV sales, BMW's annual unit sales surpassed the one million mark in 2003.

Rolls-Royce: The car of kings

Four years after acquiring the Rover Group, BMW engaged in another M&A deal: the acquisition of the British premium vehicle brand, Rolls-Royce, for 340 million pounds. BMW outbid Volkswagen to do so. Having acquired only the trademark to Rolls-Royce (Rolls-Royce's production facilities were purchased by Volkswagen), BMW built a Rolls-Royce plant in Goodwood, West Sussex, UK. The factory manufactured 3,575 handmade cars in 2013. In the early 2000s, Rolls-Royce's annual unit sales were hovering around the 1,000 mark.

Rolls-Royce was founded in 1884 when Henry Royce started an automobile company. In 1904, Royce produced the Royce 10, which was equipped with a two-cylinder engine, from his Manchester factory. That year, Royce met Charles Rolls, a race car driver of noble birth. In March 1906, Royce and Rolls launched Rolls-Royce and released the luxury sedan, Silver Ghost. The Silver Ghost was famous for having close to no vibrations and being quiet in the inside. Even while driving at 130km/h, tea cups would not shake and the only noise that passengers could hear was the ticking of watches. The media named the car "ghost," because it was so quiet. Rolls-Royce still uses ghost as a model name.

In 1915, during the height of WWI, Rolls-Royce manufactured aircraft engines. By 1931, Rolls-Royce was doing so well it acquired Bentley Motors. In 1971, the company went bankrupt in developing the engine for the supersonic passenger plane, Concorde. The British government stepped in and nationalized Rolls-Royce by taking over the company's aircraft engine, shipbuilding and industrial gas turbine businesses. The automobile division was sold to Vickers. Rolls-Royce Motors remained mediocre until it was picked up by the BMW Group. Under the BMW umbrella, Rolls-Royce began to flourish. Unit sales have improved consistently as the model portfolio was expanded to include the executive model Phantom, the owner-driven model Ghost and the Wraith, which targets younger customers. The company adopted the "bespoke system," a custom manufacturing system that reflects all of the purchaser's tastes and demands. The bespoke system has raised the status of Rolls Royce, while improving its profitability.

Mini: Nuisance becomes a cash cow

BMW rid itself of the Rover Group in 2000, but retained Mini because the company had its eyes on the marque's value. Since its release in 1959, Mini has been one of the most popular cars in the UK, as it was recognized as a cheap and practical car. British comedian Rowan Atkinson of "Mr. Bean" fame also owned a Mini.

BMW worked to improve the quality of Minis and its brand recognition, creating its own fandom, so that the brand would have a worldwide following. Today, Mini is accepted as a premium city car brand, all because of BMW's excellent marketing campaign. One of the changes brought on by BMW is model diversification. Mini currently has seven models, which includes the two-door Mini Coupe, the Mini Clubman, the large Mini Countryman and the high-performance Mini JCW. Minis come with 3-cylinder engines and turbo charged 4-cylinder engines. It also has its own 4WD system, ALL4. When all variants are taken into consideration, Mini's product line-up has over 30 models. Mini was able to satisfy various consumer tastes by offering a wide variety of products under its marque. Thanks to such strategies, Mini's unit sales surpassed the 300 thousand mark in 2013.

History also played a large part in the success of the Mini. The Monte Carlo Rally is one of the reasons Mini enjoys popularity worldwide. Mini cars were small and light. They also offered excellent handling. Focusing on such characteristics, Englishman John Cooper entered the Monte Carlo rally with a tuned Mini and won. The modified Mini driven by John

Cooper became a mass production model – the high-performance Mini JCW (John Cooper Works).

Mini also had a stint with the fashion industry. In the 1960s, British designer Mary Quant designed the world's first miniskirt after seeing a Mini. The miniskirt was extremely popular among teenagers and women in the 20s and spread to other areas in Europe. As a result, London emerged as the global fashion hub in the 1960s.

Chris Bangle innovates BMW

The resignation of Wolfgang Reitzle in 1999 triggered a "butterfly effect" that changed the course of BMW's history. To elaborate, Reitzle's decision to acquire the Rover Group in 1994 led BMW into its prime seven years later because the design innovation by Chris Bangle, own of the top three automobile designers, began after Reitzle's departure.

Bangle is BMW's first American chief of design. Bangle designed the 7 Series, which was a revolution in automobile design. When the 7 Series was first released, market response was lukewarm. The European media deemed in one of the ugliest cars and referred to the protruding rear line of the car as the "Bangle butt." Contrary to its initial reception, Bangle's design changed the course of the world's automobile designing industry.

Bangle's designs gave a new look to BMW cars, which had remained unchanged for the better half of the past century. However, Bangle's vision would never have come to light under Reitzle, who disliked Bangle's tendencies. Having the full support of the new management, Bangle established BMW's own design identity, designing the majority of BMW models – such as the 5Series, the 3Series, the 1Series, the sports coupe Z4 and the SUV X3.

Chris Bangle was born in Ohio. He studied at the Art Center College of Design in Pasadena and received a master's degree in industrial design at the University of Wisconsin. Bangle joined GM, before transferring to the

Opel Design Studio in Germany and the Fiat Design Center. In 1992, Bangle was hired by BMW.

His career as a car designer stopped at BMW. In 2009, Bangle left BMW to fulfill his new dream of designing home appliances and furniture. He founded the design consulting firm, Chris Bangle Associates, in Turin, Italy. Bangle would go on to design home electronics for Samsung Electronics.

Return to glory

Currently, the Chairman of the BMW Group is Harald Krueger, whose predecessor, Norbert Reithofer is credited as the man responsible for returning BMW to its former glory, swinging the earnings of Rolls-Royce and Mini to positive and increasing BMW's sales. Krueger was previously the chief of Mini, Rolls-Royce and BMW AS and the president of the production. He was promoted to Chairman at the age of 49, making him one of the youngest heads of a global automobile manufacturer.

BMW sold 1.13 million cars (excluding Mini and Rolls-Royce) in 2005, beating Mercedes-Benz and Audi as the leading premium automobile manufacturer. In 2014, BMW sold 1.81 million units, topping Benz's 1.72 million and Audi's 1.80 million. When Mini and Rolls-Royce's figures are included, the BMW has sold 2,117,965 cars in 2013, a 7.9% increase from the previous year. BMW has managed to maintain consistent growth, despite the slump of the European economy.

The tables were turned in 2015. After a decade at the top, BMW was pulled down to second. BMW's unit sales climbed 5.2% year-on-year to 1.91 million units, but was unable to beat Benz's explosive growth to two million. Meanwhile, Audi was pushed down to third. BMW has faltered, but is determined to regain the throne via the i-Series and other green cars that comply with rising environmental requirements. BMW rose to the top despite Benz's effort to take over the company 50 years earlier and will continue striving to become the best.

Industry-Altering Event #5

Asian Financial Crisis and the Big 6 Theory

A dark cloud loomed over the global economy as Thailand requested a life line from the IMF (International Monetary Fund) in July 1997. After abandoning the fixed exchange rate system, the value of Thai baht plunged and pushed Thailand into a financial crisis. The sinking Thai economy took down Indonesia, Malaysia, the Philippines and other neighboring countries with it. With corporations financials strained by excessive investments, Korea was not free from the fallout.

The Asian financial economy forced the automobile industry to restructure. In May 1998, Daimler acquired Chrysler and the "global big six" theory began to emerge. Daimler-Chrysler's Jürgen Schrempp proclaimed that only the big six automakers would survive. Companies believed they would not make it through the 21st century unless they had a production capacity of at least four million units. The big six automakers were GM, Ford, Toyota, Volkswagen, Daimler-Chrysler and Renault. It was natural for smaller companies to race to increase their size for survival.

Aside from Toyota, which was struggling under the Asian financial crisis, the other five companies began engaging in subsidiaries. Daimler-Chrysler, which had become a giant conglomerate following the merger, purchased Swatch's Smart stake. In March 2000, Daimler-Chrysler bought 34% of Mitsubishi stocks for 2 billion euros to begin its entry into the Asian market. That same year, Daimler partnered with Hyundai Motor, which had just acquired Kia Motors, and secured a 10.5% stake in Hyundai.

Renault was the largest beneficiary of the Asian financial crisis, as it was able to gain partial ownership of Nissan. Suffering from a string of subpar earnings, Nissan sold 36.8% of its shares to Renault in March 1999. Renault subsequently increased its stake to 43.4%. Later that year, Renault took over the Romanian state-owned automobile company, Dacia. After the acquisition of Samsung Motors in 2000, Renault-Nissan Alliance of today was formed.

Meanwhile, Ford was in the market to buy an automobile company. In January 1999, Jacque Nasser was appointed CEO. Once Nasser took office, Ford took over Volvo and established the PAG (Premier Automotive Group), which included Volvo and the previously acquired premium marques, such as Jaguar and Aston Martin. In May 2000, Ford bought Land Rover from BMW and added it to the PAG.

Numerous other companies engaged in M&As and the automobile industry was quickly reorganized. The world leader, GM, increased its stake in Isuzu from 37.5% to 49% in 2000. In 2000, GM purchased the remaining 50% stake in Saab and a stake in Fuji Heavy Industries, which owned Subaru. GM went on to take over Daewoo Motors in 2002. Volkswagen acquired Lamborghini from the Indonesian businessman, Tommy Suharto, in 1998. In Korea, Hyundai Motor acquired Kia Motors in 1998. SsangYong Motor was sold to Daewoo Motors in 1997 and was sold on the market with Daewoo in 2000.

Jaguar Land Rover

CHAPTER 32

British Luxury Marques Recover from Brink of Collapse

"The company that dominated 24 Hours of Le Mans in the 1950s, sold to Ford in 1989, continued to suffer losses and was picked up by Tata Motors in 2007."

This is how the history of the British luxury car brand, Jaguar, is summarized. Jaguar is a brand praised by the British royal family and which performed well in motor racing events, but had to endure many hardships due to financial struggles. The history has a twist, as Jaguar was acquired by automakers based in the US and India, both of which were colonies of the British Empire.

Along with Jaguars, Land Rovers reused as state vehicles by the British royal family. The SUVs made by Land Rover are so smooth and quiet that have been nicknamed "the Rolls-Royce of the desert." It is the oldest off-road vehicle marque after Jeep. It has a history as decorated as Jaguar. Land Rover vehicles are being used as military vehicles in the US, India and the UK. Yet, Land Rover was sold to the BMW Group in 1994.

The two British luxury marques have been ignored by the market due to the unchanging design and poor quality. They were pushed to the brink of collapse, but were able to stage a dramatic comeback. Thanks to the support from the Tata Group and the designs by Ian Callum, Jaguar and Land Rover have gotten back on an upward trajectory.

Distinguished marques

Among the two, Land Rover has a longer history. Land Rover's history is traced back to Rover, a bicycle manufacturer founded by John Kemp Starley and William Sutton in 1877. In 1903, Rover expanded its business to motorcycles – more like bicycles with gasoline engines. During WWI, Rover manufactured military trucks. The Land Rover prototype was developed in 1946 by the brothers, Maurice and Spencer Wilks, who were working at Rover. The 4WD Land Rover Series 1 was unveiled during the Amsterdam Motor Show. After seeing the Series 1, the British government requested that Rover modify the car to be a multi-purpose military vehicle and supply for military use. After the war, the Series 1 was sold to the general public. In 1970, Land Rover released the high-end Range Rover and targeted the more affluent segment of population.

In addition to the British royal family, Land Rover has a storied relationship with Winston Churchill. In 1954, Land Rover manufactured a special model – the UKE80 - which was given to Churchill for his 80th birthday. The UKE80 had a larger front passenger seat than the standard Land Rover vehicle and a wooden box for Churchill to store cigars. After retiring, Churchill traveled around in the UKE80 and painted landscapes. From the 1950s, Land Rovers were used as escort vehicles whenever Queen Elizabeth visited friendly countries. During her visit to the Andong Hahwe Village in Korea in 1999, the Queen used Land Rover's flagship, Range Rover, as her official vehicle.

Despite having a shorter history, Jaguar has been in the automobile business longer. Jaguar was founded as the motorcycle sidecar company, Swallow Sidecar Company, by William Lyons in 1922. The first vehicles released under the Jaguar marque are the SS Jaguar 90 and 100 of 1935. Jaguar had released its first vehicle 13 years before Land Rover. The Jaguar brand was initially named SS Jaguar, but the SS was dropped in 1945, as it created confusion with Nazi Germany's SS-Verfügungstruppe (SS Dispositional Troops).

In 1951, Jaguar won its first 24 Hours of Le Mans title with its race car, C-type. Winning 24 Hours of Le Mans is a testament to the car's performance and durability. Jaguar won the event with C-type again in 1953. The new D-type won three straight years from 1955 to 1957. Having established itself as a capable automobile manufacturer through the races, Jaguar solidified its position as a luxury car manufacturer by releasing the XK120, XK140, XK150, E-type, XJ and other high-performance elegantly designed models.

However, Jaguar and Land Rover cars were not always strong sellers. The companies went through a number of ownership changes as it suffered through the oil shocks and economic slumps. Rover was taken over by Leyland Motors in 1967. In 1968, Leyland Motors merged with British Motor Holdings – which owned Jaguar - and became British Leyland Motor Corporation. Unable to endure the oil shock, British Leyland Motor Corporation was nationalized in 1975 and became British Leyland Limited. Eleven years later, in 1986, British Leyland was renamed the Rover Group.

From Britain to Germany and to America

The Rover Group became a private corporation after being acquired by British Aerospace. Until that point, the company bounced around England. Later, the company would be forced to migrate overseas. In January 1994, BMW purchased 80% of the Rover Group's stocks for 800 million pounds, and the Rover Group became a German company. The following month, BMW bought the remaining 20% stake from Honda. Rover, Land Rover and Mini became members of the BMW Group. Jaguar and Land Rover reunited under Ford. Jaguar was picked up by Ford in 1989. Land Rover remained a property of BMW for six years, until in 2000, BMW sold it to Ford on the condition that Ford assume all of Land Rover's debts.

At first, Land Rover seemed to be well-received by the market, as its output surpassed the 100 thousand-unit mark for the first time in 1995.

Even so, Land Rover failed to be a profitable marque for BMW and later, for Ford. Ford established PAG in 1999, uniting the prestige brands - Land Rover, Jaguar, Volvo, Lincoln and Aston Martin - under a single roof. Ford appointed former Chairman of the BMW Group Wolfgang Reitzle, whom the Quandt family virtually fired, as the CEO of PAG. Unsurprisingly, Reitzle was unable to produce any significant results at PAG.

Land Rover was not a complete flop. It released the Discovery 3 in 2007, which was met with positive response in Europe. However, Jaguar could not gain traction. In fact, after its acquisition by Ford, Jaguar cars were panned for being "Ford engines and chassis covered in a Jaguar shell." The classic designs of Jaguars were unable to lure consumers into opening their wallets. In October 2006, Alan Mulally from Boeing became the new CEO of Ford and began to restructure PAG. Mulally decided to sell off all of the brands under PAG, except for Lincoln. In 2007, Jaguar and Lincoln reappeared in the market.

From America to India

While unit sales were not satisfying, Jaguar and Land Rover were compelling marques as both had a long history and tradition, and the technology and knowhow to build capable racing cars and off-road vehicles. A number of companies expressed their interest. Among those courting was Hyundai Motor, which had remained relatively indifferent to M&As. On the first day of 2008, Ford announced that the Indian conglomerate, Tata Group, would be acquiring Jaguar and Land Rover for 2.3 billion dollars. The Tata Group incorporated the two brands under a single entity: the Jaguar Land Rover Automotive PLC.

The automobile industry had a negative opinion about the Tata Group's acquisition of Jaguar and Land Rover. On the day Ford announced the sale of the marques, Tata Group's credit default swap (an indicator representing the possibility of bankruptcy) more than doubled. Balaji Jayaraman, an auto industry analyst at Morgan Stanley, critically panned the acquisition, saying the acquisition was "value-destructive given the lack of synergies and the high-cost operations involved." The prevalent prediction was that the Tata Group, which was a latecomer in the auto industry, would extract Jaguar Land Rover Automotive's advanced technology and damage its value as a luxury brand.

Ian Callum breathes new life into Jaguar Land Rover

However, there was one thing the industry overlooked: India had been a member of the Commonwealth for a long time and was plenty familiar with the culture and characteristics of the British. The Tata Group promised full autonomy to Jaguar Land Rover Automotive, and was true to its word. The two brands displayed their full potential. The Jaguar Land Rover headquarters is located in England and all key members of its executive board are British. The Tata Group spared no expense and provided Jaguar Land Rover with 2 billion pounds for developing new models.

The resurrection of Jaguar Land Rover is the feat of one man: chief of design, Ian Callum. The Tata Group gave Callum full design control. Callum had proven his prowess worldwide – namely, through his work with Aston Martin. Regarding Jaguar's mid-sized sedan, the XF, released in 2008, Callum stated that he changed everything except the name. Callum discarded all the features that defined Jaguar cars - the four round headlights and the hood ornament, which is a leaping jaguar. While such elements were removed, the XF retained the unique features of original Jaguars and was deemed "a successful modern reiteration of tradition." Unit sales also began to climb. Jaguar Land Rover sustained its sales growth with the release of Jaguar's full-size sedan, the XJ, in 2010 and Land Rover's compact SUV, the Range Rover Evoque, in 2011.

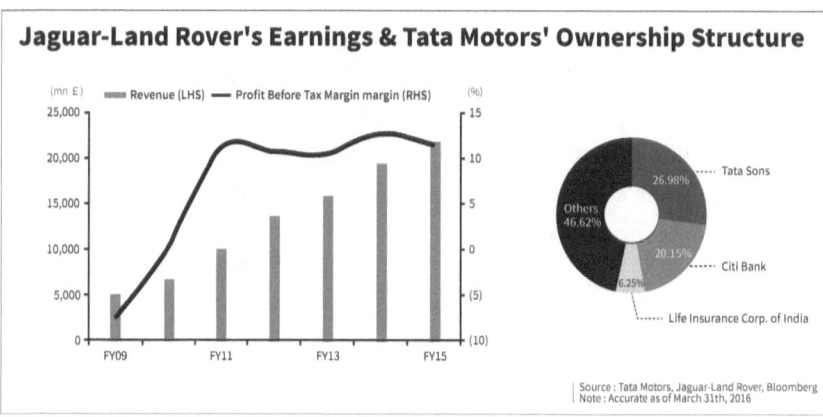

Jaguar-Land Rover's Earnings & Tata Motors' Ownership Structure

Revenue (LHS) — Profit Before Tax Margin margin (RHS)

Tata Sons 26.98%
Others 46.62%
Citi Bank 20.15%
6.25%
Life Insurance Corp. of India

Source : Tata Motors, Jaguar-Land Rover, Bloomberg
Note : Accurate as of March 31th, 2016

The Tata Group also took great measures to preserve Jaguar and Land Rover's reputation as a premium automaker. CKD versions of Land Rovers were assembled and sold only in India to avoid damaging the status and value of "Made in UK" cars.

The Tata Group's strategy translated into sales growth. After posting sales of 4.9495 billion pounds and operating loss of 402.4 million pounds for the 2009 fiscal year (April 2008 to March 2009), Jaguar Land Rover Automotive recorded sales of 6.5272 billion pounds and an operating profit of 23.5 million pounds in the 2010 fiscal year (April 2009 to March 2010). In April of that year, *Bloomberg* assessed the value of Jaguar Land Rover at 14 billion dollars, based on evaluations by experts. The company's value had increased six fold in four years. For the 2014 fiscal year (April 2013 to March 2014), Jaguar Land Rover turned in sales of 19.3386 billion pounds and an operating profit of 1.879 billion pounds.

Jaguar Land Rover is constantly attempting to make changes to ensure growth in the future. With Callum at the head, Jaguar released the F-type, the 21st century reincarnation of the E-type, which symbolized the company's heyday. The F-type was an instant hit among automobile enthusiasts. Jaguar also released the mass-production version of its compact sedan, XE, in 2014. The release of the XE implies that Jaguar will go toe to toe with BMW's 3-Series and Mercedes-Benz's C-Class. Meanwhile, Land Rover discontinued one of its flagship models, the compact SUV Freelander, and began selling Discovery Sports, the five-seater version of the Discovery, in 2015. The two brands sold 370 thousand units for the 2013 fiscal year (April 2012 to March 2013) and 430 thousand units for the 2014 fiscal year (April 2013 to March 2014). Jaguar Land Rover is expected to gain further growth momentum from the expansion of its Chinese operations. After a long, bumpy journey, Jaguar Land Rover seems to be returning to its former glory.

Groundbreaking Classics #5

The Textbook Hatchbacks, Golf

The Golf is the face of Volkswagen. The Golf is described as the "original hatchback" or the "textbook hatchbacks." Because the passenger compartment and trunk are not divided, and the trunk has a door, hatchbacks are also termed 5-doors vehicles, not four-doors. The Golf has gone through seven generations of design during its 40-year history, that begins in 1974. Throughout its time, the Golf has remained one of the best selling cars in the world. It is difficult for a car maintain its popularity across seven design generations. However, each time a new generation was released, the Golf has undergone distinct changes that differentiated it from earlier generations. As a result, the Golf began as the original hatchback, but has developed into the textbook a hatchback.

The first-generation Golf was designed by the Italian design legend Giorgetto Giugiaro. Like other Volkswagen nameplates, the Golf was named after winds or objects related to winds. "Golf" is German for "gulf," as in the Gulf Stream, the wind-driven ocean current running along the Gulf of Mexico. At one point, the car was sold as the Rabbit in the U.S. and Canada.

Unit sales testify to the success of the Golf. As of June 2013, over 30 million cars were sold under the nameplate. To put this into perspective, this means that 2,000 people purchased a Golf everyday for 39 years. The world's best-selling nameplate is currently the Toyota Corolla followed by Ford's F-Series. Golf is ranked third in the world, but first in Europe.

The most recent seventh-generation Golf is more sophisticated than the sixth generation. The seventh generation is 100kg lighter, although it is larger in size. Being lighter, fuel efficiency is 23% better than its predecessor. Based on the 1.6L diesel variant, the new Golf boasts a combined fuel economy of 18.9km/L. In other words, the Golf can drive nearly 1,000km on a single tank of fuel. Trunk capacity has been bumped up 30 liters to 380 liters.

Volkswagen is a mass brand, whereas BMW, Mercedes-Benz and Audi are premium brands. Despite being a compact hatchback of a mass brand, the Golf is compared to the likes of the BMW 1-Series, Benz A-Class and the Audi A3 by German automobile magazines, which have a reputation for having particularly high standards.

Four German car magazines, including Auto Bild and Auto Motor und Sport, test-drove the four cars and declared that Golf was the best. One advertisement slogan used for the Golf is "Oft kopiert. Aber nie erreicht."' This translates into "often imitated, but never equaled." The test drive revealed this to be no bluff. This gives substance to the fact that, in addition to being the first hatchback in history, the Golf is an icon that contributed more to the Volkswagen brand than any other car could.

EMPIRE XIII

SsangYong Motor

CHAPTER 33

The Korando Never Stops

"The Korando C will be mark the resurrection of SsangYong Motor."

At the Busan Motor Show held at BEXCO located in Haeundae-gu, Busan, in April 2010, SsangYong Motor's co-legal trustees, Yoo-il Lee and Young-tae Park, and labor union leader Gyu-han Kim introduced the company's new compact SUV concept, Korando C. The men looked nervous standing before dozens of reporters, but spoke with surety as they introduced the car. Lee, who would be appointed CEO in March 2011, proclaimed, "The Korando C is an amazingly well-composed car built on an entirely new platform SsangYong endured through hardships to develop. It is the future of SsangYong Motor."

Developed while undergoing sales, restructuring, labor strikes and other extreme difficulties, the Korando C was the last hope for SsangYong. The car was released in March 2011, six months behind schedule, because the company was unable to secure reliable parts suppliers. Despite a series of difficulties, SsangYong trudged forward. In the past, SsangYong surprised the industry with the SUV Musso and conquered the domestic high-end SUV market with the Rexton, which targeted the "top 1% in Korea." SsangYong has always been regarded as "the SUV powerhouse," which was a point of pride. The Korando is the oldest living nameplate in Korea. The Korando C was an immediate success, and SsangYong was able to get back on its aching feet.

Building cars with hammers

SsangYong started out as Ha Dong-hwan Motor Workshop. After working as a mechanic at a garage, Dong-hwan Ha jumped into the automobile industry following the Korean War. In 1954, Ha erected a tent on the front yard of his house in Changcheon-dong, Seoul. The tent was used as his workshop. Ha purchased trucks from the US military and took apart the engine and transmission axles. He cut train rails to make frames. He hammered barrel drums flat and applied them to the frame to make the so-called "drum buses."

Afterwards, his operations were relocated to Guro-dong, Seoul. On December 6, 1962, Ha officially launched his company. In July 1963, Ha's company merged with Dongbang Motor (established in December 1962) and renamed the company, Hadonghwan Motor Company. The company exported full-size buses to Vietnam and Brunei in August 1967, becoming the first company in Korea to export buses. The company was renamed Dong-A Motor in February 1972 and began constructing two factories on a 990 thousand m^2 lot in Pyeongtaek, Gyeonggi Province. This location is still used as SsangYong's production base.

The Jeep becomes the Korando

The Korando's lineage begins in 1969. Shinjin Motors formed a technological partnership with Kaiser Motors and began producing the CJ-5 in Korea. In April 1974, Shinjin and AMC launched 50:50 joint venture called Shinjin Jeep Motors and began assembling CKD parts for four different CJ models. However, AMC broke the partnership because Shinjin Jeep was exporting vehicles to Libya, which was one the enemy states of the US. Shinjin Jeep was renamed Geohwa in 1981 and began producing CJs of its own. In 1983, the nameplate was changed to Korando, which meant " Korean do it", "Korean landover" and "Korean land dominator." Geohwa forayed with the market with the Korando 4, Korando 5, Korando 6, Korando Van and other models. The number on the model name referred to the number of passengers the vehicle could carry.

The Korando manufacturer Geohwa and the bus manufacturer Dong-A became a single family when Dong-A took over Geohwa on November 20, 1984. Dong-A Motor CEO Du-seob Jeong and Geohwa CEO Gi-seob Kim co lead the company. In February 1985, Dong-A released the Korando 85 series, an enhanced version of its existing models. The Korando 85 series consisted of six models, including the Korando Family 9, the Korando Van and Korando Ambulance. The series was newly designed to prevent tipping over and was equipped with the centralized instrument panels seen in sedans, air conditioning systems and Isuzu's 2,238cc diesel engine. The 4WD system was also improved. The changes removed a great number of the vehicle's weaknesses. Later, gasoline engine variants were added.

Derailed dream of a SsangYong Dynasty

In 1988, Dong-A Motor renamed itself SsangYong Motor and took out full-page ads that said "We are now SsangYong Motor." Two years earlier, in November 1986, Dong-A was acquired by the SsangYong Group. At the time, Dong-A Motor was recording 27.9 billion won in equity capital, 135.0 billion in assets and had 2,325 employees. The SsangYong Group ventured into the auto industry by taking over Dong-A. At the orders of SsangYong Group Chairman, Suk-won Kim, the company began developing new models to increase its market presence. The most notable fruit of its labor was the Korando Family, released on November 21, 1988. The Korando Family was a 4WD station wagon using the company's proprietary technology. Thanks to its design overhaul, improved performance and superior comfort, 278 units were sold on the first day and over 20,000 were sold over a two year time period.

SsangYong began to expand to other car segments and emerged as a major threat to Hyundai Motor and Kia Motors. The Musso, released in 1993, dominated the SUV market with its superior design and performance. In 1994, the Musso entered the 13th Pharaohs Rally and won first place in the 4WD segment and placed second overall. That year, 139 vehicles from 30 countries took part in the Pharaohs Rally, which began on

October 2nd at Alexandria. The race took participants across a 4,710km course across the desert terrain of the Sinai Peninsula.

Around the time it released the Musso, SsangYong formed a technology partnership with Mercedes-Benz. The Musso and the 9-seater New Korando Family released in 1995 were equipped with Benz's 2,300cc engine, which produced 79 horse powers. In 1996, SsangYong completed an engine factory in Changwon, South Gyeongsang Province. The plant produced 10,000 large-size diesel engines per year. The technology partnership was a part of SsangYong's diesel engine partnership with Benz in 1003. The six-cylinder 11,000cc and eight-cylinder 15,000cc engines were used on buses, trucks and semi trucks.

The partnership with Benz also resulted in a full-size luxury sedan. From 1993, SsangYong spent 450 billion dollars over four years to release the Chairman in October 1997. The Chairman employed the same platform as Benz E-Classes, while using technologies infused in Benz S-Class vehicles.

Unfortunately, SsangYong's bold investments and new model developments strained the company. Due to the financial drain, the Asian financial crisis of 1997 and the ensuing demand for restructuring by IMF, the SsangYong Group began to topple crumble. The SsangYong Group, which was the fifth largest conglomerate group in Korea, fell into financial troubles, and SsangYong Motor was sold off to the Daewoo Group after its 11-year stint with the SsangYong Group.

Short-lived dream

On December 8, 1997, the Daewoo Group held a press conference at the Namdaemun Hilton Hotel in Seoul and announced that it was acquiring SsangYong Motor. The contract was signed on January 9th of the following year. The Daewoo Group and the SsangYong Group agreed that Daewoo would purchase 51.98% of SsangYong Motor's outstanding stocks from the SsangYong Group for 64.2 billion won and assume half of SsangYong

Motor's 3.4 trillion won debt. Among the 51.98% stake, Daewoo Motors bought 48.01% and Daewoo Heavy Industries the remaining 3.97%.

Daewoo Group Chairman, Woo-jung Kim, immediate moved to globalize the Korando. Kim weighed the feasibility of establishing a plant in Europe dedicated to the production of Korandos, while preparing to sell Korandos in North America. The project was named K115. Preparations for Korando's foray into North America were completed and in late 1999, the company was adjusting its schedule for the Korando's debut. However, the project came to an abrupt halt as the 12 Daewoo affiliates were put into workout programs. The Group was forced to transfer ownership of Daewoo Motors to its main creditor, Chohung Bank, in 2000, three years after Daewoo Motors took over SsangYong Motor.

SAIC controversy

Chohung Bank decided to sell off SsangYong Motor. Experiencing difficulties in reaching agreements with GM and PSA, Chohung Bank began negotiating with the Chinese state-run petrochemical company, China National Blue star. Ultimately, SsangYong Motor was sold to Shanghai Automotive Industry Corporation (currently, SAIC Motor). Between the time SsangYong parted with the Daewoo Group and was sold to SAIC, SsangYong employees focused their efforts on normalizing operations. In June 1999, the efforts resulted in the 7-seater Musso, which came in 2,300cc and 2,900cc turbo-intercooled diesel engine variants. In November of that year, the Korando entered the Baja 1000 in Mexico, in which 167 teams from 38 different automakers around the world - including Ford, Toyota, Honda and Nissan – competed in 18 different classes. The Korando prevailed over 4WD vehicles from Ford and Isuzu and won the Stock Mini class.

SsangYong unveiled its luxury full-size SUV, Rexton, at the Hilton Hotel in Seoul on August 30, 2001. The Rexton immediately gained traction in the Korean premium SUV market. Even today, many SsangYong employees will testify that one of the busiest times for company's assembly lines was right after the Rexton was released. In 2002, the company added the pickup, Musso Sports, to its line-up, bringing it another step closer to normalization.

However, the company's fate took another downturn when it was placed in the hands of SAIC in 2004. Management discontinued the steady-selling Korando nameplate and succeeded it with the Actyon. The Actyon was a flop; its design did not appeal to consumers and the perception of it being a Chinese car created a so-called "China discount," which impeded sales. The government's fuel tax adjustment plan of 2007 also dealt a significant blow to the sales of the diesel vehicle Actyon. As a result of the fuel tax adjustment, the price of diesel fuel shot up from around half to nearly 85% of gasoline prices.

With the sales of Actyon, Actyon Sports, Rodius and other new models stalling, SsangYong decided to revive the Korando nameplate in 2006. The goal was to release a fully changed fourth-generation Korando by 2009. However, the financial crisis engulfed the world in 2008, and SAIC applied for SsangYong's court receivership in early 2009. SAIC had abandoned SsangYong in five years, triggering controversy that SAIC had drained SsangYong's technology and hung it out to dry.

The court appointed SsangYong Motor executive vice president Young-tae Park and former Hyundai Motor CEO Yoo-il Lee as the co-legal trustees. Park and Lee came up with plans for enterprise value calculation and restructuring. The restructuring plans infuriated the labor union. Conflict escalated quickly when the unionized workers occupied SsangYong's plant in protest. The strike was prolonged and reached a point where law enforcement was called in. Production was stopped for 77 days and caused over 300 billion won in losses.

Korando continues forward

Even during the labor strikes, engineers continued to work on the new Korando. The result was the Korando C, which was introduced in 2010 and sold from March 2011. Mahindra & Mahindra became the new owner of

SsangYong Motor in 2010, causing the company's nationality to change from Chinese to Indian.

SsangYong stepped up its efforts to develop and sell new cars. Following the successful Korando C, the company unleashed a barrage of new models, including the Chairman W (partial change), Korando Sports (pickup), Rexton W and Korando Turismo (minivan). Thanks to the array of improved models, unit sales began to rebound. After plunging from 154,307 units in 2003 to 92,665 in 2008 and 35,296 in 2009, unit sales bounced back to 145,649 in 2013 and remained above the 140 thousand mark in 2014 and 2015. Sales peaked at 3.4255 trillion won in 2005 before dropping to 1.0668 trillion in 2009 and recovering to 3.4849 trillion in 2013 and 3.3901 trillion in 2015. The company had recovered to normal levels on paper, but its Korean SUV market share has yet to recover to levels on par with those before its acquisition by SAIC. SsangYong Motor's SUV market stood at 59% in 1999, but dropped to 40% in 2003 and 27% in 2004. It continued to plunge, reaching 15% in 2008 and 7% in 2009, but recovered to 17.3% in 2013.

In January 2015, the company rolled out the Tivoli (project name X100), a model crucial to its goal of reaching 300,000 in unit sales. The Tivoli is an SUV, one size smaller than the Korando C. The company spent 41 months and 350 billion won to develop the model. The model took the market by storm and sold 63,693 units (45,021 in Korea with 18,672 exported), accounting for over 40% of the company's overall sales. The Tivoli commanded 55% of the Korean compact SUV market in Korea. The success of the model allowed the company to record an operating profit of 21.8 billion won for the fourth quarter of 2015. This marked the best performance since SsangYong was incorporated into the Mahindra Group in 2011. SsangYong released Tivoli Air, the five-passenger long-body version, and plans to yield at least one new model each year.

Since its birth as Ha Dong-hwan Motor Workshop in 1954, SsangYong Motor's history has been an endless string of trials that have made the company stronger each time. Having become a more formidable organization, SsangYong is growing at an increasing pace. The Korando will continue to push forward.

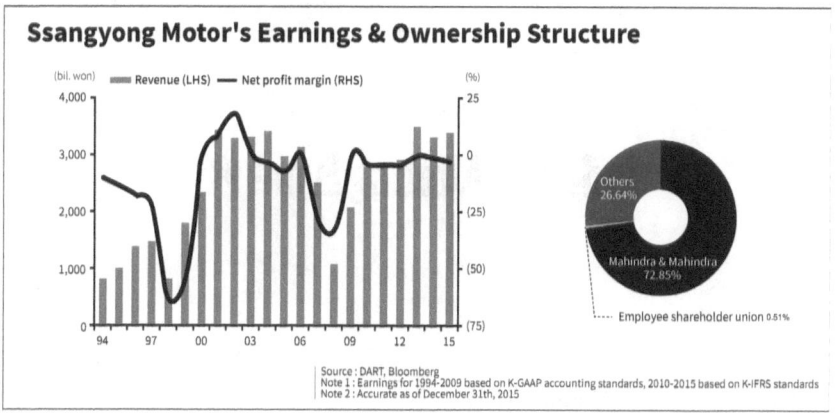

Ssangyong Motor's Earnings & Ownership Structure

Source : DART, Bloomberg
Note 1 : Earnings for 1994-2009 based on K-GAAP accounting standards, 2010-2015 based on K-IFRS standards
Note 2 : Accurate as of December 31th, 2015

Industry-Altering Event #6

The 2008 Global Financial Crisis

If the Asian financial crisis in the late 1990s shook the automobile industry, the global financial crisis in the late 2000s dealt it a heavy blow. The global financial crisis was triggered by the subprime meltdown in 2007. Subprime mortgage loans are home mortgages given to low-income households with poor credit ratings. Reckless subprime mortgage lending bankrupted the Lehman Brothers in 2008. The collapse caused the world's largest automobile market, the US, to contract quickly. US automobile sales dropped 35.4% from 16.15million units in 2006 to 10.43million in 2008. With its home base in shambles, GM, Ford and Chrysler had to undergo rigorous restructuring processes.

GM and Chrysler were hit especially hard. With the economy failing, dormant problems began to surface. GM's full-size sedan sales took a nosedive as oil prices surged, while its financial subsidiary GMAC received a direct blow from the subprime meltdown. The company's financial condition was further damaged by retiree medical benefits and life-long pension programs, which were established at the UAW's behest. By 2009, GM was forced to file for Chapter 11 bankruptcy protection and received a 50 billion dollar loan from the US government. This was the splitting image of how Asian automakers crumbled during the Asian financial crisis.

True to the expression "too big to fail," GM was different. The government loan and swift restructuring was able to salvage it from its pending doom. However, the restructuring resulted in the sales of Saab and the dismantling of the Hummer, Pontiac and Saturn marques. GM also sold off its interests in Japanese companies, like Fuji Heavy Industries, Isuzu and Suzuki. The NUMMI plant in Fremont was also shut down, ending its 25-year history.

Chrysler, which was picked up by Daimler at the time of the Asian financial crisis, was sold to Cerberus Capital Management in May 2007. Once the financial crisis broke out, Chrysler's earnings deteriorated further. By April 2009, Chrysler was filing for Chapter 11. The Fiat Group used the opportunity to acquire Chrysler. Fiat, which had been struggling during the early 2000s, had improved its financial health enough to engage in cross-border deals.

Unlike the other two American automakers, Ford was able to avoid bankruptcy because it had already gone through intense restructuring. During the Asian financial crisis, Ford dismantled the PAG and sold off all of its marques, aside from Ford and Lincoln. Asian companies became the beneficiaries of Ford's restructuring. The Tata Group of India acquired Jaguar and Land Rover, while Geely of China gained ownership of Volvo.

EMPIRE XIV

Renault-Samsung

CHAPTER 34

Samsung's Unfulfilled Dream Attempts Comeback under Renault

"Samsung Motors is applying for court receivership."

On June 30, 1999, the Samsung Group announced that Samsung Motors was entering court receivership. This implied that the Samsung Group was withdrawing from the automobile industry in less than two years, since it released its first model in 1997.

Under the leadership of Chairman Kun-hee Lee, the Samsung Group spent a decade preparing for its debut in the auto industry, but made a bitter retreat in less than two years. Samsung Motors had the funding and fully committed employees. It was going to display a new paradigm that distinguished it from Korea's existing car industry.

As it turned out, the auto industry was not easy to penetrate. Samsung was initially confident about its endurance, but it decided to cut its losses before it caused any catastrophic damage. It was one of the largest failures in the Samsung Group's history – one that would haunt it for years to come.

Longing for an automobile business

In the early 1990s, there were four automobile manufacturers in Korea – Hyundai Motor, Kia Motors, Daewoo Motors and SsangYong Motor. All four companies exported more cars than they sold in Korea, but the domestic market was still crucial. Given that approximately a million cars were sold each year in Korea at the time, competition for survival was intense. Amid such conditions, the four established companies vehemently condemned the Samsung Group's decision to join the industry. Samsung was launching an automobile business in a hostile environment.

Headed by Samsung C&T, which was Korea's leading company in terms of sales, and the up-and-coming Samsung Electronics, the Samsung Group's foray into the automobile industry was relatively late. Yet, Kun-hee Lee had a vested interest in the auto industry and saw great growth potential. Lee's decision to enter the industry was supported by the fact that information technology would soon grow into a significant aspect of car manufacture.

The Samsung Group made various attempts to get started in the industry. In 1990, Samsung Heavy Industries formed a partnership with Nissan Diesel to obtain technology for manufacturing commercial vehicles. However, its technology import declaration was rejected by the government. Two years later, the company decided to invest 72 billion won to begin producing 4,800 large-size (8-tons or larger) commercial vehicles per year from 1994. By November of that year, Samsung received approval to launch a venture into the passenger car market. Due to its determination to enter the automobile industry, the Samsung Group was considered one of the top candidates for acquiring the struggling Kia Motors. In 1993, Samsung Life Insurance and Samsung F&M Insurance accrued a combined 10% stake in Kia Motors.

Lacking the technology to manufacture cars, Samsung formed a technology partnership with Nissan - similar to when Hyundai Motor's seeking help from Mitsubishi to learn engine manufacturing technology, and Kia Motors from Mazda in the early days. Just as Hyundai and Kia moved on to developing original models and technology, Samsung needed to develop its own technology to survive in the industry.

In March 1995, Samsung Motors was launched with 100 billion won in capital. By 1996, the company completed a factory in the Sinho industrial complex in Busan. Samsung affiliates were assigned to provide assistance. For instance, Samsung Electro-Mechanics would supply parts from its plant in the Noksan industrial complex, while Samsung C&T was entrusted with sales and repair services. The company established the goal of becoming an automobile manufacturer churning out 1.5 million cars per year by 2010. In February 1998, Samsung Motors released its first mass-production mid-size sedan, the SM5, which was based on the Nissan Cefiro. In November of the same year, Samsung Commercial Vehicles began selling the 1-ton truck, Yamousine, which was based on the Nissan Atlas.

Korean financial crisis and the big deal

The auto industry is a process industry, requiring a large amount of startup costs. Cash reserves can be depleted instantly if only one or two new models do not sell well. There are many instances in which conglomerates expand to the automobile industry based on their success in other sectors and just break apart. Such examples are Daewoo Motors and SsangYong Motor. Despite being one of the largest conglomerate groups in Korea, Samsung Group nearly collapsed because of its automobile venture.

To be fair, Samsung's dalliance could not have come at a worse time. The Asian financial crisis had nearly crippled the Korean economy.

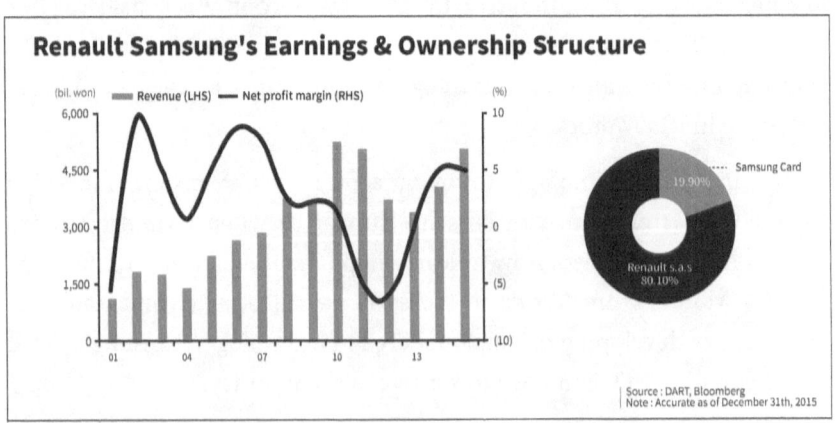

Meanwhile, the automobile industry had just heard of Jürgen Schrempp's big six theory and automakers believed they would not be able to survive unless they achieved critical mass. Immediately after Samsung Motors released the SM5, Korea requested a bailout from the IMF. In December 1998, the Korean government claimed, due to their high debt ratios, the top five conglomerate groups must undergo restructuring. To this end, the government proposed a "big deal" plan, in which the groups would be given exclusivity to industries they excelled in – similar to the 1980's measure to have each automaker specialize in a single car segment, but at an industry-level scale.

As a result, the consensus was that the newest entrant, Samsung Motors, should withdraw from the auto industry. This claim was supported by the Samsung Group's failed attempt to take over Kia Motors in October 1998, just before the "big deal" plan was proposed. The company was forced into a restructuring program less than a year since it officially began selling cars. Due to many complications, the Samsung Group was unable exchange Samsung Motors for Daewoo Electronics and in June 1999, Samsung Motors was placed under court receivership. Lee promised to compensate the creditors' losses incurred by court receivership using 20% (3.5million shares) of his 26% stake in Samsung Life Insurance, after it went public. Each Samsung Life Insurance share was deemed to be worth 700 thousand won. The Samsung Group agreed that Lee and Samsung affiliates would repay Samsung Motors' 2.45 trillion-won debt to its creditors and compensate for any additional losses incurred.

Renault picks up Samsung Motors

Creditors were considering the liquidation of Samsung Motors, but decided on selling the company. Busan citizens requested that Samsung Motors be spared to save the local economy. The committee to resolve the Samsung Motors issue was headed by Busan's prominent human rights lawyer, Moo-hyun Roh, who would later become president.

Samsung Motors entered negotiations with Renault, which expressed its desire to take over Samsung Motors in early 2000. By April 2000, the deal was closed. Renault-Samsung was launched that September with 440 billion won in capital. Renault owned 80.1% of the company and Samsung Card the remaining 19.9%, which remains unchanged to this day. The Samsung Group allowed Renault to use the Samsung brand in exchange for receiving 0.8% of sales as royalty each time the Renault-Samsung turned in an operating profit. Renault seems to have agreed to these conditions because, although Renault was a multinational company, Samsung had stronger brand recognition in Korea. Having not been acquired by Renault, Samsung Commercial Vehicle went bankrupt in late 2000. Samsung Commercial Vehicle's assembly lines and machineries were sold to a company in Vietnam.

Renault-Samsung released the compact sedan SM3 in September 2002, the full-size sedan SM7 in 2004, the mid-size SUV QM5 in 2007 and the CUV QM3 in 2013. Sales peaked at 516.8 billion in 2010, before taking a downturn.

In accordance with the Renault-Nissan Alliance's policy, any new model released by Renault-Samsung after the QM5 would be based on Renault cars and modified to comply with the taste of Korean consumers. As a result, the company's connection with the Alliance was changed from Nissan to Renault. The decision was made by Chairman Carlos Ghosn of the Renault-Nissan Alliance. At the time, Nissan was recording brisk sales thanks to the yen depreciation and the recovery of the American automobile market, whereas Renault's sales were stalling because of the sluggish European economy and it desperately needed to unload its inventory. Ghosn seemed to have decided to push Renault's piling inventory out through Renault-Samsung. Due to the increasing use of parts made in Europe, Renault-Samsung's earnings were heavily affected by the won/euro exchange rate. From 2014, Renault-Samsung also began producing Nissan's mid-size SUV, Rogue, in order to maximize on the tax benefits arising from the Korea-US FTA.

Aftermath of the Samsung Motors sale

Even after Samsung Motors was placed under court receivership and subsequently sold, the Samsung Group was not freed of its failed venture, because the IPO (initial public offering) for Samsung Life Insurance was delayed. The social consensus was that the assets of a life insurer belonged to policy holders, creating controversy over the fact that the majority shareholder stood to gain from the IPO. Ultimately, Samsung Life Insurance went public at an initial price of 110 thousand won in 2010, allowing the Samsung Group to discard all of its financial obligations related to Samsung Motors. The 3.5 million Samsung Life Insurance shares set forth by Lee were split into 35 million shares (70 thousand won per share).

Though it no longer manufactures cars, the Samsung Group remains associated with the auto industry by producing batteries for eco-friendly cars. In 2008, the Samsung Group launched a 50:50 joint venture with Bosch called SB Li Motive, which makes batteries used in electric and hybrid cars. In 2012, Samsung brought out Bosch and is supplying electric car batteries to BMW, Volkswagen, Chryslers and other auto companies. Thanks to the increasing application of electronics, the Samsung Group's participation in high-tech automotive electronics is growing. The Samsung Group is unlikely to give automobile manufacturing another try, but its influence in the auto industry is expanding.

Daewoo Motors

CHAPTER 35

Daewoo Motors: The Withering Empire

"We will be selling our flagship subsidiaries. In addition to the Group's 13 trillion won in assets, I will give up my personal wealth of 1.3 trillion won and inject the money into the automobile business."

Daewoo Group Chairman Woo-jung Kim's voice trembled as he read the restructuring plan, which included a promise that he would give up the personal wealth he spent his entire life accumulating. Having built his business through manufacturing and exports, Kim was a living legend among white collar workers in the 1970s. On July 30, 1999, Korea's second largest conglomerate group, Daewoo, collapsed after expanding at a fast rate for nearly 30 years.

The culprit for the demise of the Daewoo Group was Daewoo Motors, Korea's second largest car manufacturer at the time. Under its corporate value of "global management," the Daewoo Group emerged as the largest multinational conglomerate based in an emerging country. For Daewoo, the automobile business was its main growth engine and the cause of its doom.

Relationship with GM

The root of Daewoo Motors is traced back to Shinjin Industrial established by Chang-won Kim in 1955. Shinjin was a service shop repairing US military vehicles damaged during the Korean War. Along with repairing vehicles, the company also modified and sold military vehicles. Shinjin Industrial began manufacturing cars after acquiring Saenara Motor in November 1963. Saenara Motor was founded by Japan-born Korean No-jung Park in 1962, immediately after the Korean government announced the first 5-year economic development plant. Saenara Motor built a plant in Bupyeong-gu, Incheon, and imported, assembled and sold SKD versions of the Nissan Bluebird. The Bluebird is Korean first passenger car manufactured through a modern assembly line. However, Saenara Motor closed after nine months due to a shortage of foreign funds, leaving behind speculations of providing political funds.

Saenara Motor was acquired by Shinjin Motor, which was the only government-authorized passenger car manufacturer. The government wanted Shinjin Motor to develop original technology and cars, but Shinjin seemed indifferent to developing technology, as it formed a technology partnership with Toyota and focused on importing and assembling SKD versions of the Publica and the Corona. In response, the government cleared Hyundai Motor, Asia Motors and Kia Motors for passenger car production.

Years later, Shinjin Motor was unable to produce Toyota cars. Toyota had withdrawn from Korea when Chinese Premier Zhou Enlai announced a foreign trade policy which stipulated that China would not engage in any businesses with companies operating in Korea and Taiwan. Lacking the capacity to build its own cars, Shinjin focused on establishing ties with GM instead of developing its own technology. Shinjin Motor gave GM 50% of its stocks and was renamed GM Korea. And so, the company's ties with GM began in 1972.

The partnership with GM was no pleasure cruise. GM Korea was unable to record significant profits, as it had to pay 750 thousand dollars in annual instruction fees and 3% of sales as royalties to GM. While Hyundai successfully developed the Pony, GM Korea was only assembling the Chevrolet 1700. To make matters worse, the oil shock broke, causing sales of gas-guzzling cars to plunge. GM cars were the very definition of gas-guzzlers. In 1976, GM Korea was placed under the control of the Korea

Development Bank. It maintained its relationship with GM and was renamed Saehan Motor.

Journey into the world with the Daewoo emblem

In 1967, at the age of 30, Chairman Woo-jung Kim founded Daewoo and expanded the company by taking over financially troubled companies. Daewoo took its first step into the automobile industry by purchasing 50% of Saehan Motor from the Korea Development Bank in 1978. The Daewoo Group gained control of the company in 1982 and renamed it Daewoo Motors. Thanks to the heavy and chemical industry rationalization measure of 1980, Daewoo and Hyundai were the only companies authorized by the government to manufacture passenger cars, allowing Daewoo to profit significantly. Yet, even then, Daewoo was more interested in importing cars of foreign automakers than developing its own cars and engines.

As a result of GM's "world car" project, Daewoo Motors released LeMans in June 1986. The LeMans was the Korean version of the Opel Kadett. Daewoo's initial goal for the LeMans was to produce 300,000 units per year, but managed to sell only 536,254 units in Korea and export 516,099 units during the 11 years after the release of the model. The figure represented a little over 30% of the company's target. Placing more emphasis on comfort than performance, Korean consumers did not find the LeMans appealing. Daewoo also needed GM's approval on where the car was exported. In the US, GM agreed to sell 100 thousand LeMans per year using Pontiac's dealership network, but struggled to recover initial costs due to the car's poor sales. In 1990, Daewoo Motors released the Espero, a partially modified version of the LeMans, despite protests from GM.

Meanwhile, the Daewoo Group decided to form a partnership with Suzuki to develop a 2 million-won city car. Being a motorcycle powerhouse, Suzuki had world-class technology in small-size engines. The problem was the partnership was discovered by GM, which owned 5.3% of Suzuki. GM, which also owned 50% of Daewoo Motors, demanded that

Daewoo stop the development of its small-size passenger cars. Suzuki piled on, saying that it could not develop a city car with Daewoo engineers, who only had experience in mid and full-size sedans. Ultimately, the Daewoo Group decided to develop a city car through Daewoo Shipbuilding & Marine Engineering, not Daewoo Motors. The resulting car was the 796cc Tico. Daewoo Shipbuilding & Marine Engineering built an assembly plant in Changwon in April 1989 to manufacture Ticos. The plant was completed in May 1991. With the success of the Tico, the Daewoo Group was finally able to earn some real money. In 1992, the Daewoo Group used the funds to buy back the 50% stake held by GM.

Daewoo did not release any notable models aside from the Tico. The draught continued until 1995. The mid-size sedans, Brougham and Prince, were merely successors of the Royal Salon in 1980 and the Royal Prince in 1983. Daewoo Motors offered interest-free installment plans for models that did not sell, because it had to sustain the utilization rate of its plant.

While Hyundai Motor became diffident after closing the Bromont plant in 1993, Daewoo Motors aggressively expanded overseas. In 1995, it outbid GM and acquired the Polish automobile manufacturer, FSO, which was capable of producing 300 thousand units per year. FSO was founded by the Polish government in 1951. Following the acquisition of FSO, the western media nicknamed Chairman Woo-jung Kim "Kimghis Khan," in reference to the Mongolian warlord, Genghis Khan.

Between 1995 and 1996, Daewoo Motors established production bases in Eastern Europe and Southeast Asia. Plants were constructed simultaneously in Romania, Uzbekistan, Ukraine, Iran, Vietnam, Indonesia, the Philippines and other such countries. The plants were mostly SKD assembly lines. Instead of Daewoo Motors directly establishing local presences, the Daewoo Group had the overseas offices of Daewoo Corporation, Daewoo Heavy Industries and other subsidiaries raise capital through loans in Korea and raise remaining funds through local financial institutions. The Daewoo Group chose this method because Daewoo Motors was financially unstable. Daewoo Motors's projects were almost fully leveraged. By 1998, Daewoo Motors was capable of producing a million cars in Korea and another million through its overseas production bases. However, with the exception of FSO, none of the factories was operating at even 30% capacity.

Amid the vacuum of new models, Daewoo Motors acquired Worthing Technical Centre of the British design firm International Automotive Design in January 1994 and began the development of three cars – the Lanos (subcompact), the Nubira (compact) and the Leganza (mid-size). These original models were released in 1996 and 1997. In 1998, Daewoo released the Matiz, the successor of the Tico.

Having a solid line-up in the smaller passenger car segments, Daewoo Motors turned to SUVs and full-size sedans. To this point, the company had yet to develop 1,800cc or larger engines. It was buying larger engines from Holden, which was detrimental to profitability. It was at this time when a company that could fulfill Daewoo's needs was put up for sale. That company was SsangYong Motors. Despite its poor financial state, Daewoo Motors acquired SsangYong in December 1997, which proved to be a bad move. The Daewoo Group even made a push to acquire Kia Motors in August 1998. As previously stated, M&As sometimes fill voids for the acquirer, but in other situations, push the acquirer into an abyss. For the Daewoo Group, M&As turned out to be the latter.

One of the world's largest companies goes bankrupt

As Korea was receiving relief funds from the IMF in late 1997, a large number of Korean companies were undergoing rigorous restructuring processes. Daewoo Motors was financially strained as its financial sources were blocked. The company's decision was to reunite with GM by selling 50% of its stocks for 7 billion dollars. At the time, GM was anxious, because it was suffering in Europe due to Opel's lackluster performance and Ford had beaten GM to the Chinese market. Even so, GM did not draw a conclusion about Daewoo's financial situation despite numerous inspections of Daewoo Motors.

In July 1999, the Daewoo Group announced plans to restructure, mainly around Daewoo Motors. The Group attempted to apply for court receivership, but its creditors opted for a workout program in late August of that year. As of end-June 1999, the Daewoo Group possessed 91.9 trillion won in assets, making it one of the world's largest corporate bankruptcies of the time.

In its collapse, Daewoo Motors dragged its affiliates, which were in better financial health, down with it. This was a fallout that resulted from favoring joint ventures and acquisitions over focusing on core capabilities while being financially stretched. Another detrimental factor was that the Group had clashed with economic bureaucrats who had the power to decide the company's fate during this desperate situations. The irony of history was that following the regime change, Woo-jung Kim's Daewoo dynasty was dismantled by the Dae-jung Kim Administration and the Financial Supervisory Commission headed by Hun-jai Lee. Woo-jung Kim was the closest thing to an economy tutor for Dae-jung Kim and was the sponsor of Hun-jai Lee, the former CEO of Daewoo Semiconductor and the future finance minister of Korea.

GM takes over Daewoo Motors

In February 1998, GM and Daewoo Motors signed a memorandum of understanding (MOU) following the stake transaction. As a result, GM had exclusive negotiating rights for taking over Daewoo Motors until November 1999. On December 13, 1999, Louis Hughes, the executive vice-president of GM's overseas operations, secretly sent the Korean government a letter of intent for acquiring Daewoo Motors. GM's conditions were that it would take full control over Daewoo Motors, but would not assume Daewoo's 5-6 billion dollars in debt. Negotiations dragged on until in June 2000, the Korean government selected Ford, which had placed a 7.7 trillion won-bid (SsangYong Motor included), as the preferred bidder. The Daimler-Hyundai consortium was reported to have offered 5-6 trillion and the GM-Fiat consortium 4-5 trillion.

Ford desired to increase its presence in Eastern Europe and Asia through the acquisition of Daewoo Motors. However, Ford forfeited as it was unable to raise enough funds to acquire Daewoo due to a number of issues, including the decision to buy back its shares in the wake of the Firestone tire recall in the US. The Korean government searched for a new potential buyer, but no one stepped forward. Hyundai Motor was unable to place an aggressive bid, as it was financially strained by its recent acquisition of Kia Motors. GM was also undergoing a restructuring program, which resulted in the dismantling of the Oldsmobile brand and the closing of the Vauxhall plant in Britain.

The tide seemed to tip in GM's favor as time passed. After various twists and turns, GM took over Daewoo Motors in October 2002 and renamed it GM Daewoo. GM bought Daewoo Motors for 1.36 billion dollars, which was around 14% of price it had initially negotiated with Daewoo (50% stake for 7 billion dollars). In the end, GM actually paid only 400 million as the 1.36 billion included Daewoo Motors' debts. It was a bargain for GM. After the acquisition, GM held paid-in capital increases for Daewoo Motors on October 17th and 24th. As a result, GM's Australian subsidiary, Holden, owned 44.6% of Daewoo Motors, its Japanese subsidiary, Suzuki, 14.9% and its Chinese subsidiary, Shanghai Automotive, 10.6%. Korea Development Bank held a 29.9% stake at the time.

Daewoo Motors fades into history

The acquisition of Daewoo Motors paved the path for GM's excursion into China. The Daewoo Nubira (renamed Lacetti in Korea after the acquisition) was released in China as the Buick Excelle by Shanghai GM. The Nubira/Excell was a major success in China, generating around 70% of GM's Chinese sales. The Daewoo Matiz debuted in China as the Chevrolet Spark. The Chevrolet Sail, Shanghai GM's bestselling model among its city car line-up, was based on the technology fused in the Daewoo Lanos. GM is currently competing against Volkswagen to become the leading automobile manufacturer in China.

The Chinese automaker, Chery Automobile, benefited substantially from the downfall of Daewoo Motors. From 2003, Chery fueled its growth through the production of the QQ, which is regarded as a copy of the Matiz. According to Michael Dunne, author of *American Wheels, Chinese Roads: The Story of General Motors in China*, Chery manufactured the QQ with a Matiz diagram, which was leaked into Taiwan while Daewoo Motors was going through its workout program in 2001.

In 2011, GM Daewoo was renamed GM Korea, and its cars began bearing the Chevrolet marque. As a result, the 33-year-old Daewoo name was removed from the automobile industry. Thanks to continuous investments from 2002, GM Korea's unit sales increased from 377 thousand to 1.96 million (CKD models included) over a 12-year span. There is still a lingering chance that GM may sell or retract GM Korea in accordance with its global restructuring strategy. However, the Korea Development Bank signed an agreement with GM in 2010. According to the agreement, GM Korea would be given permanent ownership of technologies, and if sold, its production technology and domestic and overseas sales rights would be relinquished to the new owner. This clause is the only safeguard to preserve GM Korea, the successor of Korea's first car manufacturer, Saenara Motor, and allow Daewoo Motors, which was once a pillar of the Korean automobile industry, to live on.

Groundbreaking Classics #6

S-Class, the Standard of Luxury Sedans

The Mercedes-Benz S-Class reflects the wealth, social status and power of its owner. Most countries around the world use S-Classes to transport visiting heads of state. There are numerous luxury brands producing full-size sedans that are the amalgamation of their own technologies. However, the Mercedes-Benz S-Class remains the one vehicle they all compare themselves to and strive to beat. This indicates that the S-Class' long-standing history of innovation and value makes it worthy of being the standard of all full-size luxury sedans.

The S-Class first came into existence in 1903 with the release of the Mercedes–Simplex 60hp. The car was equipped with a four-cylinder engine and infused with all the cutting-edge technology of the time, such as overhead intake valves and a honeycomb radiator grille. During the early 20th century, cars usually generated around 10 horsepower. However, the Simplex could spill out 60 horsepower and reach a top speed of 109km/h. Mercedes-Benz presented a W08 (released in 1928) as a gift to the Pope, earning it the nickname "Pope Mobile."

The S-Class name was first used in 1972. The vehicle also bore a number of state-of-the-art technologies, including four-spoke safety steering wheels and shock-resistant fuel tanks. In 1975, the S-Class was equipped with a 6.9 liter eight-cylinder engine capable of producing 286 horse powers. It had the largest engine displacement in Germany. The S-Class was also the first vehicle to come with anti-lock braking systems and turbo diesel engines (1977).

The second-generation S-Class featured various high-tech safety devices, which was a turning point for all sedans. Airbags were first installed in the 126 model released in 1981. By 1988, airbags were installed for all passenger seats. The third-generation enhanced driver convenience – GPS navigation system, sensor-base parking assistance system, lane sensors and other gadgets. In 1998, the elegantly designed fourth-generation was released. Among new features was the active dampening air suspension, which controlled the vertical movement of suspensions in accordance to road conditions. Other new additions were the active body control system, the 4Matic (all-wheel drive system) and other functions that enhanced safety and comfort. By the fifth generation, all features were improved.

The sixth-generation S-Class, released in 2013, came with the "Magic Body Control: system, in which the vehicle reads the surface of the road and automatically adjusts the height of the suspensions in accordance. It is also the world's first car to come with a hot stone massage seats. Mercedes-Benz develops technology and designs with the sole purpose of satisfying its high-class consumer, and such efforts leads the trend of automotive technology and guide the course of the industry. This is the role that the flagship sedan of a prestige brand should play.

About the Authors

Eric Junghyuk Choi, Equity Analyst at Shinhan Investment

Eric Choi began his career as an analyst in 2009 after graduating from Sungkyunkwan University with a degree in Business Administration. Since 2012, Eric was chosen as the best analyst of the auto/tire industry by Maekyung Economy and by Hankyung Business Weekly for three consecutive years. Eric built his career working at a global investment bank and a newspaper company.

In 2011, after two years as an analyst at LIG Investment & Securities, Eric transferred to the Research Center of Shinhan Investment, where he has worked as the topflight analyst covering the automotive, auto parts and tire industries. He contributes articles to the Hankyung Business Weekly, Maekyung Economy and Motor Trend. While in college, he founded the university's finance society, *"The Corner."*

Richard Jin-suk Choi, Reporter at Korea Economic Daily

Richard Choi graduated from Sungkyunkwan University with a degree in Korean philosophy. He started his career at the Korea Economic Daily in 2007. Since 2011, Richard has been covering the automobile industry in the newspaper industry. He also contributes articles to the Hankyung Business Weekly and the online automobile news outlet, Road Test. Richard is also a regular panel of an automobile program at YTN Radio. He is also an amateur race car driver, who has competed in the 2014 Nexen Speed Racing and 2014 Yamaha SL Cup. In addition to managing the popular automobile blog Nichado Gear, he is the author of *My Car Mini.*

Reference

- AlfredSloan 《My years with General Motors》 (DOUBLERDAY, 1990)

- Jennifer Clark 《Mondo Agnelli: Fiat, Chrysler, and the Power of a Dynasty》 (John Wiley&Sons, 2011)

- Michael J. Dunne 《American Wheels, Chinese Roads: The Story of General Motors in China》 (John Wiley&Sons, 2011)

- Hideo Kobayashi 《The Day Hyundai Beats Toyota》 (21st Century Books, 2011)

- Byeong-wan Kim 《How Kia Overcame Crisis》 (Chamdol, 2013)

- Seong-hong Kim, Sang-min Lee 《Mong-ku Chung's Venture》 (Gods Win, 2005)

- Woo-jung Kim 《Large World with a Lot to Do》 (Gimmyoung, 1989)

- Jung-sik Kim 《Tata Group's Trust-based Management》 (Random House Korea, 2011)

- Tae-jin Kim 《Toyota: The Strength that Withstood Japan's 10-year Slump》 (Wisdom House, 2004)

- Tae-jin Kim 《Honda: Belief in the Power of Dreams》 (YBMSISA, 2004)

- Daniel Goeudevert 《 Wie ein Vogel im Aquarium: Aus dem Leben eines Managers》 (Chamsol, 1999)

- Kazumasa Takeuchi 《The Ambition of Elon Musk》 (EZ Book, 2014)

- David Margee 《Ford Tough》 (Vision Korea, 2005)

- David Kiley 《Driven》 (EZ Book, 2005)

- David Harding, Sam Rovit 《 Mastering the Merger: Four Critical Decisions That Make or Break the Deal 》 (Chungrim, 2008)

- Digital Naeil 《Hyundai Motor's Global Leadership》 (Human&Books, 2004)

- Lee Iacocca, William Novak 《Iacocca: An Autobiography》 (Hwangso Jari, 2005)

- Miguel Rivas-Micoud 《The Ghosn Factor: 24 Lessons the World's Most Dynamic CEO 》 (Ilshin Books, 2008)

- Micheline Maynard 《The End of Detroit》 (Indi Book, 2004)

- Byeong-jae Park 《New Brilliant Company》 (Maeil Economic Daily, 2012)

- Bob Rutz 《Car Guys vs. Bean Counters: The Battle for the Soul of American Business 》 (Business Books, 2012)

- Thomas Ammann, Stefan Aust 《 Die Porsche-Saga: Eine Familiengeschichte des Automobils 》 (Shwim Book, 2013)

- Jang-seob Shin 《 Talk with Woo-jung Kim: Large World with a Lot to Do》 (Book Corps, 2014)

- Asahi Shinbum 《Toyota Next One》 (Joongang Books, 2013)

- Asia Economic Daily 《MK Leadership》 (Akyung Books, 2011)

- Won-cheol Oh 《Korean Economic Construction 4》 (Korea Institute of Economic Policy, 2002)

- Hiroyasu Otomi 《Carlos Ghosn: Success from Change and Reform》 (Samho Media, 2002)

- Ulrich Viehöver 《Der Porsche-Chef: Wendelin Wiedeking》 (Econ, 2006)

- Jong-hun Yun, Ho-jun Lee 《M&A Strategy and Case Studies》 (Maeil Economic Daily, 2005)

- Shinya Iwakura, Masaki Iwatani, Shinya Nagasawa 《Design Management Seen at Honda》 (Human&Books, 2005)

- Wu-kwang Lee 《Toyota: Winning the Respect of People》 (Salrim, 2009)

- Im-kwang Lee 《Mong-ku Chung, Hyundai and Kia: Race for Change》 (Thought Map, 2007)

- Eiken Itakaki 《Miracle Maker: Carlos Ghosn's Leadership》 (Dunan, 2002)

- Nikkei 《Carlos Ghosn: Revolutionary Leader of Nissan's Revival 》 (Young Books, 2001)

- Se-yong Chung 《Make Your Own Future》 (Hangrim, 2000)

- Il-goo Chung 《Manufacture, Supervise and Manage like Toyota 》 (Sidae Books, 2004)

- Ju-yung Chung 《Hardship, but not Failure》 (The Third, 2001)

- Ju-yung Chung 《Born in Korea: Autobiography》 (Sol, 1998)

- Hui-jeong Jin, Yong-ju Gwon 《The Power of Hyundai Motor》 (Myungsung, 2006)

- Jin-suk Choi 《My Car MINI》 (EZ Book, 2014)

- Carlos Ghosn 《Renaissance》 (Ire, 2002)

- Ferdinand Piëch 《Auto. Biographie.》 (Thought Tree, 2004)

- Yozo Hasegawa 《COO Carlos Ghosn and Nissan》 (EZ Book, 2002)

Photo Credits

- Empire 1 Courtesy, Volkswagen of Korea

- Empire 2 Courtesy, GM Korea

- Empire 3 Courtesy, Toyota Motor Korea

- Empire 4 Courtesy, Renault Samsung Motors, Nissan North America, Inc

- Empire 5 Courtesy, Hyundai Motor Company

- Empire 6 Courtesy, Fiat Chrysler Automobiles

- Empire 7 Courtesy, Ford of Korea

- Empire 8 Courtesy, Honda Korea

- Empire 9 Courtesy, Hanbul Motors Corp

- Empire 10 Courtesy, Mercedes-Benz Korea

- Empire 11 Courtesy, BMW Korea

- Empire 12 Courtesy, Jaguar Land Rover

- Empire 13 Courtesy, Ssangyong Motor Company

- Empire 14 Courtesy, Renault Samsung Motors

- Empire 15 Courtesy, GM Korea